ADVANCE PRAISE FOR
60 STORIES ABOUT 30 SECONDS

"In *60 Stories About 30 Seconds*, director Bruce Van Dusen's quick wi
keen observations, and entertaining behind-the-scenes anecdotes serv
as a delirious love letter to his lifelong passion—making television con
mercials. A truly delightful read."

—Meredith Vieira, Broadcast Journalist a
Television Persona

"Written by a man who describes himself as 'a toxic mix of insec
and headstrong,' *60 Stories About 30 Seconds* is a joyful romp—a mi
stories about idiotic mistakes, surprising successes, and business and
lessons well-learned. Reading it is about as much fun as you can pos
have while sitting quietly and learning new stuff."

—Richard Davies, Former ABC News Radio An
Co-host of "How Do We F

60
Stories
about
30
Seconds

60 Stories

about

30

Seconds

How I got away with becoming one of the biggest commercial directors of all time without losing my soul (or maybe just part of it).

A PRETTY BIG

Bruce Van Dusen

Post Hill
PRESS

A POST HILL PRESS BOOK
ISBN: 978-1-64293-402-1
ISBN (eBook): 978-1-64293-403-8

60 Stories About 30 Seconds:
How I Got Away With Becoming a Pretty Big Commercial Director Without
Losing My Soul (Or Maybe Just Part of It)
© 2020 by Bruce Van Dusen
All Rights Reserved

Cover design by Alexander Smith/Smith Design Office
Interior design and layout by Sarah Heneghan, sarah-heneghan.com

Post Hill Press
New York • Nashville
posthillpress.com

Published in the United States of America

Dedicated to Joel Brodsky

TABLE OF CONTENTS

You live in a deranged age, more deranged than usual because in spite of great scientific and technological advances, man has not the faintest idea of who he is or what he is doing.

—WALKER PERCY

I Know He's Crazy. Is He Alive?

CRAZY EDDIE WAS THE FIRST PERSON TO HIRE ME TO DIRECT A COMMERcial. Crazy Eddie himself. He didn't actually say, "You're hired," because his jaw was broken, and he was attached to some life-support machines. His ad manager translated his grunts. But I'm getting ahead of myself.

In the late '70s, his commercials were everywhere. And terrible. They featured an actor named Jerry Carroll, who spent all thirty seconds screaming into the camera about low prices. Spittle actually flew from his mouth during some of the spots. Viewers thought Carroll was Crazy Eddie. Not true.

Crazy Eddie was really a guy named Eddie Antar. A Syrian Jew who, through a combination of chutzpah and what would later be revealed as illegal bookkeeping of epic proportions, created an enormous electronics retail chain. And, as I said, Eddie made a lot of commercials.

I had graduated from Boston University with a degree in film and television production a year ago and moved to New York. I understood the basics of how to use a camera and edit, but I'd learned nothing about getting paid for it. My friends think I'm just fucking around, having fun,

1

chasing girls, one day away from realizing I should do whatever it is real people do. My parents think "the film business" is some marginal, seedy, vaguely illegal industry that is dominated by people who changed their names to sound either less Jewish or less Italian.

My career path was weird. I never worked in a restaurant or a bookstore or a movie theater. I never looked for that kind of job because I thought anything like that would be a detour from being a director. After two production assistant jobs, a wannabe producer hired me as a director/salesman at his wannabe commercial production company. I should write the job titles in reverse order because all I really do is sell. Me. I'm hustling all the time. I've learned that getting work is all about contacts and connecting the dots. A year ago, I had zero contacts and no dots. But I'm figuring out how to be an operator, always listening, watching, plotting. One thing is working great for me: the dress code. Or lack of. I live in blue jeans, T-shirts, and cowboy boots. My hair is down to my shoulders. I smoke Camels. I go to work in a scuzzy building on 45th Street just off Sixth Avenue. My new friends are photographer's assistants, wannabe musicians, unemployed actors, roller skaters, and bartenders. I am struck by how none of them have any idea how they're going to turn whatever they're doing into something big and real and rewarding. No plan. I'm all about the plan. Maybe too all about it. I'm living *What Makes Sammy Run*, but a version written by John Updike.

I am never *not* looking for work. I treat any social event as desperation networking. Somebody put me in touch with the guy who buys the television time for Crazy Eddie. I ask him to set up a meeting for me with the Crazy Eddie people. He does. Thank God. I need to make something happen. Now. I've only brought in one job in the last six months. A commercial that was basically a shot of a milk carton that we got paid $1500 to do. I proudly told people I directed that. I'm walking around like it's all good, everything's working out fine, but I'm panicked. The guy I'm working for has to be thinking he's wasting his $100 a week on me. I'm having a hard time taking myself seriously.

One day in late February, I take the subway out to Avenue U in Sheepshead Bay. It's a section of Brooklyn that's half Italian and half Middle Eastern. Half residential, half business. The Crazy Eddie empire is headquartered in a nondescript cinderblock building that looks like one of those garages near Shea Stadium where Dominican guys pound dents out of your Buick. The place is totally unmarked. Telling. When I finally find it, I buzz a jury-rigged doorbell, it buzzes back, and I go in.

I'm in one large room filled with seventy-five beat-up, battleship gray, government-issue desks. All of them are covered with leaning towers of papers and takeout glatt kosher food. Every stoop-shouldered clerk in the place looks nauseated because of the sickly green tint cast by the fluorescents overhead. The work force is mostly men. All dressed in various versions of Orthodox attire. Some with *tzitzit*. Some in black suits, white shirts, and fedoras. Some with *peyas*. The random davening guy over by a cinderblock wall swaying back and forth. A *goy* like me walking in probably set off an alarm.

A chubby little guy in an unbuttoned vest approaches.

"Can I help?"

"Yeah. I'm looking for Larry Miller."

"He's expecting you?"

"Yeah. I have a one-thirty appointment."

The little guy beckons me to follow. He leads me through the mess of desks to Miller's office and parks me at the door. Miller's inside sitting at his own shitty desk also covered in crap. He's in his mid-thirties, kind of disheveled, with a put-upon, defensive posture. Which makes sense. If you have his job, when you go to a cocktail party and tell people you're the ad manager for Crazy Eddie, they'll think you're a total asshole.

It's immediately clear he has no interest in me or this meeting.

"What d'ya want to talk about?"

For some reason, I have total confidence that he's interested in the opinion of a twenty-three-year-old long-haired kid. I hold forth like I've done this a million times before.

"Your ads could be a lot better."

"Who the fuck cares? They work."

"People think they're kind of obnoxious."

I probably could have been subtler.

"So what? We sell a ton of shit."

"Okay. But don't you think it might be possible to be effective and less annoying?"

"Like I said: who cares?"

I actually have an idea of how to do this. But, in the real world, like on Earth, commercial directors don't stroll into your office and pitch you ideas. Ad agencies come up with the ideas. And agencies spend time developing the ideas, not thinking them up on the train ride out to Sheepshead Bay. I don't know enough to know how many rules I'm breaking, so I plow ahead.

The idea's simple and not at all original. Take scenes from famous movies with famous songs. "Follow the Yellow Brick Road" in *The Wizard of Oz*. "As Time Goes By" in *Casablanca*. Re-create the scenes. But, instead of having them sing the famous song, have them sing the Crazy Eddie jingle rearranged in the film's musical style. Funny, maybe. Less obnoxious, definitely. More effective, we'll see. I don't even process the fact that these ideas don't use Jerry Carroll. I've jettisoned their spokesperson without bothering to explain why.

The ad guy reflects for less than five seconds.

"Stupid. It'll never work."

Compared to what they're doing, it's genius, but I'm not going to correct him. He tells me he'll pass it along to Eddie and be in touch. I know what that means. Fuck off. I leave through a parting sea of observant bookkeepers/embezzlers and hop the Q train back to Manhattan.

Two weeks later, the ad manager calls.

"Can you come over tomorrow and present those ideas to Eddie?"

Shit, I'll come right now if that works better for you.

"Yeah. Sure. When?"

"Two."

"Out to headquarters?"

4

"No. At Roosevelt Hospital."

"What?"

"Long story. Let's meet in the lobby. Two o'clock."

Roosevelt Hospital is in Hell's Kitchen. And Hell's Kitchen is a tough fucking neighborhood. This is not the kind of health care facility you're going into by choice or if you have insurance. I'm pretty confused as I get out of the cab and walk through a crowd of smokers dressed in hospital gowns, pushing IVs on rolling poles on my way toward the lobby.

Miller's waiting inside the revolving doors. As soon as he sees me, he turns and heads for the elevators. I follow.

"What're we doing here?"

"Eddie's upstairs.

"What happened?"

"He got stabbed."

"He did?"

"Yeah. Like sixteen times. And a lot of broken bones."

"What?"

"He was installing a sound system in a disco and got ambushed when he left."

"Maybe this isn't a great time to do this presentation."

"It's a great time. Eddie wants to stay busy and thought this would be entertaining."

Great. I'm the fucking clown who does balloon tricks for the terminally ill kid.

We head through a portion of the ground floor where the emergency cases are clustered. People slumped in chairs. Lying on gurneys. There's a lot of screaming and moaning. Much of it's in Spanish, so I can only assume these people are saying something about being in indescribable pain. The blood-soaked clothes and sheets would kind of speak to that too. We get in an elevator, and Miller punches the button for the sixth floor.

It's slightly calmer up there. We go down a hallway and into a private room. Jesus.

Eddie's in the bed. At least, Miller says it's Eddie. What I see is a chubby, hairy-as-a-bear guy attached to two IVs, his torso wrapped in gauze, wound seepage stains everywhere, one arm in traction, the top of his skull wrapped in more gauze, one leg in traction, inflatable cuffs on his ankles, two blackened eyes, and an oxygen line in his left nostril. The guy is totally fucked up. It doesn't seem appropriate to try and shake hands. In fact, I'm scared to get too close to the guy for fear I'll catch something. Like a stab wound.

Miller makes a quick introduction then tells me to start.

"Make it quick. He hasn't got all day."

He doesn't? Whatever. I try to figure out which of Eddie's blackened eyes to aim my gaze at and dive in. I explain the movies, the scenes, the jingle. I state confidently, with no backup, that the ads can be a little less intrusive, my euphemism for stone-cold obnoxious, and still sell tons of stereos and televisions. I finish my spiel and Eddie grunts. Like three grunts. His mouth is all fucked up from the beating, so it's impossible to understand him. I'm pretty sure his jaw is broken too. Miller understands him. He turns to me with the translation.

"How much to make one? Not all. Just one."

I'm not prepared for this question. I figured, if everything went great, I'd hear back in a few days and then we'd talk money. So I fumble and throw out a stupidly low number. A number so low, even if you didn't make television commercials, you'd pay me to make one just to show your friends. Eddie grunts again. Miller seems to understand him.

"Got it. When?"

Grunt, grunt, slight arm gesture, which stops abruptly when Eddie screams in pain. But he's apparently just given us the go-ahead to make a spot.

Two weeks later, I make a take-off of *Casablanca*. That ridiculously low estimate I threw out on the fly has left me with such a tiny budget that I can only afford to build half an arch in the set, which is supposed to be Rick's Café Américain. I spend the biggest part of the budget on a low-rent Bogart impersonator. He makes more than me. Having never directed a commercial, I desperately try all sorts of things to make myself look experienced. I wear a suit and tie to the set, certain it'll make people overlook the fact that I'm twenty-three. It probably makes them notice it more.

The ad goes on the air a month later. *The Village Voice* writes an article about it. With a picture from the spot of Sam and the Bogart imper-sonator draped over the piano. The writer says Crazy Eddie has done something interesting with its advertising. Which is like saying the guy who always shows up for church drunk managed to grab a shower before this week's services.

Whatever. I'm now a New York commercial director.

Fast Forward.

THIRTY YEARS LATER, I'M DRIVING FROM MY HOTEL IN WESTWOOD TO Pasadena. It's 5:30 in the morning, but it'll still take for-fucking-ever to get there. Since I did that first job for Crazy Eddie, I've directed almost a thousand commercials, some of which you might even remember, like ones for Ford, AT&T, Bell Canada, and NY Telephone. I work all the time. Half the jobs I get I don't even bid on; the agencies just give them to me. I know now that I know what I'm doing. Whether I like it is another story.

I'm in the fifth day of an eight-day shoot for TD Waterhouse. The Canadian financial services giant is moving into the US market, and the commercials I'm doing are announcing it. We're using athletes, movie and television stars, and expensive locations, and employing a crew of eighty people. It's one of those jobs where you have everything you want. The money is stupid. I'm trying to put as much of it as possible on the screen instead of in my pocket.

I turn into the public parking lots at the Huntington Gardens. Production has taken over the biggest one for the trucks, motor homes, and crew parking. I pull in by the production motor home. I figure out what I should take with me. It's a sunny day, so sunglasses and a baseball cap. It's so director. I'll be different and not wear it backwards. The cap.

I stop at the craft service truck. There are two long tables set up with every kind of baked goods, fresh fruit, cereal, juice, nondairy milks, teas, and cold beverages imaginable. And there's a food truck where you can order a custom breakfast. Most of the crew eats big. Burritos, pancakes, omelets. I get a coffee and a donut.

My assistant director, Steve, joins me.

"Morning, sir."

"Morning. How we doing?"

"Fine. Talent's in makeup. Wardrobe's dressing the extras. Art department is working on getting the horses and carriages in position. Camera says they should be ready by eight. Anything you need?"

"I'm good. I'm gonna go introduce myself to Geena."

"You want me along on that?"

"Do your thing. Do I need to check in with camera first?"

"You're okay. I'll have someone find you if Vilmos has a question."

"Thanks."

I've worked with Steve on the last twenty jobs I've done in LA. He's young but very solid. Disciplined, thinks ahead, manages the crew well, walks the line between tough and charming. He'll go far.

On a movie, you assemble a crew and they're together for months. They have time to develop a rhythm. On a commercial, you put together a crew for a few days. They have to gel instantly. When you shoot a lot, you figure out who the best people are and try to book them over and over. Good people, even if they don't know each other, gel quickly. Especially in this line of work.

I walk over to the talent motor home where the actors are being dressed and made up. I've worked with the makeup woman for years. She makes every actor she touches walk on the set confident and happy. She makes them feel like they're the best. I've never worked with the wardrobe lady. She's won two Academy Awards, so she obviously knows what she's doing. My only fear is that she'll be some prima donna and make the job all about her. I'll find out.

There's a production assistant at the trailer door.

"Morning, sir."

I've never figured out where this "sir" shit comes from. Maybe it's as simple as production assistants don't always know directors' names, so they just opt for formal.

"Morning. All good?"

"Seems to be."

I climb the three steps into the motor home. The interior is spacious. The area where I enter has two big Formica-covered work tables and six chairs. Various production people work on computers and do paperwork.

"Morning, sir."

"Morning, sir."

"Morning, everybody."

To the left is a long counter where the makeup department is set up. We have three chairs and three makeup artists today because we have a cast of ten principals. At the far end, behind some sliding doors, is a separate area where actors can get dressed or get some privacy. Or where you can park a celebrity. I go there.

I stop at the sliding door and knock.

"Morning."

Geena Davis faces the mirror and sees me framed over her shoulder. She's won an Academy Award, been nominated for another, is purported to have a genius IQ, is an Olympic-level archer, and is probably getting paid a million bucks to be in this ad. The premise is she's starring in some period-piece film, keeps trying to get on her laptop to do a trade, can't because the set is too disorganized, so she grabs a bow and arrow, fires it at an apple, cutting it in half, and it hits the mouse and executes the trade. A little complicated, but it's a sixty-second spot, so we have tons of time to tell the story. And the agency has given me total freedom to do whatever I want, otherwise known as just enough rope to hang myself. She's wearing an elaborate Elizabethan-style gown we've had shipped in from London. It's an enormous, multi-layered brocaded dress with silver filigree woven through the seams and some complicated thing around her neck that looks like the bellows of an accordion. Her hair is pulled into a braid wrapped around her head. She looks unbelievably great.

"Wow. I'm at a loss for words here."

I come around, so we don't continue the conversation into the mirror.

"I'm Bruce, the director. Very nice to meet you."

"Nice to meet you, Bruce."

"I found out we have a good friend in common."

"Right? Small world. I was on the phone with Craig yesterday."

"I've never understood how such a nice guy became an entertainment lawyer."

Okay. Good. We now have the six degrees of separation thing going. The comment about our friend Craig is just to prove I'm normal too. So many of the guys who do what I do are pretentious idiots who actually think they're fucking artists. If they're working with a famous actor, they explain how they aren't "like most commercial directors and this isn't just some commercial; this is way more cinematic and it'll be amazing, and I love all your work and what I'm envisioning is a mashup of *Rashomon* and *The Lives of Others* and *Blazing Saddles*." Commercial directors get so little respect for a good reason. They're desperately insecure and broadcast it. I always go for the "this is just a stupid ad, it'll be easy, and I'll get us out of here before five" approach. It works.

"This'll be way simpler than a movie. I break everything down into very short scenes. We'll do most everything in sequence. We can be very loose with the lines. The cast around you is great. Very funny and quick. You'll have a good time."

I'm hoping Geena sees I'm going to be easy to work with.

"Oh. And you're going to look amazing. Have you ever worked with Vilmos?"

Vilmos Zsigmond is the Academy Award–winning cinematographer who's shooting this job.

"No and I'm so excited. One question: Should we go over anything about the bow and arrow stuff with the art department?"

"I think we're good. We'll work it out when we get to that shot. In the meantime, just let us know what you need. We'll be ready in less than an hour."

"Really?"

"Yup."

I leave the trailer and walk across the parking lot to an area where another trailer and pair of tables have been set up by the art department. This is where we'll do a scene with Geena working on her computer and the actor playing an AD coming over to bring her to set.

It's the first shot of the spot, so I want to give it a little scope. The camera's mounted on a Technocrane fifty feet up in the air. Four grips stand around the base of the crane, and Vilmos is looking at a video monitor to see what the camera sees and set the shot. Steve calls action, and the grips pull the crane down quickly toward the set. It looks majestic.

"Morning, guys. Morning, Vilmos."

"Hey, boss."

Better than sir.

"What do you think?"

"It's great. You vant to see motor home or garden behind her? I think motor home is better."

Vilmos left Hungary as a teenager when the Soviets rolled in. He still sounds a little like Henry Kissinger. He's a charming, gracious man. He treats me as seriously and respectfully as he would Steven Spielberg, Woody Allen, Brian de Palma, Robert Altman, Michael Cimino, or any of the other directors he's worked with. Who the fuck knows why?

"Maybe the motor home, so we know we're on a set? Does that work for the light?"

"Yeahyeahyeah. It'll work."

"When are you set to go?"

"Whenever she's ready, we shoot."

Not all big-time cinematographers are this chill. Some make the job all about themselves. They slow-walk, they get snippy, they change their minds, they tell you what you can and can't do. Vilmos is not that guy.

I look for the agency. They're nowhere in sight, so I keep working. Halfway over to the other set, I find Susan, my script supervisor. I have worked with her for almost fifteen years. She is smart, funny, quick, and becoming a director in her own right. She has as good an understanding of what needs to be done on a job as I do. Sometimes better. This job has been pretty free-form. I have the actors change the dialogue take to take, encourage them to improvise, and play with the blocking. It works because the end product will look like two hours of footage has been cut down to sixty seconds of greatest hits. Continuity isn't an issue. But someone needs to write down who's in a scene, who walked into it when and from which side. That's the script supervisor.

"Morning."

"Morning, sir."

"All good?"

"I think so. Question: There's a sequence in the shooting board where Geena's walking away in frame two and then, in frame three, she's already in the scene they're shooting. I know we're not worried about continuity, but is that going to be jarring so early in the spot? Do you need something in between?"

"Yeah, maybe. A slate. Someone's face. The camera guy speaking in Russian. Something. Make a note we need a frame two A."

"Got it."

"And remind me to do it because I'll forget."

"I'm going for a tea. Can I get you something?"

"I'm good. Thanks."

Where the fuck is that coffee and donut? I must have left it in Geena's trailer.

The AD catches up with me.

"Let's take a look at the carriages and the horses. If we put 'em in the wrong place, they'll take a fucking century to move around. Plus, the fucking horses'll shit everywhere."

Most of the action in the spot is set around a line of horse-drawn carriages with Geena trying to get in one. Problems ensue. The door jams. Actors faint. Clouds come in so the director of photography storms onto the set demanding that the cameras cut. I hope it'll be funny.

The carriages look fine. The thirty extras are already there in the Elizabethan costumes. They look great, even with half of them smoking or on cell phones.

"Did Vilmos sign off on where he wanted these?"

"He's good. He figured we'd be here by ten and the sun'll be behind us from then until two. We'll do lunch at two then go in for the close-ups."

The lead prop guy joins us.

"Morning, sir."

"Hey there."

"Just confirming what you want on the door gag. You want it to really jam, right?"

"Yeah. Better if the actress really struggles with it."

"Copy that. Thanks."

The AD's walkie-talkie crackles. He's got his earwig in, so I don't hear what's being said to him, just his responses.

"Geena's ready. What d'you think?"

"Let's do it."

Steve and I walk back to the parking lot where we've got the motor home scene set up. Geena is escorted over to the set by three wardrobe women. They move around her like ladies-in-waiting, keeping the hems of her voluminous skirts aloft and her veils from catching. Someone's holding an umbrella over her to keep the sun off.

"Someone find the agency and tell them we're about to start shooting."

I introduce Geena to Vilmos. I explain the action: she's at a table, the actor playing the AD approaches, the crane descends. I realize I'm telling two Academy Award winners what to do. And they're listening. When I first started directing, I was twenty-three. The actors and crew members thought I was a production assistant. I overcompensated by acting ridiculously confident. Now I actually know what I'm doing. But, fuck, these two *really* know what they're doing. The thought doesn't go too deep. Better to believe I'm their equal.

I see the agency take their places around the video monitor. I wave to them and walk over to mine.

I think of something and go over to Geena.

"Tom, the AD? You kind of hate him. Be a little annoyed."

"How annoyed?"

"Take three, you're a bitch."

"Got it."

Walking back to my seat, I see thirty crew people standing at film set attention, ready to make the adjustments that happen between takes: move props, adjust clothes, reposition lights and flags. Fifty yards away, I see another thirty guys working on the next set: touching up paint on the carriages, raking the lawns, adjusting lights, moving cables. It's a circus.

As I pass the AD, I say quietly, "Let's shoot."

He calls for a sound roll, a camera roll, slates and yells, "Action." The guy playing the AD ambles into the scene, all officious and smug, Geena's buried in the computer, the camera floats down out of the sky. It works. We do two more takes. Then I have an idea. First shot of the day, might as well break the ice a little. I get out of my chair and walk over to Geena.

"We're good."

"He's very funny, so I can play with him, right?"

"Absolutely. Tell you what: this time, instead of just being a bitch, when he says it's time to go, tell him to go fuck himself."

"Literally? Like actually say, 'Go fuck yourself'? Can you say that on TV?"

"No. But say it anyway. It'll wake the agency and client up. And the AD will give us a very natural reaction of shock and terror. Always good to have in editing."

"Okay. I'm great at telling people to go fuck themselves."

"Good to know."

We're getting along great.

I'm working on an enormous job, surrounded by Hollywood big shots, getting paid a fortune, and having a blast. I'm going from one job to another, people are letting me have my way, and I actually, finally, at long last, have complete confidence in what I'm doing. What could possibly go wrong?

Dawn of Man.

ONE CHRISTMAS, MY FOLKS BOUGHT MY YOUNGER BROTHER AND ME A super 8mm movie camera. Working it didn't take a lot of skill. You loaded a film cartridge into the back, pointed the lens at what you wanted to shoot, and pulled a trigger. The cartridge let you shoot three minutes of film. When it was used up, you sent it off to Kodak. They mailed back the developed film a week later. I was always frothing at the mouth to see "the movie" I'd made. Once, I shot three minutes of our dog staring into the lens. Another time, it was my little brother waving at me then getting bored and leaving to do something else. Great stuff.

After a couple of cartridges, I figured out that, if I wanted to make something that looked like an actual movie, I'd have to come up with some kind of story and add specific kinds of shots. Like close-ups and cutaways. I didn't know what those were called, but, from watching television shows and comparing them to my shitty films, I figured out what they did.

I started making three-minute masterpieces about psychotically violent ten-year-olds settling scores. I'd put together a cast of six or seven of my pals. The sequence of shots was pretty simple. Cast stands around looking nonchalant. Then a bad person shows up and does something threatening. This was confirmed by the cast looking into the camera and imitating Munch's *The Scream.* Then there's an explosion. Bodies fly through the air. They land in such a way that their lifeless forms spell out T-H-E E-N-D. Amazing I didn't already have a three-picture deal at Fox.

I set a lot of my films at John's Pizzeria. I was a very good customer, so John let me use the place. An essential member of the cast was some-one's older brother who had a driver's license. I'd tell him he could play the bad guy if he brought his folks' car. All he had to do was pull up in front of the pizzeria, get out of the car, and look menacing. That sounds simple but can be hard for a self-conscious sixteen-year-old boy with eruptive skin issues. I had props to help with the threatening part: fake sticks of dynamite I'd laid in for some Halloween event. I put them in the trunk of the kid's car. All he had to do was pull them out and wave them around and you knew he was up to no fucking good.

I get the first minute of the movie done pretty quick. Troupe of inno-cents milling around. Bad guy pulls up. Pops trunk, reveals dynamite. Troupe does the Munch faces. Now it's time for the explosion.

I had an M-80 left over from July 4th. Who didn't? I needed to make this explosion shot look big. Like it could kill seven or eight kids. My way of solving this was to try to make the M-80 itself look big. Using my limited understanding of optics, I figured I'd put it close to the lens. Really close. So I lay down on the parking lot asphalt, put the M-80 a foot in front of me, wedged it in place with some pebbles and sand, then placed the camera, and therefore my face because I was looking through the viewfinder, right over the thing and lit the fuse. Platinum-level dumb. Which was obvious to everyone but me. The cast ran for cover, hiding behind cars or inside the pizzeria. I was out there on my stomach inches away from an explosive like some midget reenacting a defusal sequence in *The Hurt Locker.* Anyway, the thing exploded, and I got the shot. The only side effect was mild deafness in my left ear for the rest of my life.

Then I did the shots where the bodies go flying. The troupe launched themselves through the air sideways, grabbing their stomachs to hold in their severed guts. They somersaulted, ass-over-teakettle, and crumpled as if their legs had been blown off. They keeled over backwards like they'd been shot through the heart. They wound up all clumped together, a pile of dead, smirking ten-year-olds. The bad guy looked on, happy he'd killed them all. Then some quick shots of the bodies spelling out "T" and "H" and all the rest. Like a live-action *Looney Tunes* signoff, but with corpses.

I found that I could keep the kids in my little troupe involved in the movie for as long as I kept coming up with new ideas and shouting out commands. If the momentum slowed, they'd space out or just go into John's and order a slice. I could never convince anyone who was in the middle of a slice to come back outside and rejoin the death reenactment scenes. So I learned to keep things moving. Talking, giving orders, explaining, telling jokes, giving compliments, getting mad, pretending that I knew how the camera worked, pretending that I knew how to make a movie. Once in a while, someone would just walk away and disappear. We were ten-year-olds. I'd just keep my focus on whoever was left. Moving fast solves a lot of things. Mainly people don't get bored. Twelve years later, when I started making real films, I learned boredom on the set is a director's biggest enemy. I didn't let it happen when I was ten, and I still try to not let it happen today.

Everyone had a couple of laughs watching the films when they came back from Kodak. They could sit through two, maybe three, viewings. Actually, it was only my parents who could endure three viewings. They were trying to encourage any activity where I didn't swear. I could sit through them fifty times. It was proof that I could create something. From nothing. Think up some idea, corral my friends into playing along, see the results. That was a big deal for a ten-year-old. That made me feel good. And it must have been a giant distraction because, as I started to get into this stuff, my grades started to go down. By eighth grade, between sports, band practice, the movie camera, and girls appearing on the horizon, whatever academic promise I'd shown started to fade. I lost interest. I went from the honor roll to Bs and Cs.

I was also starting to get a glimmer of what kids five years older were doing. They were reading things like *The Prophet*, *Slaughterhouse-Five*, and *Naked Lunch*. They were listening to Hendrix and The Who. They were going to concerts in the city at the Fillmore. It all sounded way more exciting than Latin II homework. I didn't fail. I just did a lot less schoolwork and spent a lot more time doing what interested me. What interested me looked to my parents like extracurricular activities. To me, they looked like a way of life.

Bad Influence.

MY MOTHER'S COUSIN MARRIED A PHOTOGRAPHER NAMED JOEL BRODSKY. He and his wife, Val, lived in New York City with their three daughters. They'd come out to our house in Connecticut every year for Thanksgiving. Joel was the coolest almost-relative I had. And he was also the only one who did something different than going to an office. I was fascinated by how a guy could support a wife and three kids by taking pictures.

I was also fascinated by how my second cousin, Val, had moved from Grosse Point, Michigan, to New York City right out of college, started working as a fashion stylist, and married a Jewish photographer from Brooklyn. While I had Jewish friends, my world was made up of people who married people from their town or prep school or college. It was pretty narrow. Joel was a breath of fresh air. And he was willing to answer any and all questions I had about what he did. I had no questions for any of my parents' friends about what they did.

When I was fifteen, I called Joel and asked if he'd let me work in his studio during my summer vacation. I'd do anything for free was the basis of my pitch. He said yes. My parents were uneasy about the whole thing.

For good reason. They didn't like the idea of my taking the train to the city every day by myself.

I loved it. I'd be dressed in jeans, a T-shirt, and cowboy boots and sit surrounded by men in gray flannel suits. I'd grab a window seat, read the paper, and smoke. Everyone smoked. I felt very grown up. When we got to Grand Central, I'd run downstairs, hop on the 6 train, get off at 28th Street, and walk two blocks west to the Albans Hotel. It was a dump. Basically, an SRO hotel. The tenants were mostly old guys who flopped there until they died of cirrhosis or TB. There were also a lot of prostitutes. I'd take the elevator to the tenth floor, nod hello to whichever hooker was standing there smoking, then climb a flight of stairs to Joel's studio. You opened the door and walked into a big, open space with an entire wall of north-facing windows. There were darkrooms on the left, makeup and dressing rooms down the hall, and a kitchen.

Joel didn't give a shit what he was hired to shoot, as long as he was getting paid. He worked for Revlon and Estée Lauder. He shot catalogues. He did annual reports. He also worked for record labels. That was the fun stuff. A lot of covers he shot became seminal art of the '60s and '70s. Albums for The Doors, Tom Waits, The Stooges, Aretha Franklin, MC5, The Ohio Players.

I was a useless but enthusiastic intern, relegated to holding Hasselblad film magazines until Joel asked for a new one and phoning in orders to the corner coffee shop. When I was given a more technical task, like holding a fill card beneath a model's face, I often got distracted. Once, because a model claimed, falsely, I was looking up her skirt. Another time, because another model claimed, also falsely, I was looking down her shirt. Honestly, I was too cowed by these famous girls to do anything other than look at my shoes. Most of the musicians were pretty laid back. But a few were complete psychos. Jim Morrison would show up drunk. Phil Ochs didn't want to hold a guitar. Aretha Franklin obsessed about what color fur coat she'd wear. I loved all of it.

One thing I saw over and over that summer really stuck with me: Joel was never in awe of any of these people. The musicians, the models, the clients.

He did his job and didn't particularly care about developing relationships with any of them. The only thing he really cared about was sports. If he'd had to take a picture of Roger Maris, he would have shit himself. But, if Jim Morrison was sitting in front of him, which he was on more than one occasion, Joel just treated him like a mook in a turtleneck whom the art director was hoping they could make look like a hot gay Jesus.

Some of these famous folks were assholes. But, when they worked with Joel, this sort of awkward Jewish guy from Brooklyn with a quick but slightly too loud laugh, who took great pictures and wasn't interested in being friends with them or hitting them up for tickets, they pretty much behaved themselves. A number of them would even request that Joel always shoot their covers.

At the end of this summer job, I had an epiphany. You could make a living doing something fun. A shaky part of the epiphany was that it was based on seeing only one guy do it.

But what a fucking amazing world this was. You didn't sit at a desk in a cubicle in an office building. You didn't wear a tie. You smoked and swore and told jokes. There were tons of girls and black people and gay guys around. A normal day had you dealing with Spanish-speaking coffee shop delivery guys, hookers, Korean fabric merchants, stylists, record company A&R guys, famous and not-so-famous rock musicians, drug dealers delivering to those musicians, and models who were as self-involved and uninteresting as people say. There was planning and organization and schedules but very little was written down, you never went to a meeting, and really good music played all day on the huge stereo system.

I was interested in making movies, not taking pictures. But director and photographer struck me as being similar jobs. You came up with ideas, got a crew together, did some casting, made decisions, solved problems, and created things. Okay, so directing movies in front of John's Pizzeria wasn't quite comparable to telling Jim Morrison which way to turn his head, but it kind of was.

And it looked like you got paid to do something that no one in their right mind would describe as work. I was in.

Tom Waits.

JOEL IS SHOOTING THE COVER FOR A NEW TOM WAITS ALBUM, *SMALL Change*. In keeping with Waits's persona as a street poet, the label wants him photographed in a stripper's dressing room. Apparently, real strippers' dressing rooms didn't look sufficiently sleazy, so we're at the Truck and Warehouse Theater, a tiny off-off-Broadway place in the East Village.

The theater's running a show called *Women Behind Bars*. It's the first time Divine, the Baltimore transvestite famous for eating dog turds in John Waters's movies, has acted on stage. We're using his/her dressing table. The cold cream containers, the lipstick tubes, the wigs, the shoes, the falsies are all tremendous. Like something an enormously overweight clown would wear. It should be a little titillating to be around all this women's underwear. But it turns out XXL Maidenform brassieres hanging from hooks next to cheap, horse-hair wigs don't have the same effect as scanning the pictures in *Penthouse*.

Joel first got big doing portraits of musicians like Aretha Franklin, Iggy Pop, Isaac Hayes, and Albert King. He's just done The Doors' cover for *Strange Days*. Acrobats, a strongman, street musicians, a midget, and a juggling mime pose in a mews on East 38th Street. So now the labels want the covers to tell stories. Which is why we're backstage at the Truck and Warehouse. To tell the story of a street poet sitting at an obese transvestite's makeup table.

The room is tiny. The dressing tables have mirrors bolted on them, framed with small, frosted bulbs. The table surfaces are littered with personal crap like postcards, photos, toys, and candles. Joel thinks it all looks great and leaves everything alone. The stripper shows up. A brunette from Queens. Joel has a brief conversation with her, they discuss the outfits she's brought along, and he decides she'll wear pasties and a thong. It's a bit disconcerting to listen to my sort-of uncle having a totally mundane conversation with what I'm sure is a prostitute about pasties.

Waits hasn't shown up yet, so Joel has me sit in for him. I perch on the stool at Divine's dressing table. I try my best not to overtly ogle the pretty-much-naked woman visible behind me in the makeup mirror.

Waits arrives. There's no entourage, just him and a friend. Waits is pretty much as advertised. His hair is filthy. His clothes are filthy. There are stains on his shirt and trousers. His shoes barely have soles. He actually smells pretty funky. He smokes continuously. The person from the record label tries speaking to him, but he's not interested in replying. Joel explains the shot to him, and Waits shuffles over and sits at the makeup table. Joel starts shooting.

Waits doesn't do much. He sips from a pint bottle of cheap whiskey. He lights a Chesterfield nonfilter. He leans his forehead into his greasy palm, looking like he's suffering a migraine. He throws his feet up on the table. He lights another Chesterfield. He does not interact with the girl. He's in his own head.

The dressing room is really starting to smell rank. This guy must take his art super seriously. Which somehow involves not showering or, at a minimum, not using soap when he does.

When we're done, Waits picks up his pocket-sized pint of Four Roses, does a little bow to everyone and no one, and walks out into the East Village afternoon. Because I'm fifteen and a little unclear on the economics of the music business, I think it's pretty cool that a guy who's got to be making millions of dollars is walking around like a bum, smelling like shit, pretty much drunk on a Tuesday afternoon. That said, the part I want is the million dollars and strolling around on a Tuesday afternoon. The b.o. and Four Roses I can do without.

I loved working for Joel—which drove my parents crazy because they had some fantasy I should be a lawyer. Apparently, my ability to mouth off like an arrogant putz had them convinced I'd be a great litigator. And lots of my relatives were lawyers, so, using a sketchy understanding of WASP genetics, they just assumed I'd go in that direction. I didn't.

Don't Do It.

I WENT TO FILM SCHOOL AT BOSTON UNIVERSITY. I LIVED IN A DUMP ON the backside of Beacon Hill. If you went out the front door of my building and tripped, you'd roll down Grove Street into the emergency room at Mass General. My place had two rooms. A bedroom with my waterbed taking up every square inch and a kitchen/living room/bathroom where I ate, showered, and worked. My desk was against the wall. It was a one-by-eight piece of lumber balanced between a pile of milk crates and the edge of the tub. The desk held a typewriter and a super 8mm film editing setup. The editing equipment was tiny. Two plastic reels to hold the film and a sprocket-geared device with a lens to view the film. A girl I'd gotten up to my place and was trying to impress asked me if Fisher-Price made it for ages two to four.

In the early '70s, if you wanted to learn how to make movies, you didn't have many options: NYU, USC, UCLA, and BU. There were other programs, but you'd only learn film history or how to write film criticism. I didn't want to move to Los Angeles, so I applied to NYU and BU.

I'd spent my first two years in college at the University of Colorado in Boulder. Taking English classes about pretentious books I claimed to understand like Joyce's *Ulysses* and Pynchon's *V*, poli-sci courses on the history of war, working in a Headstart classroom in a Chicano neighborhood, and playing in a band. Compared to high school, Boulder was easy. So easy I'd write my friends' English papers for them to give me something to do. By the end of sophomore year, all of it seemed stupid. Most of my friends had no idea what they were doing. Boulder was beautiful but pointless. I was living with a girlfriend who would throw plates at me when she got mad. Amazing, considering she didn't get high. I wasn't getting high either. But everyone else in Boulder was. I decided to leave Colorado, get a job somewhere, save some money, then go to Europe on whatever I'd been able to bank and try to figure out where to go back to school. The plate-throwing girlfriend would stop throwing plates and come along. When our summer jobs ended, we flew to Munich. We lasted until a giant plate-throwing episode in the tiny coastal town of Nerja, Spain, five months later. She went back to the States. I stayed a few more months then went home with the plan for film school. I'd gotten into both NYU and BU, so I went to visit both. At NYU, all the equipment was reserved for juniors and seniors and they still had to wait months to use the cameras and editing tables. At BU, there were unused cameras sitting in closets and workspaces full of Steenbeck editing tables with no one using them. BU was the place for me.

The film department was part of the School of Public Communication. About fifty of us were in the film department. Another fifty wanted to learn about journalism. Some were only interested in radio, like my classmate, Howard Stern. The faculty wasn't great about teaching us the actual technical skills required to use cameras and editing tables. But it didn't matter. Learning by doing is the only way to learn this stuff. Books are of no help whatsoever. Using a camera or an editing deck is like playing a musical instrument. You do it over and over and over and, eventually, you get the hang of it.

I was a quicker study than a lot of my classmates. Maybe all the little super 8 films I'd made had helped. My classmates all wanted me to help shoot their films or be involved in post-production. The more I did, the more I learned.

The spring of my junior year, I applied for an internship at a local TV station, working as a sort of a jack-of-all-trades on their daily newscast. Channel 56, WLVI, was a really low-rent Kaiser Broadcasting station. They ran old movies and syndicated game shows. About the only original programming they had was this half-hour late-morning news show that they had to air in order to keep their license. It had one reporter who wrote all her own stories and did the newscast at eleven thirty in the morning. When I showed up, she happily shoved most of the writing, editing, and guest booking into my lap. I'd drive to work at 4:00 a.m., fly through the *Herald*, the *Globe*, the *Times*, the *Journal*, and the *Courant*, clip whatever was interesting, and manually cut and paste ten minutes of stories together for her. At one point, she went on vacation and told me I would anchor the show for three days. I went to a barbershop and asked the guy to make me look like a newscaster. The haircut he gave me was so shitty my girlfriend dumped me. I put on the suit I graduated from high school in and wrote and read the news for three days. Why station management allowed this to happen is a mystery. Maybe because they knew no one watched the show, so it didn't matter who was doing the news. Anyway, when my boss returned, I was full of beans. I asked if I could do a short documentary. Since this would also help Kaiser satisfy their license requirements, she said yes. I took the old, wizened union cameraman out with me and did a story about economic inequality on Beacon Hill. I interviewed this nice rich couple my ex-girlfriend babysat for and the old Italian couple who ran the deli across from my apartment. The cameraman/editor somehow put it together into a coherent ten-minute film.

I shot two friends' senior films and then directed my own about an angry breakup between a boy and a girl who both smoked a lot. But, after the experience at the TV station, I started thinking I wanted to make documentaries. Change the world. Maybe rule it if things really worked out.

$$O \quad O \quad O$$

In 1975, there are four documentary gods: D.A. Pennebaker, the Maysles brothers, Michael Apted, and Frederick Wiseman. I think Wiseman's the best. He goes into an institution, like a high school or a police station, and films what happens. Then he constructs a story in editing. There's no narration explaining things. There's just what is. And it's riveting. He's great. And he lives in Boston. And his number's in the White Pages. So, today, I'm going to call him.

I picture Wiseman in some cool office over in Cambridge. Probably a floor or two in a townhouse. High ceilings. Fireplaces. Editing tables in one room. Young assistants doing research. Him sitting at a big old desk thinking about shit. Being paged to come to the editing suite and take a look at a new sequence. Probably not entirely accurate, but, no question in my mind, it's close. He's got a lot going on, running a big show.

I slide the ripped, red, plastic-upholstered kitchen chair I found on the street twelve inches over to my one-by-eight desk, pick up the phone, and dial. I'm sure I'll have to deal with a receptionist who'll officiously protect Wiseman and pretend to take down my name and number. I may have to call more than once. I'm ready for that.

A woman answers. Yup. She's officious. I ask to speak with Mr. Wiseman, please.

"Who's calling?"

"Bruce Van Dusen." I think my inflection was more question mark than period.

"Hold on."

I wonder how far she has to walk through the townhouse to find him be…

"Hello?" A man's voice.

Jesus Christ. Wiseman. What the fuck.

"Mr. Wiseman?"

"Yeah."

"My name is Bruce Van Dusen."

"Okay."

A better-prepared person would assume the party they're calling might answer the goddam phone. Said better-prepared person therefore wouldn't have to scramble to piece together a coherent sentence.

"I'm graduating in two weeks."

"From college?"

"Yeah. BU."

"Okay."

"And I'm moving to New York."

"Great. Did you call to tell me that?"

"No. Thing is, the reason for my call, I'm moving there because I want to work in documentaries. And I thought you might be able to give me some advice. That's why I'm calling."

I'm expecting him to say, *Listen, kid. I'm busy. Move to New York, good luck, have a nice day.* Instead, Wiseman actually gives me some practical advice.

"You ever made a documentary?"

"Kind of. One. For the television station I've been working at."

"Okay. So they paid for it, right?"

"Yup."

"That'll never happen again."

"What d'you mean?"

"No one will ever again just hand you money to make a film. When you want to make a documentary, you'll have to go out and convince someone to give you the money to make it. Money you'll need to buy film and pay the crew and the editor and the lab. Making a film costs a lot of money."

This must be where he shares his secret formula about fundraising with me.

"Okay. How do you get the money?"

31

"It's complicated. Most important thing I can tell you is I spend a lot more time raising money than I do making films. I spend years groveling for money. Literally. It's no fun."

"But you're so well known, you must have people, backers who..."

"Wrong. Every time I make a film, I have to start from scratch. It's hard. And it never gets any easier, no matter how many times I do it."

"I see."

"Anything else you want to know?"

"Um, no, I don't think so. You've been really helpful."

More like grimly pragmatic.

"This business is not that fun. I hope you have a lot of determination. You'll need it."

I hang up and slump over my one-by-eight, milk-crates-and-bathtub desk. I'm now seeing my idol differently. Like that townhouse is not a townhouse. Instead, he's in a shitty little kitchen just like mine, and the receptionist is an unpaid intern sitting at the table right across from him, smoking a Marlboro and reading the *Boston Phoenix*, and Wiseman's looking at a pile of unpaid invoices, trying to figure out whom he can call today to scrape up some money to finish the film he's working on.

Thank God Frederick Wiseman took my stupid phone call. Someone finally told me the dirty little secret of filmmaking: It's hard to find someone to pay you to run film through a camera. Really hard. And even harder to find someone to tell you that it's almost a fool's errand to think you can make a living in the film business. It never came up once in any of the classes I took. If I'd been a little smarter, I would have realized that the reason all these so-called filmmakers were standing in front of me teaching was that they weren't on a set somewhere getting paid to make a film. But that would require a pretty brutal level of honesty. The teachers would have to tell you that you're going to pay twenty grand a year to go to film school and the chances that you will ever make a nickel in the film business are pretty much zero. No one in their right mind would take that deal.

Special Skills.

I FINISHED SCHOOL A SEMESTER EARLY IN DECEMBER 1975. NO ONE ELSE IN my class was done. This had its benefits. When I was working on my student film, the black-and-white opus about a guy and girl who smoked a lot, I was six months ahead of everyone, so I had a lot of the equipment to myself. And access to equipment basically determines your happiness in film school.

I found a guy who was finishing his master's midyear who also wanted to move to New York. We decided to live together. Jeff had gone to NYU undergrad as a film major and was dead set on us moving back to his old stomping grounds in the Village. I was partial to no neighborhood other than a cheap one. After a three-day apartment-hunting whirlwind all over the city, we found a place on East 74th Street. He thought the neighborhood sucked. Which it did. But the apartment was big, had two bedrooms, a living room, a separate kitchen, and a little balcony overlooking a garden of sick trees. And it was cheap.

We drove down from Boston in a U-Haul. I thought it was odd that Jeff was bringing large, plastic plants. And I found it challenging that he played Dylan cassettes on a small, battery-operated player for the entire six-hour drive to New York. Clearly, it was the soundtrack of his life. How the plants fit into the picture, I didn't know.

We immediately started looking for jobs. I discovered *The Yellow Book*, a trade publication that listed every film production, equipment, and editing company, their address, and phone number. It was done alphabetically, so I spent a day re-sorting it by address, so I could be efficient and walk east to west, north to south to every company listed. I walked into places unannounced, asked to see someone, anyone, and prayed somebody would give me five minutes of their time. I'd tell my story, try to convince them to look at my 16mm film of the bad breakup, and leave a résumé.

I got nowhere. I knew no one in the industry. I had no contacts. There was no one I could turn to for advice. I had one hundred and seventy-five dollars in the bank. My half of the rent was a hundred fifty bucks. After three weeks, I hadn't had one offer. I needed work.

One night, Jeff walked in the door with a little smile on his face and announced he'd gotten a job. He bopped triumphantly over to the stereo and put on a Dylan record. Of course. I'd asked that we have Dylan breaks, but it was no use. It was driving me insane. As "Highway 61 Revisited" blared, he told me he'd been hired by a company that made television commercials to drive a truck around Manhattan and pick up props. Jeff was a really quiet, taciturn guy. Like, truly boring and enormously uncharismatic. I couldn't believe he'd gotten a job before me.

The next morning, a little after 9:00, I was sitting at the kitchen table eating a bowl of cereal, getting ready to head out on my job search, when the phone rang. Jeff.

"Do you know how to drive a stick shift?"

Of course I do. I'm a guy.

"Yeah. Why?"

"I don't. This truck has a stick shift. Can you come down here and take over?"

I was employed.

One guy with a master's. One with a bachelor's. Necessary job skill for first gig: mastery of a clutch.

The lessons just kept on coming. When I got to the garage, the attendant wouldn't let me take the truck because the production company was three months behind on their bill. So my first call to someone called a production manager involved explaining that I'd replaced my roommate who, I lied, had gotten sick and, oh yeah, there was some sort of money issue at the garage. The production manager had me put the garage guy on the line. They worked the bill out. The garage guy handed the phone back, and the production manager told me to drive to the office so he could give me a list of pickups.

I drove the van up to their office on East 57th Street. It was in a six-story office building across from Tiffany. Big, busy place. Lots of people running around. Behind the offices in front, there was a sound stage where a large set was being constructed. I was sent to the production manager's office. He tossed me a sheet of paper with a list of stores and addresses. There were about ten on the list.

"Make sense?"

"Yeah. Where's Columbus Avenue?"

If, a decade later, I'd been asked that question by someone whom I'd just hired to drive around Manhattan, I'd have quickly found something else for that person to do. But this guy just looked at me like I was stupid, told me where Columbus was, and sent me on my way.

I got the pickups done. When I returned to the office, I snuck into the sound stage to see what was happening. There were at least thirty people at work. A kitchen and a dining room had been built. It was beautifully done. Furniture was being unwrapped and placed in the rooms. Guys in jeans and T-shirts were hanging lights from the overhead grid. Off to one side, an enormous Mitchell camera on a Moviola dolly was pointed at a curved piece of white paper. Seven guys milled around the dolly. I walked closer. I noticed a box of Minute Rice on the white paper. What I was watching was a director, a director of photography, an assistant cameraman, an assistant director, and a couple of gaffers and grips doing a product shot. That's the scene at the end of a commercial where they show the product and an announcer says something catchy. Who knew it took seven guys to do that?

I asked the production manager if he needed me the next day and he said no. I was crushed. I'd rallied from a bad start and gotten all the pick-ups done right and fast. I really needed another fifty bucks. And I wanted to see how a commercial was made. I had no idea how these thirty-second films came together. Being on the set for this few hours revealed that it was way more complicated, expensive, and technical than I'd ever imagined. Because film school is all about making you believe you're some kind of fucking artist, this segment of the business had never even been mentioned. Even though I'd learn it's one of the best ways to see how films are made. Probably a sign of how out of the loop my teachers were. They didn't seem to have a clue about any part of the film business where you got paid, and they certainly had no fucking clue about commercials. The production manager told me to keep in touch. I could tell he didn't mean it.

As I was leaving, I walked by the director's office. He was on the phone, saying something about a problem he was having with the engine of his Maserati. The red one, not the silver one.

I didn't give a shit about cars. I didn't know shit about commercials. I totally gave a shit about feeding myself and having a roof over my head. And it sounded like directing commercials was a really good way to make that happen.

Honor Among Thieves.

AFTER THE MINUTE RICE COMMERCIAL, MY JOB PROSPECTS DIDN'T improve. So I kept walking the streets, dropping into production companies unannounced, trying to show somebody my film. Once in a while, someone would be kind enough to meet with me. I wasn't a particularly good interview. I was looking for the lowest job on the totem pole, production assistant, but I'd always feel compelled to tell whoever was interviewing me that, actually, I was a director. Already? Yeah. I've made films. Want to see one? Bad interview.

One day, I was in an elevator on West 44th Street. Two women behind me were talking about getting someone to run a video camera and manage a casting session. I turned around and, without even bothering to introduce myself, said I could do that. For some reason, they didn't think I was a lunatic. We got off on their floor, had a quick conversation about what was required, and they hired me. It probably helped that I didn't try to show them my film.

I had four days of work. This month's rent was covered.

I managed to run the sessions efficiently, keep accurate logs, and not erase the tapes. The best young woman who auditioned was an unknown who I thought was great. I made a note that the client should cast her. Her name was Pam Dawber. Two years later, she would be cast as Mindy to Robin William's Mork.

During the four days I was there, I had a couple of conversations with the woman who owned the place. At the end of the casting job, she offered me a position as her assistant. Real money. Somehow, I knew this wouldn't be a good move. I told her I was grateful for the offer, but I wanted to be a director, and this didn't seem to be the right path. Riding the subway home that night, I didn't feel so great.

As my drive-by résumé drops continued, one took me to the top floor of a building on West 45th Street. Five companies were jammed into a rabbit warren of little offices. They were all involved somehow in film and music. The man who had the lease and sublet space to everyone else was a Dutch guy who was basically a criminal. He ran various scams, all of which were film-related, which, I guess, made him think it was necessary for him to wear a safari jacket to work every day. In scam one, he took pictures of rich people's estates from a single-engine Cessna he rented by the hour. He'd make prints then go to the rich people's houses and try to sell them the pictures. In scam two, he did screen tests for naïve, young actresses and put the moves on them. They paid him for this harassment. During my job interview, he excitedly described all these endeavors, offering them as proof of his genius. At scamming, I guess. One of the guys he rented space to was a down-on-his-luck music manager. His big, actually only, moment in the sun had been an appearance as a singer on *American Bandstand* when he was fifteen. Once in a while, he'd wear the outfit he'd worn on the show to work. He didn't fit in it anymore, so it looked ridiculous. But you had to say something about the get-up and that would get you sucked into ten minutes of *Bandstand* stories. In the last room down the hall was a guy named Paul. He did slide shows, corporate videos, and radio spots. It wasn't much of a business. Its real reason for being seemed to be keeping him out of the clutches of his family, who wanted him to join their kosher food company.

I went through my pitch, showed him my film, underlining the fact that I was already a director. He had an idea. Why didn't I join him as a director with the proviso that I'd also be my own sales representative? In the normal world, directors had sales reps who acted as their agents. But Paul wanted me to sell myself. Which is kind of what I'm learning is the day-to-day reality of anyone trying to make it in the film business. And he'd pay me a hundred bucks a week.

Done.

The office was one room with a desk. He sat on one side of it, and I sat on the other. I used *The Yellow Book* again because it listed all the ad agencies in New York and who the producers were. I started making phone calls. Once in a while, I'd get through to a producer or an assistant and try to make an appointment to screen a reel. I was completely naïve. I actually believed something would come of my efforts. I got up every morning, took the 6 train to Grand Central, walked west for three blocks, and spent the day cold calling people I didn't know. I even bought a safari jacket, though I didn't wear it that often.

I was positive something good would happen. How could it not? I had unlimited energy, a totally inflated vision about my skill set, a very crude picture of how sales reps sold directors' work, and a lonely boss who bought me lunch every day. I was certain that, if I kept showing up, the stars were going to align. I was less certain about keeping the safari jacket.

Something Good Did Not Happen.

I WENT TO THE TINY LITTLE OFFICE ON 45TH STREET EVERY DAY. I couldn't get us any work. But my boss wasn't panicked. He was just glad to have someone to talk to. My real function, I came to understand, was helping him rationalize why he wasn't joining the family business. And, for a hundred dollars a week, I was glad to rationalize the shit out of it with him.

Early in the summer of 1976, I got a call from my friend, Billy Jones. During my freshman year in Boulder, we'd been in a band together. We weren't terrible. We rehearsed a lot, played intermittent gigs, and took it seriously. But not seriously enough for Billy. He was dead set on being a working musician. When two guys from his old band in Tampa asked him to come back there and join them, he was ready. He asked me to go with him. The new band was slated to have three guitar players. I'd be the third. This was difficult to process for a couple of reasons. First, I was a freshman in college. Second, it would mean dropping out of school and moving to Tampa with no backup plan. And, third, I wasn't a good enough guitar player. Billy was. I'd watch the guitar players I admired and realize, instantly and viscerally, I didn't have it. So I said no. In fact, the afternoon before he left, I had Billy drive me to Denver, so I could sell my amp at a pawnshop. I was done with music.

○ ○ ○

Four years later, I'm going to a shitty little office trying to sell my services as a director. Of anything. Billy is coming to New York with his band, The Outlaws. They're opening for The Who at Giants Stadium.

I meet Billy at the Holiday Inn on West 57th Street. Certainly not the Ritz, which makes me feel somewhat less jealous. When, definitely not meaning it, I suggest he come over for dinner, he accepts immediately and asks if he could bring his partner, Huey. So much for the fancy expense account meal I'd been counting on. That night, Billy, Huey, and I are sitting around the card table in my third-floor walk-up, eating weird-ly-colored Nicaraguan lobster tails I splurged on. I learn a lot. Arista, their record label, gives them each an allowance of a hundred bucks a week. Shit, that's what I make. The band owes Arista something like two hundred grand, plus interest, for the costs of making the first album. Even with a hit song that summer, they're making shit off record sales because Arista deducts what they're owed first. And, even with staying in Holiday Inns and cadging meals off guys like me, touring isn't gener-ating much money, so they've barely made a dent in paying Arista back. It's so bad, Billy's wife is selling weed back home to pay their rent. This is hugely enlightening. When Billy and Huey leave that night, I'm not so depressed about the decision I made to be a director. Until the next day.

I meet them at 4:00 p.m. at the Holiday Inn. We climb into a black stretch limo. They're all dressed up in western shirts and cowboy hats. That's the band's look. After a half-hour drive, we pull into a cor-doned-off parking area at Giants Stadium. We go backstage. Little Feat is in one dressing room. Lowell George is behind those doors. Fuck. The Who is in the other dressing room. Pete Townshend is in that room. Fuck again. This is seriously depressing. I try to make myself feel better by doing a mental spreadsheet of the band's precarious financial situation. But my gloom doesn't lift. An hour or so later, I walk with them through the bowels of the stadium, and then I stop in the wings as they hustle out on stage and rip into their hit single. The crowd goes crazy.

I think I made the wrong call.

Off and Stumbling.

BEING THE RECEPTIONIST/SALESMAN/DIRECTOR/CERTIFIED SOCIAL WORKER at this barely functioning production company sucks. The Crazy Eddie thing has happened, and I've brought in a few other jobs, but nothing's really changing. I feel stuck, and stuck inside a shithouse, so I ask my boss for a raise.

"Can't afford it."

I rephrase the question.

"We've done three jobs. Jobs I brought in. I directed those jobs. I edited those jobs. I think I'm worth more than a hundred a week."

"Can't do it. Maybe next year."

My thought process actually goes through a list of adjectives involving "fairness" and "merit." But I'm so angry, I just put on my jacket and walk out of the office.

On the subway home, I decide *fuck it, I'll open my own company*. I don't know how to do that, but the guy I was working for was so stupid, I'm sure I'll be able to figure it out. I get home, call the phone company to order call waiting, then call my boss. He's the receptionist now.

"Have you calmed down?"

"Completely. Mail me my last check."

"C'mon."

"I quit."

Three months later, he closes the company and goes to work for his father selling kosher chickens. The two hundred bucks I have in my checking account won't last that long.

Self-Promotion.

I HAD NO IDEA HOW TO RUN A COMPANY. BUT OPENING ONE WAS A SNAP. You go to a lawyer, pay him a few hundred bucks, and sign a lot of papers. Two weeks later, you get a fancy three-ring binder with lots of documents and stock certificates and a metal stamping contraption that lets you emboss your corporate seal on shit. And then you go to a bank, show them the incorporation statement, and open an account. You're in business.

"In business" didn't mean I *had* any business. I had me. I answered my phone, "Van Dusen Films." My friends, who were the only ones calling for a long time, thought that was hilarious.

I understood the basics of looking for work. Cold call agency producers and try to set up a screening of my reel. Which wasn't much to look at. It was now my student film, the spot I'd made for Crazy Eddie, and another one I'd done for a mattress retailer. Almost a joke. But it was a definite conversation starter. How did you make this? And, always, always, they'd ask, "How much did you make it for?" Like an idiot, I'd tell them the real numbers. Which were so low that the producers were fascinated. This taught me something.

If low prices were so important to them, maybe that was my way in. No one was quoting prices as low as mine. If someone asked a production company executive how much to do a spot, he'd scribble a six-figure number on the back of an envelope. I'd be happy scribbling five. Or four.

If I got a screening a week, that was great. Often, I'd spend the whole day on the phone and reach no one. I wasn't a director. I was a salesperson. Forty years later, I think it's the best lesson I ever learned about business. That I always needed to rely on myself to hustle up work. No one else was ever going to be as concerned about me as I was.

The other thing I learned during the first years of being on my own was about advertising. Not about directing ads. But about advertising myself. There were a number of trade publications that focused on the commercial industry. The biggest was *Backstage*. It came out weekly and was usually forty to fifty pages thick. Filled with news, PR pieces, and ads taken out by production companies touting what they were doing. The awards they won. The big campaigns they'd just shot. The new director signings. A quarter-page ad conveyed little company. A half page, sort of a big company. Full-page ads, especially a series of full-page ads that appeared week after week, meant the company was a big deal. Established. Financially solid. And in demand. All the things I wasn't. But, if I started running full-page ads, then maybe people would think I was. When I called the ad manager at *Backstage* to see what this would cost, he quoted me some outlandish number to run an ad once. I asked what happened if I ran four ads. Ten ads? Fifteen ads? The price per ad dropped. A lot. Being the glass is half-full/dumb guy I am, I agreed to buy twelve—one a month for a year. I only had enough money in the bank to buy three ads, even at the heavily discounted rate. But I was sure as shit that I'd get some work if these fuckers ran, so I'd be able to pay for the next nine from future earnings. You can diagnose this as confidence. I'd go for naïve. Or nuts.

I hadn't shot anything worth publicizing. I hadn't won any awards. And I didn't have a stable of famous directors. So I made the ads all about me.

The first ad was a picture of me with a noose around my neck. The headline was, "Try and ignore me." The second was me handing out flyers in a seedy section of Times Square with the headline, "Check it out." This was the phrase uttered by nickel bag dealers and pimps to get your attention. Classy but real. The third one was me on a skateboard holding a storyboard as I zoomed past the lens. "Great with boards." I negotiated that the ads would run somewhere in the first six pages of the issue and on the right-hand side, which someone had told me was important.

Let's just say the phone didn't ring off the hook. In fact, the only direct response I got was a piece of hate mail criticizing the grammar in the first ad. Apparently, I should have written "try to ignore" instead of "try and…."

But I noticed that more people started taking my calls. More people started seeing me. And, maybe because I got more polished in my sales pitch or maybe because of the ads or maybe because of both, I started bidding on jobs inside big agencies. I looked legit. I sounded legit. I mean, fuck, here's his ad in the trade. A full-page ad for God's sake. Bid the guy.

No one had any idea that the company was just me. That the company was a Crate and Barrel desk that doubled as my dining table in my one-bedroom apartment. That my phone didn't have multiple lines, only call waiting. No one had a clue that I was doing it all with mirrors. But I was doing it.

Polishing Turds.

I TAKE THE 6 TRAIN TO ASTOR PLACE. IT'S EARLY, BEFORE 7:00, AND ST. Mark's Place is temporarily free of junkies, dealers, and stick-up men. New York in the late '70s is totally fucked up and totally fucking great. It's filthy, there's tons of crime, there aren't too many jobs in any industry and virtually none in film, but it's New York and it's where you want to be. You avoid certain neighborhoods and then, after a few beers and a couple of lines, you change your mind and stroll right into them. Everything is happening below Houston Street except the comedy clubs, which are in Times Square and on the Upper East Side. One night, you're at CBGB's watching the Ramones and Television. They are nobody. You stand two feet away from the stage and see up close what a terrible guitarist Johnny is, but that Richard Lloyd is a genius. The next night, you're at Catch a Rising Star seeing Robin Williams or Steve Martin. They are nobody. Everybody you're hanging around with, drinking with, sharing lines with is nobody. I met a girl at a party. She told me she was an actress who'd just moved here from LA. I asked her where she collected unemployment. She said she had a job on a new show.

Saturday Night Live. I'd never heard of it. It had only been on the air for a month. She gave me a ticket to see it the next week. Now I knew an actual somebody: Laraine Newman. But I was still nobody. Which is still okay in New York City. There are no velvet ropes anywhere yet. It didn't matter how you looked. It didn't matter where you were from. Everyone did weird things to pay the rent and support whatever it was they really wanted to do. I had a company, I directed commercials, so I qualified as one of the most stable people in any group.

The night before, I'd seen Peter Gabriel at the Bottom Line. He performed his first solo album dressed in miner's garb, and I sat in the back, snorting lines off my table, the coke making me invincible and all-powerful when I let myself think, *I'm the shit. Look at me, I'm twenty-five, I have two people working for me, I'm paying my bills, running those full-page ads, figuring out the basics of the business.*

◯ ◯ ◯

That feeling is shot to hell the moment I walk through the front doors of Mother's Sound Stages. In the lobby, there's a chalkboard on the wall that lists which production company's shooting what product on what stage that day. I scan the board and see: PfeiferStory – Hanes – Stage 3, Gomes/Lowe – John Hancock – Stage 2, and Van Dusen Films – Ex Lax – Stage 1. Enough said.

This spot is very simple. A woman delivers a thirty-second monologue looking directly into the camera. This extreme close-up, monologue thing is trendy this year. And advertising is all about trends. Following them. The cooler brands rip things off first. That's how music video–style editing might appear in a Nike ad. Or why a cool color correction and camera technique might be in an Apple spot. By the time creatives working on laxatives start mimicking a trend, it's late in that trend's life. Really late.

Somehow, we've lucked out and cast an actress who's playing the lead in a hit Broadway play. She is very nice. Intelligent. Certainly skilled enough to take any script and make it sound interesting. Even this one.

The script is seventy-five words about peristalsis. That's the scientific term for taking a shit. The word peristalsis is in the script twice. I don't think there's any need to dwell on its meaning when I go through the script with the actress. She'll get it. I'll talk about tone and speed and leave the rest in her very capable hands.

When you're working on commercials for certain products, you separate your brain from what you're doing. If you're making tampon commercials or adult diaper ads or Viagra spots, you just do your work. If there are parts of the script that require an actress to go into detail about stuff like heavy flow or a guy about persistent erectile dysfunction, you don't chortle like some idiot frat dude. You get technical. Create a nice image and pay attention to timing, rhythm, and energy. The only people on the set who might be embarrassed by the product they're selling are the actors. A grip doesn't care if his time card has the word Ex-Lax on it. Part of the director's job is to help the actors get through it. At a minimum, you don't want to amplify their discomfort.

Someone doing a thirty-second monologue about not being able to move their bowels is probably not going to savor their time in front of the camera. And, if you're the star of a Broadway play, you're not just uncomfortable; you're also furious with your agent who somehow convinced you to audition for the spot. Yeah, yeah, yeah. You're going to make fifty thousand dollars in residuals. But the time spent shooting this spot, speaking these words, is unsettling. At best.

I could read the regret on this woman's face from the moment I said hello to her in the makeup room. I've done everything in my power to make sure we'll get done quickly and painlessly. I've arranged to have a teleprompter on the camera, a device that enables a performer to read a script while looking right into the lens. With the teleprompter, she'll never flub a line. Because there's only one shot, the extreme closeup, the lighting doesn't take long. We rehearse a few times and establish the tone the creatives want to hear. I shoot a few takes, get some suggestions from the agency folks, make a few adjustments, and do ten more takes. The actress makes a ridiculous script sound almost profound. Amazing. Seems to me we're done.

Which is when the copywriter appears at my side. Furrowed brow. Stroking his chin. Like he's a therapist or something. This doesn't bode well.

"I don't think she gets it."

"Gets what?"

"How bowel movements work."

OhmyfuckingGod. This guy has got to be kidding.

"I'm sure she gets it."

"She doesn't. She doesn't understand peristalsis."

"How could she not?"

Now he's got his hands on his hips. Pear shaped, of course.

"Someone's gotta explain it to her."

That's going to be either him or me.

"You want to tell her how to take a shit, be my guest."

I could have phrased that better.

I am about to learn my first lesson about the conch. Directors have most of the power on the set. Call it the conch. Sometimes it's theirs by default; other times they've wrested it away from someone. Rarely do they willingly hand it over to someone else. Too many risks. Directing can't be done by committee. Or shouldn't be. But it seemed there were no risks on this one.

So I let the writer take control, temporarily. He walks over and stands intimately close to the actress. He lowers his voice. He folds his script in quarters and puts it in his back pocket. He brings his hand to his chin. Then earnestly explains to her how we take a shit. The actress is a pro, so she nods her head, gives him a few "uh huhs" and, after what seems an eternity, he stops, touches her shoulder as if to baptize their time together and walks back to video village, confident he's schooled her in the finer points of defecation.

Letting him do this was a necessary political move on my part. If I hadn't let him take charge for that moment, he would have stopped all forward motion on the job. And we would have been shooting all night. Or so I thought. I may have succeeded in keeping the momentum going.

But I've failed the actress. By not warning her about what this imbecile was about to do.

I go over and apologize.

"I'm sorry I wasn't able to head that off."

After my lame mea culpa, she looks away and speaks.

"Let's finish this."

We shoot ten more takes. The copywriter now feels things are absolutely, 100 percent better. She is really understanding what she's saying. She sounds so much more knowledgeable than in the early takes. We're done before lunch. The actress isn't interested in hanging around to eat with us.

A decade later, when I've gotten a little better at this, I realize there's a smarter way to manage the conch situation. If the creatives become adamant about speaking directly to the actors, I let them do it. But, first, I signal to the soundman to kill the mics and walk over to the actor. Now the ten or twenty agency people and clients wearing headsets won't be able to hear me.

"That was perfect. I'm happy. My opinion, we're done. But now we have to do this thing called advertising. That's where all those people in video village chime in. So. We'll shoot the scene ten more times. Maybe twenty. Everything I ask you to do will make no sense whatsoever. That's okay. What they're asking me to tell you doesn't make sense to me either. Don't worry about it. Just power through it and we'll be outta here in no time."

Then I signal the sound man to turn the mics back on and wave whichever agency person is most disgruntled over, so he can say whatever he wants to the actor.

It works well. Agency people have even said to me after a shoot that they enjoyed "our collaboration." We didn't, but that's okay.

Behave.

We're shooting at Boken Studios, one of the tinier New York stages. It's right next to the Scientology headquarters on West 48th Street. As I walk by it on my way to the stage, I like to peek through the windows and clock the outfits the people who run the welcome desk are decked out in. They look like stewards for a really low-rent cruise line. They also have terrible haircuts. The upside is there's always a ton of free reading material out on the street by the front doors. L. Ron Hubbard seems to never stop typing.

I use Boken a lot because it's cheap. It's also really small. I've made an unfortunate mistake on this job because I've forced the set designer to put seven small sets in a space that really can't fit more than three. But I couldn't afford a bigger stage. The result is an impassable labyrinth of cables, stands, lights, and set walls. This morning, I've put the camera in the middle of a bathroom set looking across the tub toward a kitchen set where the actress is. It's a mess. The agency thinks I've cheated them somehow. I haven't. I've just made a bad decision on stages. It'll work out. But I feel this vibe of regret coming from their side of the room and it's making me crazy. Actually, that vibe is emanating from a country porch set where I've got them jammed together in front of a television monitor.

Because I started directing so young, I am a toxic mix of insecure and headstrong. The insecurity is entirely rational. I don't always know what I'm doing. And I'm nervous I'll be found out. By the creatives, by the clients, by the fucking caterer. But I figure that, as long as I have an answer for every question and carry myself confidently, I can fake my way through anything. But the whole thing falls apart when I get challenged by an agency person. When that happens, I jump to the conclusion that that person's onto me. That "fraud" is stenciled across my forehead, like I'm a Jenny Holzer installation. I'm less nervous it'll happen with the technicians. Which is dumb because they're in the best position to know how inexperienced I am.

Most commercials are shot in 35mm. Like movies. I'm still working on lower-budget jobs, test commercials, smaller products. So I use 16mm. I take it personally. It makes me feel like I'm not a real man. And, when the agency people who hire me see that smaller 16mm camera instead of a hulking Panavision rig, they start acting like what we're doing is pretend work instead of the real thing. That feeds perfectly into my toxic insecurity loop.

I'm sitting on the dolly, trying to frame a shot over in the kitchen and avoid the tiled walls and lamps in the bathroom set the camera's buried in. I don't have many options. The dolly's in pretty much the only spot it can be in. The agency producer appears next to me.

"I don't like this framing."

"I don't either. I'm trying to work it out. Give me a minute."

"Why did you pick this stage? It's fucking tiny."

"I picked it because it's the only one the budget would allow."

It's a little after 9:30 in the morning. This is the first time I've ever shot for this agency. For me, it's a big job, and I want to do it well. But I haven't even gotten the first shot, and I'm already pissing people off. Specifically, the people who are paying me. I often start shoot days like this: thin-skinned, saying very little to the agency, avoiding the clients, exhibiting a kind of touchy body language when they speak to me. By lunch, owing to my expertise at this masochism, a lot of them sort of dislike me. Even if what's happening in front of the camera is good. I am so desperate to prove I am in charge that I create an environment where everyone feels uncomfortable. I exclude them and send a pretty clear message that I know what I'm doing and they don't, so leave me the fuck alone and let me do my job. Terrible bedside manner.

But I do it for a reason. I have trouble respecting these agency people—these regular folks who've hired me. I'm working on the lowest rungs of the business. The budgets are minuscule. The people giving me orders are often inexperienced or they're hacks. Or they're both. The art directors are supposed to come up with the visuals for a spot. But the majority of them can't draw. Many have a hard time verbalizing their thoughts. About locations or clothes or action or any of the other stuff an art director is supposed to weigh in on. They often tell me they're not happy with what I'm doing, so I better show them something else. No coherent thoughts about what's right or wrong. Jesus. You'd be more helpful with a shoe salesman. And the copywriters depress me. They have terrible jobs. Writing sentences that are rewritten by lawyers, the true experts at bad writing. Very few of them read. Anything. Or want to write something bigger or better. Once in a blue moon, someone jumps out of the business into Hollywood. But we're talking blue moon. And the agency producers rarely help things. They're supposed to guide the creatives through the production process. What I deal with are men and women who dress up like directors, bollocks up the shooting days because they don't really understand much about shooting or editing, and then, when they get to the editorial phase, move in to some poor editor's office for a month, ordering breakfast, lunch, dinner on the editor's tab and town cars to take them home at night while the editor stretches out work on the dumb spot, which could really be finished in a day or two. The agency creative side has a very low bar of entry. To keep this rant equal opportunity, let me add that the bar for directors is even lower.

That's my opinion. And it's as harsh as it is because I have come into directing from nowhere. And at the bottom. Most commercial directors start out as agency art directors or copywriters. So they're used to all the bullshit. They must have been the cream of the crop because they had enough oomph to get the fuck out of the agency side and start shooting. But, if you come in as I have, via film school, and a little production work but no agency experience, working with these people is crazy-making.

Two grips see me struggling to find a frame. Irish guys related by marriage. The film unions are loaded with the members of about thirty Irish and Italian families. The technicians know how green I am but often help me out of my messes. Maybe because I'm paying them. One of the grips ties a rope to the ceiling lamp hanging down in my frame and pulls it out of the way. The other finds a furniture jack, lifts the tiled bathroom wall onto it, and slides it two feet to the right. Now I have a nice frame of a young mother in a kitchen who's going to discover she's got a stain in her armpit because her deodorant isn't up to snuff.

I make my way through the kitchen, the mudroom, the bedroom, the garage, and, finally, to the porch where the agency and client are jammed together looking at the video monitor. All ten of them put on uncomfortable smiles. I point at the image on the monitor.

"Does that work?"

They look. They think. They look at each other. Finally, the producer speaks.

"Can we get any wider?"

"A tiny bit."

"That'd be good."

"Let me shoot this first and then we can try that."

"Okay."

The actress does a great job of looking surprised when she notices her damp underarm. As is normal in advertising, a subtle reaction isn't what the clients want. They're thinking she should look crestfallen when she sees the stain. Or maybe we can try shocked? How about humiliated? What they'd really be happy with is if I had the young woman threaten to kill herself after clocking the stain. As I shoot more takes, I have her gradually amp up her reactions, in the end, exaggerating everything so much I know they'll never use that.

"We love that last take. Let's move on."

People who do what I do develop reputations. Agency people compare notes on the different directors they've worked with. It's amazing that I was able to feed my family for forty years with "insanely difficult," "skilled but arrogant," and "great but evil" as the subject line of the emails written about me. Somehow, I got past it.

Where I Pretend I'm Not From.

WHEN PEOPLE WOULD ASK ME WHERE I WAS FROM, I'D ALWAYS SAY DETROIT. This is true, but not the whole story. I was born in Detroit. The City of Detroit. Harper Hospital. But my folks lived in a place called Metamora and then Grosse Pointe. When we moved to Connecticut, we moved to New Canaan. Rich people towns. Old money. Snobs. Trust funds. This did not work with the image I wanted to present to people. Especially people in the film business. I didn't want to be seen as some spoiled punk who was able to stay afloat in this industry because he could fail and still have a roof over his head. Because I couldn't.

When I was a kid, we were "comfortable," as they say in New Canaan where no one talks about money except to complain about how expensive the things they can easily afford are. I went to a private day school, where I had to wear a coat and tie to class, and, after that, to Deerfield, a boarding school. My father and his five brothers had all gone there. I didn't know what legacy meant. You didn't think too much about this stuff. You just did it. My parents' financial fortunes changed quickly and dramatically when I was in college. The short version is they spent more than they had. By the time I got out of college and moved to New York with $175 in my pocket, I was on my own. There was no well to go back to.

Which was fine. It certainly stopped me from ever looking back over my shoulder when things went badly, as they did once in a while, wondering if someone could save me. I could look back all I wanted, but there was nothing there. The only thing I could do was stare straight ahead and keep going. If I thought too much about it, it was scary. But fear is a big motivation to make something happen.

I was the kid who was never living up to his potential. Not even getting close. I could get better grades in school. Work harder. Make better friends. Get summer jobs that would lead to something. Basically, my whole childhood, the people around me were asking me to do better in life.

No matter what I did, playing guitar, interning at a magazine, directing a play, no one in my family understood these were things you could make a living doing. I barely did. But the things that interested me were jobs no one in my world did. So no one got it. Which was also fine. I wasn't looking for their approval.

They got curious about how it all worked when I started to get successful. Suddenly, the production business, which had been both impossible for them to figure out and kind of icky because of the types of people in it, looked interesting. My family started treating me like they would a successful circus performer.

I didn't look successful. I dressed like a bum. I swore like a fucking truck driver. I had hair down to my shoulders. But, underneath it all, I still looked like a WASP. And, if people knew I was from Grosse Pointe, Michigan, and New Canaan, Connecticut, and had gone to Deerfield, I figured they'd think I had it all handed to me. Which wasn't the case. I was inventing a career, pulling jobs out of a universe I didn't understand, meeting a payroll, doing things not many people my age had done, not necessarily very well but doing them nonetheless. No mentor, no trust fund, just me.

I've never learned to tell the whole truth about where I'm from. Someone asks, I still say I was born in Detroit. Harper Hospital. The person listening now thinks it's fitting. Some foul-mouthed guy with a nasty sense of humor who fought his way up in a brutal, mean, dirty business and became a big success. From Detroit. Yeah, makes a ton of sense.

I Will
Not Be
Undersold.

I'M BACK WORKING ON THE STAGES AT MOTHERS. IT'S CHEAP. AND, SINCE most of the stuff I'm shooting is low budget, I can't afford the nicer stages. The agencies that are hiring me understand that my unbeatable low prices come with some concessions. One being dirty, beat-up stages in the heart of the crime-ridden East Village. The producers who have heroin problems love it, though.

I'm in a year-long rut of shooting crap. Actually, it's been a five-year rut. And little do I know that it's going to last another ten years before something changes. There *is* an upside: directing crappy commercials forces you to be creative. Every part of what the agency hands you sucks, so you have to figure out a way to make it better. Because, in the Russian firing squad logic of advertising, if you don't, they'll blame you for the piece of shit they wind up with. Not that you wrote a word of it or came up with any of the settings. Avoiding those bullets is forcing me to get better at my craft. So there's that.

I think that I'm good enough now to start getting some okay work. But it seems the only way I can get it is to give the jobs away. Meaning charge nothing but my costs and not make a dime myself. Agency creative people are generally not savvy business people. But they are very smart about one thing. They know when they've come up with a commercial that will get some attention. Okay, that's a one-in-a-million occurrence. But, when that happens, directors circle them like starving sharks. They'll do anything to get one.

Creative people can be annoying to work for. Directors included. Especially when they get a little hot because they then can become really arrogant. Like they're fine artists or some shit. One campaign that's all over television, a couple of write-ups in the trades, and, bingo, they're Jesus. And, when that happens, if you're a normal, working director, it's impossible to get them to even look at you. They only work now with whoever's on the top of the heap. Geniuses like them. Everyone else is crap. It's painful.

The tables turn when they don't have money. Because the directors on the top of the heap that month won't work for free. All of a sudden, the agency needs assholes like me who'll work for nothing. Well, a version of nothing. Because I get something of value out of the deal, even though I don't make a penny. I get to put this spot on my reel and show people I work with great agencies and the geniuses they employ. I'm on a heap. Of some kind.

I'm shooting for Cliff Freeman & Partners. Cliff's the guy who came up with the "Where's the Beef?" commercials for Wendy's. One of the creative directors there knows he can make me dance like an organ grinder's monkey if he offers me one of his no-money jobs. The campaign's for Little Caesars Pizza. One spot is a sight gag with a dog. There's no directing involved. I'll just film a dog sitting next to a sign while a hand rewrites the sign. The other spot involves very minor directing. A guy gets handed an enormous cup with a straw in it. He's excited. So excited, he squeezes the cup and water squirts in his face. I've convinced myself that this is great creative and worth my (uncompensated) time. I ignore the fact that the bit, like many advertising ideas, is stolen. This time from either the Three Stooges or the Marx Brothers.

When ad guys steal someone else's bit, which happens a lot, they call it "my idea."

When I walk on the stage, the crew is setting up the lights. Ten minutes later, Cliff, the name on the door, comes in.

I say hello, we grab coffees, and go sit by the monitor to figure out how we'll shoot these things. It's the first time I've met Cliff. Easygoing, nice. I can't help noticing that his blue jeans are covered in ink. Doodles. Wait. His pant legs, from the knees up, are covered in doodles. Makes no sense. As if on cue, Cliff takes out a Bic pen and starts doodling on his pants as we talk. Okay. That explains that. What kind of fucking quirk is that?

After a few minutes, the client from Little Caesars arrives. She's loud and brassy. She doesn't fit the image for who'd be hired as the marketing director for a food company that uses the hottest agency in New York. She doesn't fit that mold because, turns out, she got the job because her dad owns the company. She knows less about advertising than she does about how to get dressed. But she's the client. And, like on every other job I will do as a commercial director, a person with no knowledge of filmmaking will have final say on lighting, blocking, wardrobe, tone, and performance. She'll work this all out with a guy who doodles on his fucking pants.

I wanted this job. I got it.

I excuse myself, walk off the stage, and wander into makeup. Because this job is on a really tight schedule, we cast this actor from an audition tape. There was no callback session so no one's seen him in person. But I'm not concerned. All he has to do is look in the camera while he's holding a giant cup and squeeze it hard enough that he squirts himself in the face. Any schmo can do this.

My makeup woman, Jane Forth, is getting him ready. Jane was the third makeup person who ever worked for me. After I met her, I never hired anyone else. Makeup people tend to do too much, making actors look like they're either in a casket or starring in a Spanish-language soap opera. Jane has a very light touch. I like having her around because of her weird history. She'd worked at Andy Warhol's Factory and starred in *Trash* and a few of the other Warhol films. Commercials for her are just a gig. A refreshing point of view. And she's also responsible for my son's name. She and I were in a crew van driving to location one day and, out of nowhere, she told me, if I ever had a son, I should name him Zane. Because Zane Van Dusen was a great name. Not only did I remember this, I did it.

So Jane's working on the actor. He's sitting in the chair with a bib around his neck, so the powder doesn't get on his clothes. I say hi to Jane then reach to shake hands with the guy. His hand comes out from under the bib, we shake, and I sense something's not right. It's *so* not right that I have to tell myself not to grab his hand with both of mine and take a gander at it. Instead, I have to act like nothing's wrong and nonchalantly sneak a peek. Which I do. Wow. The fucking actor is missing his middle finger. Which, when he takes hold of the Big Gulp cup, will be instantly apparent. Finger, finger, no finger, finger, thumb. Fuck.

When actors audition, they slate. That means the casting director takes a closeup shot of their face, they say their name, then bring up both hands in front of their face. I always thought this was stupid. Any actor going out to audition is going to have all their extremities.

Turns out that's not true.

Because I'm pretty sure he won't grow a new finger in the next hour, I head back to the stage to tell the agency we have an issue.

I find the producer. This woman's been treating me like a second-rate dick for the last few days. Because she normally works with A-list directors. She's actually said this to me. More than once. I find her over by the craft service table. I ask if we can have a word. She follows reluctantly. What the fuck does a second-rate dick of a director have to say?

"What?"

"I went back to see the actor."

"And…?"

"So there's a bit of an issue."

"Yeah?"

"Yeah. He's missing a finger."

"What?"

"Yeah. He doesn't have the middle finger on his left hand."

"What's he got?"

"Like a nub."

"A nub?"

"Yeah. Like the little piece of the finger that'd be left after you had an accident. Like with a lawn mower."

"Yuck."

"Yeah. Well, anyway, he doesn't have a finger and he has to hold the bottle and squeeze it so we might see it, or we might not, depending, but I thought you should know, so, if the client notices it, you can say you knew and we're cool and it's fine."

I pick up a water bottle and grip it like the guy will grab the Big Gulp. It's pretty easy to hide one of my hands entirely behind the bottle. Whether our guy can do this, I don't know, but I'm demonstrating there's a way out of the mess.

"All right. Did you tell Cliff?"

"No. I figured you'd want to."

"No way. You cast the guy."

This is a specialty of agency people. They want to be in charge of everything. They have to approve everything. Then, when something goes to shit, it's you, the director, who fucked up. They never take responsibility and never say thank you.

Which is why I get paid. Not on this job. But in general.

So I go over to where Cliff's sitting with the client, take him aside, and tell him what's going on. He's surprisingly chill about the whole thing and says, "Whatever. Let's just try not to see it."

When we shoot that scene, the daughter/marketing director is so focused on a Barney's catalogue, she never notices the few times when the actor brings out his hand with the missing digit. He does the squeeze thing really well, soaks the shit out of himself four or five times, looking like that's exactly what he thought would happen, and we decide we're good and move on to the spot with the dog.

When we're done and the producer's leaving, she reminds me how lucky I am to have shot this job. A lot of people wanted it. "A-list" people.

Every time I watch a casting tape and the actors bring their hands up in front of their faces, I can only think of two things. The missing finger and Cliff Freeman drawing Kilroy faces on his pants.

Normal Girl.

I RAN INTO BLANCHE ON 56TH AND SEVENTH AVENUE. SHE WAS WALKING home from the grocery store, loaded down with shopping bags.

"That's a lot of food."

"I'm a caterer."

"You are?"

"I am on Saturday."

I'd met Blanche Baker two years before when she was dating an acquaintance of mine. She was, at twenty-three, an accomplished actress. She'd been Lolita on Broadway, done a couple of movies, and won an Emmy for her role in *Holocaust*. The relationship with the acquaintance had ended a while back.

"I'm throwing myself a birthday party Saturday afternoon. Come."

"Okay. How old are you?"

One of my best almost opening lines. Ever.

"You're not allowed to ask a girl that."

I showed up on Saturday. Her apartment was full of actors. I only knew one. Kate Capshaw. She'd done a lot of commercials, dated a commercial director, and was trying to make the switch into movies. Kate and I spent a while talking. Suddenly Blanche joined our conversation. And then Kate left, and Blanche stayed. I was glad. I was very interested in her. I had no idea if she was interested in me.

Interested enough to take me up on a dinner invitation. Then another. And another. We'd just talk. Blanche was smart and funny and knew what she was doing. She'd been a bio major at Wellesley before leaving a year early to start acting. Not your normal actress.

Blanche was the straightest girl I'd ever met. She didn't get high. Didn't drink much. For some insane reason, one Saturday at dinner, I mentioned I had two hits of acid in my wallet.

"What's it like?"

"Kind of great. Life becomes amazingly interesting."

"I think we should do it."

"Really?"

"I'm not going to die, am I?"

"Nah. You'll be fine."

For eight hours, we wandered all over New York City. Into bars, bowling alleys, restaurants, book stores, arcades. I dropped her off around 3:00 in the morning. When I got home, I called to make sure she was okay.

"I'm fine."

"Drink water. That helps."

"I had a lot of fun."

"Me too."

"And I beat your ass in Foosball!"

"I let you win. See you later."

We kept having dinners. Kept talking. Nothing but talking. We talked a lot about what we wanted out of life. My goal was stability. A wife, kids, financial security—predictable and boring. I'd had a pretty normal upbringing. My parents had been married for thirty years. There'd been ups and downs, but, big picture, it was solid. I got stability.

Blanche's life was another story.

Her mother was Carroll Baker. A Hollywood movie star. She'd been in *Giant, How the West Was Won, The Carpetbaggers.* Most people knew her from *Baby Doll.* I'd never heard of Carroll Baker. Never seen her in a movie. Never seen her in a magazine. I don't think Blanche believed me when I told her this. And the life she'd had as a movie star's daughter was nuts. The parents divorced when she was nine. Carroll put her and her brother in a Swiss boarding school, where she sometimes forgot to pick them up for vacations. They move to Rome, and Carroll starts making movies there. Riding the bus to school, Blanche would see huge movie billboards with her mother's face and the word "Orgasmo" stenciled over it. When Carroll's work in Rome dried up, they moved to London, Carroll checked out, the kids kind of raised themselves for two years, got themselves into Wellesley and Yale, and came back to the States. Normal was never part of their life. And Blanche was now dead set on making her life normal as shit.

We got married in Cancun, Mexico, in 1983. Carroll had decided Cancun was the most convenient destination for her large, cosmopolitan coterie of friends. The hotel referred to the wedding as the "Carroll Baker Wedding." The pictures were handled by *Us* magazine. Carroll was in most of them.

Twelve months to the day after we got married, our first kid was born. We were having a lot of fun, a lot of battles about balancing work and family, and we were figuring it out. Semi-successfully.

Cameo.

THE EIGHT GUYS IN THE R&B BAND CAMEO STAND IN A V FORMATION under the marquee of the Orpheum Theatre. They're dressed in identical outfits. Baggy, shimmery, silver pantaloons, and blue sleeveless shirts with plunging necklines made from the same material as the pants. Earth, Wind & Fire meets MC Hammer. It's their look.

It's an early Thursday evening in mid-July. The East Village sidewalks are jammed with people on their way home from work or going out to eat. This being New York, not many even give a second look at these flashily dressed black guys.

For the past two days, we've been roaming around the city, shooting a music video. MTV has happened, and every band wants to be in their rotation. They all need music videos. Anyone who can spell the word "director" is jumping into this market. Photographers, choreographers, movie directors, other musicians are all shooting videos. Some are doing spectacular work, working with great bands, making tons of money, overwhelmed with offers and even signing movie deals. I'm not one of those guys. I'm a B-level commercial director with no distinctive style whom no one's heard of. But it's clear as shit to me that music videos may be a way out of ads and into something else.

Getting one is kind of similar to how you get a commercial. You pitch your ideas. But to the bands and record executives and managers instead of agency people. Often the bands come up with some story and you riff on that. Sometimes you just shoot the band lip-syncing a song. Sometimes you shoot a little movie with actors and intercut it with the performance footage. Sometimes the band members want to be the actors. The whole business is being invented as it goes along, so I figure I can shove my way in. One of my many dots is a guy who'd come into my office a year ago looking for a job in production. We became friends and, when he went into the talent management business instead, his first client was Cameo. They needed a video, and I was the only director my friend knew.

Cameo is great. Everything they do on stage involves choreography and movement. For the video, no matter what I suggest, they have a great move. And, because they're pros, they don't have any qualms about dancing in the middle of a Second Avenue sidewalk on a Thursday night wearing odd costumes while hundreds of people walk past them. They're totally at home being the center of attention.

I don't have a lot of money for this job. Certainly not enough to rent the crane I need to do this shot. So, instead, I've got the camera bolted onto the end of a one-by-ten piece of lumber that's balanced over a pipe. It looks like a seesaw with two muscle-bound grips on one side and an Arriflex 3 camera on the other. What I call a film school solution. It'll work just fine. I show Larry Blackmon, the guy who leads the band, what the camera will see, and he works out some steps to cover four bars of the song. The band walks into frame with their backs turned, pivots on cue, then starts hopping like bunnies away from the camera. If I did this, it'd look idiotic. They look cool.

I'm ready to try a first take when two burly guys wearing Naugahyde jackets and loafers with curled-up toes appear next to my jury-rigged crane. They are just close enough to the action to force us to ask them to move. They don't. Instead, they ask to speak to "who's in charge."

Judging from their squat builds, fat fingers, shitty shoes, choice of rings, and blown-dry hair, I'm guessing they're Teamsters, the mobsters of organized labor. Unfortunately, I'm right.

I know, if I get near them, I'll blow a gasket. I hate these people. My producer sees what's happening and comes over.

"You guys okay?"

"You the guy in charge?"

"Yeah."

"How come you don't have Teamsters on this job?"

"We don't need 'em."

"Yeah, you do."

"We're not a union job."

"Yeah? Well, that's a problem."

For us. Because now they demand two grand, cash. Now. Never mind that we don't have a contract with the Teamsters. And, therefore, no legal obligation to employ Teamsters. Their threat is simple. Pay us off or we'll call in more of our guys and fuck up your whole night.

Larry comes over next to me. He notices this little discussion going on and that the crew's stopped working.

"We cool here?"

"Yeah. Just stupid union shit. Give us a minute."

I'm paying forty people to work on this video, and these two goons are telling us we need a bigger crew. My producer leads them around the corner. He'd like to be shaken down in private. What really singes my drawers is the righteous patter about their union brothers and how that solidarity disappears the second we fork over the money. I hate Teamsters.

I'm particularly happy when I hear stories about them getting hurt. Teamsters are truck drivers. They drive shit from here to there and unload it. They have absolutely bizarre work rules such that they usually start their days in double overtime and finish it that way. They wind up making fortunes for doing pretty much nothing. On one job, the Teamsters had demanded we hire four more guys than we already had. Because they're basically the Mafia, you do it. Anyway, these four mooks who've been shoved down our throats drive up to location an hour and a half late. We're sitting around with our thumbs up our asses because these "professional" drivers can't read maps. My producer decides, as retribution, to make the fuckers do some actual work. He orders them to unload everything on the truck. The two ignoramuses driving seem confused by how the truck works. One goes over to the rear lift gate, hits a button, and is immediately clobbered by the gate, badly bruising his shoulder. The other goes to a side panel on the semi, throws the winch arm to let the door swing open, and is buried under fifty sandbags that fall out of the shelf they're stored on in the truck. One idiot with an enormously swollen shoulder. The other flat on his back covered in sandbags. The joke was on me. They were already in triple time.

Meet the Beatles.

CARIBOU RANCH IS A RECORDING STUDIO ABOUT FIFTEEN MILES OUTSIDE Gold Hill, Colorado. It has become a popular and pricey destination for bands who want to make a record in some place cooler than New York or Los Angeles. Stephen Stills, Elton John, Phil Collins, Tom Petty, Billy Joel, and many others have been here. Lesser-known acts that can wrangle a big enough recording budget from their labels are here too. Like Shooting Star, the first American band signed to Virgin Records. They've already released two records and had some solid airplay. They tour constantly. They open for John Mellencamp, Jefferson Starship. They're here recording their third album, and I'm here to make the video for the first single. The songs are all fine. But there isn't anything unique in their look or sound. They must be aware of this because, while I sit with the guys in an empty dining room waiting for dinner, they describe what they're hoping for in the video.

"Make us look like the Beatles."

"Okay. Are there some specific Beatles' visuals you're thinking about?"

There are. The lead guitar player takes a stick of incense and a pack of matches out of his backpack. He lights the incense. The bass player slides his chair over next to him, and they put their heads together, faces almost touching. The guitar player's holding the incense down below the table edge, the smoke's wafting up in front of their faces.

"See?"

"See…?"

"It's like *A Hard Day's Night.*"

They tell me the shot they're referring to is one of the close-ups of Paul McCartney and George Harrison singing a backup vocal. The smoke in that shot is coming from a cigarette Harrison is holding below the mike. It's a nice shot. But its impact has to do with the fact that you're looking at McCartney and Harrison. Not the smoke. I can do exactly that shot with these two guys. But no one will be reminded of *A Hard Day's Night*. Not even if these two play a Beatles song, wear lapelless jackets, and get haircuts with bangs.

I haven't shot anything yet, but I'm pretty certain no one will be happy with this video.

When I finish three days later, I'm pretty sure we haven't done anything even remotely like *A Hard Day's Night*. We did shots of them walking around an abandoned silver mine. We did a shot in a barn. We did one with them singing on the porch of one of the ranch buildings. Then we did a lot in the recording studio. The guitar player came prepared to do the incense gag. It turned out like I thought it would. Thin plume of smoke. Not as thick as what would have come from a cigarette but the guys in the band didn't smoke. Exact same microphone. Sennheiser 814. Similar white acoustic tile board in the background. Same extreme close-up of the two guys. Just like McCartney and Harrison. But not.

I should have told the guys during that first dinner that I couldn't make them look like the Beatles. Because they weren't the Beatles. Not their fault. Or mine. But by nodding my head, aiming to please, and agreeing to do the incense and microphone thing, they must have gone to bed each night in their fancy Caribou Ranch bunkhouse convinced that this video was finally going to make girls start chasing them around Cleveland. I should have told them there probably wouldn't be any girls.

The end product was kind of boring. The song wasn't ever going to be a hit, but what I shot didn't help matters. I am seeing that music videos are like commercials. If you work with a bad idea or a so-so band or a weak song and you do so-so work and don't come up with some amazing visuals or a mesmerizing edit, the result is going to be…bad. And the person who'll get the blame is you, me, the director.

The guys who are getting ahead of me in the world of videos are working with cooler bands, pretty good ideas, great songs. But they also know how to create great visuals, which often involves hiring a fancy cinematographer from the movies. My talent is that I can make interesting things happen with actors in front of a lens. But I'm also insisting on operating the camera myself, on being my own director of photography. It's essential to my image of what I do. But the truth is: I'm afraid if I bring in one of these seasoned pros, I'll be exposed as a fraud. So I don't hire them, which is dumb.

Even dumber is that I don't see how much it's holding me back.

Maybe I'm Not Good Enough.

THE FIRST FEW YEARS I'M IN NEW YORK, EVERYONE I HANG AROUND WITH is defined by what they want to be. It's like the scene in *Serpico* where Pacino is at a party and, when he asks people what they do, they'll respond, "I drive a cab but I'm really a poet," or, "I work as a waitress but I'm an actress." I have friends like this. I feel embarrassed for them. On the other hand, when I answer, "I'm a director," and people ask of what and I add "commercials," I'm embarrassed for myself. I exaggerate the shit out of my tiny successes to make my life sound better. I'm a director of ten-second milk spots and test commercials for Crisco. My sense of self, for all the cool and bravado I try to exude, is shaky enough that I'm sure the ones driving cabs think *I'm* the pathetic asshole. Which I understand. I'm making things people hate.

There's a reason people get up and leave the room when the ads come on. Most are bad. Everything's totally fake. A lot of them are cast with women who look and act like Stepford Wives. Men might hang around to watch a beer ad if some athlete is in it. More often than not, they'll go take a leak. My friends and I are typical. We have nothing but snickering loathing for all things normal. Like commercials.

But I'm trying to make them. Not just make them but succeed at it. Be recognized. In a field that everyone—even me some of the time—thinks is beneath contempt.

While no one in the real world knows directing commercials is a business, the people in the business do. They're constantly appraising who's on the way up, who's on the way down, who's making money, who's getting the work they want. There's a constantly changing hierarchy. The way you sort yourself in the commercial-directing food chain is based on the products you're shooting, the agencies you're working for, and the budgets. At this point, I'm shooting things like Tampax for mediocre agencies with medium budgets. The guys I want to be are shooting Coke or American Express or AT&T or IBM. For big agencies, with big budgets. I'm starting to think that those flashy products and cool agencies are never going to want my services. I don't have whatever skill is required to be in that club.

Except that maybe I do.

The first sign comes when one of the biggest companies in the business asks if I'm interested in joining them. The guy who runs the place has seen my full-page ads and, just like I hoped, assumes I'm way bigger than I am. He explains he runs the commercial production company version of the Dallas Cowboys and he's looking to expand his roster. Can we meet?

When I walk into his office, he's on the phone with an agency producer. I'm only hearing one side of the conversation, but the thrust is that the director the agency wants isn't available, but the guy I'm meeting has another guy on his roster who is; he's great, give him the job. There's a bit of back and forth and, after ten minutes, that's what happens. For me, this is like watching a dream. To even have a chance of getting a Dawn dish soap ad, I have to go through three or four phone calls with creatives, explaining each time how I'll make their spot better with casting or some camera trick or a little piece of business I suggest for the storyline.

It takes days. The guy in front of me gets one of his directors a job by saying he's a good substitute for the director they really want. When he hangs up, I ask if that's how it always happens. He says always. People want his guys. Whatever guy is available. And I could be one of his guys. He then adds that he likes working on the couch he's sitting on because it's great for getting blow jobs. Weird business.

I meet this guy a few more times. Once, he has his driver pick me up and bring me down to his office for lunch. Another time, he meets me for dinner and brings along an as-yet unknown Sean Young who's wearing an unbuttoned shirt she borrowed from him. When we finish dinner and he's ready to go home to his wife, he leaves Sean with me. I take her roller skating. He calls the next day to thank me for looking after her and guarantees my fortunes will take off like a rocket if I join up with him. I'll start getting all the jobs I'm only dreaming about. I'm sure he's right.

But I know something he doesn't. That I'm not a very good director yet. I've made a few memorable spots, but what I mostly do is take terrible ads and make them slightly better. Which I call polishing turds. But I would be in over my head if I was directing a Coca-Cola ad or a Ford ad or a Mastercard ad. I don't yet know enough about how to do my job. And I'm convinced, if I was put in the deep end of the pool, I'd blow it. So I say no.

It's funny. All my bravado, the act I put on every day to help me get work I think I'm unqualified for. Now, when the act is working and putting me in a position to leap ten steps forward and really create a career, I don't do it. I think I'm being pragmatic.

Independent Filmmaking.

I GET OFF THE ELEVATOR ON THE FIFTH FLOOR. CALL TIME IS 7:00 A.M. Usually, I'd show up for work around 8:00, but it's the first day of shooting on my first movie, so I'm anxious and early. But working hard to look serene. I don't think I'm pulling it off.

I've been shooting commercials, music videos, and corporate films for six years. Somehow, I keep managing to come up with another job. I'm not getting rich. But I'm getting paid. And saving. And learning. Not enough to lose the feeling that I'm going to be found out on the next shoot, but I'm a little more secure.

I've always operated under the hazy premise that there was a path that leads from commercials to movies. You shoot a lot of ads, someone realizes you're a fucking genius, agents compete to sign you, studios line up to fund your film, and you make a movie. Since nothing even close to this has happened for me and I'm impatient, I decide to do it myself. Write and direct a movie. Note that "edit that movie" is missing because I only have enough money to shoot it. I'll figure out how to pay for the editing later.

I've written a script designed to be shot very inexpensively. Small cast, not too many locations, all in New York City, so no housing or per diem costs. I can pay everyone, rent the equipment and locations, and get the thing done for about a hundred grand. Everyone gets paid. Except me.

No one's ever invested in me. No one's ever backed me. The risks have been all mine. Quitting a job and opening an office. Buying full-page ads. Hiring employees. Paying everyone's health insurance. I live on whatever's left over after all the bills are paid. I can buy dinner, pay my rent, go to a concert. But I save a lot. Because I'm convinced this will all come crashing down at any moment. But the rainy-day fund's gotten kind of big. Maybe it's time to invest in myself.

I'm twenty-eight, simultaneously invincible and clueless and some-how able to convince myself this is a sound business move. A sure thing. In reality, I'm risking everything on a single throw of the dice.

I get out of the elevator and go right, down the gray carpeted hall. The developer hasn't spent two nickels converting the place into apart-ments. The hallway paint job is already cracking, the carpet's coming unglued, and the power cords for the track lights bolted to the ceiling are haphazardly nailed into the wall joins. Shitty but the norm for early '80s downtown conversions. I picked this loft because it's big and has four different-looking areas I can use for filming. That saves me from having to move from one location to another and wasting a lot of time. I can accomplish in two days what would normally take four. Saving two days matters because I'm making this movie with my own money. I don't tell anyone that. I just say I'm also one of the producers.

The door to the loft is wedged open with a pile of sandbags. From ten feet away, I can hear the voices of crew people and the crackle of walkie-talkies. The floors are covered in thin cardboard to protect them from getting banged up by light stands and camera equipment. I say hello to two prop guys who are laying plates, glasses, and silverware out on the dining room table where we'll shoot scenes in the afternoon. Breakfast, a real breakfast ready to be eaten, is set up in the kitchen. It's a bag of donuts, some fruit, and an urn full of coffee. Again, my money, low budget.

I go over to a small bedroom where makeup and wardrobe are set up. The kid who sleeps in here really likes patchouli. The crew has opened the window wide to try and get some fresh air in to dilute the stench. Griffin Dunne is in a director's chair getting worked on. He's playing Tom Christo, the male lead whose marriage is falling apart. In the other chair is Blanche Baker, who's playing Leslie, his about-to-be-ex-wife. Blanche is also my girlfriend, but we're trying to keep that under wraps. I think it looks kind of pathetic when a director hires his girlfriend. Particularly bad for the reputation of the semi-famous girlfriend. Blanche doesn't need this job. She's been on Broadway, won an Emmy, done a few studio movies, so her involvement is a favor to me and helped to give this tiny film some legitimacy. Which I figure would evaporate if people knew she was my girlfriend.

Griffin is a very nice guy. And a very good actor. Easygoing. Smart. Funny. I'm lucky to have been able to cast him. He's just been in *An American Werewolf in London*. Another plus for a tiny movie written and directed by an unknown guy who makes commercials. Griffin also seems to be, in life, exactly the character that he's playing in the movie. Verbal. Quick. A little sarcastic. And charming.

Two weeks before we started shooting, I rented a small rehearsal space in the West Fifties. An empty room with four folding chairs and windows that overlooked Broadway. It was sandwiched between two rooms where tap dancers were rehearsing what sounded like a musical about firing squads. I had Griffin and the female lead, Marissa Chibas, read the key scenes. They were great. Everything sounded perfectly real. I'd try to come up with some comment about timing or tone. But I didn't think they needed to change anything. Once, I asked them to walk around the room as they read a scene. Halfway through, Griffin stopped and said it felt stupid to be doing that, so they sat down in the folding chairs and finished. As I walked home that night, I realized I was in over my head. I was concerned that Griffin and Marissa thought this too. My experience has been solely in commercials. The actors in spots are often very good, but what they're doing and saying is fake. I've learned enough tricks to help them sound real. But I don't know if I have the chops to do that with movie performances. By the time I got to my apartment, I've got a plan. Have confidence in the casting and keep the rest of it simple. Basically, do nothing.

I discovered another problem during the rehearsal day. Every word Griffin and Marissa spoke sounded great. Every single word. Oh. Wait. I wrote this stuff. My objectivity is ten feet up my ass. In addition to doing nothing, I'm going to have to constantly remind myself that my judgment stinks.

At least I know this. I spend a lot of time in movie theaters watching small films. Some are good, some are bad. What they all have in common is long, boring passages. It's easy to understand why. Small films are often made by people who wrote and directed the movie themselves. It's their baby. They don't want to cut anything. When I watch someone else's film, it's easy to see what should be cut. For me. Now I'm that guy, the director who can't give up anything. I need to remember that. But my judgment is also skewed because the story has some similarities to how my relationship with Blanche came together. I've taken plenty of license, but I've also got moments in there that, while they happened to us, I think will resonate with anyone. I figure, at worst, I'm going to make a sweet romantic comedy. At best, it has a few interesting insights and observations that'll make it stand out. But who knows? The only people who read the script before I started casting are Blanche and me. This is not what you'd call great due diligence.

I go into the living room to set up the first shot. In the scene, Griffin is sacked out in a sleeping bag on the floor and Blanche is talking to him from their bedroom. They've had a fight the night before and slept separately. I want the camera to just observe Griffin's sleepy face as he tries to deal with a woman who is clearly a handful.

I put the camera on the floor, take a look through the lens at Griffin's face. It's covered in a day's worth of stubble. His hair is messed up. He's half in and half out of a sleeping bag, wearing a Sandinista T-shirt and boxers. The scene is going to run for a while, so I need to add some visual interest. Widening the frame should do it. The simple way to accomplish this is with a zoom lens. But, in order to save money, I have not rented a zoom lens, just fixed focal length lenses. If I want to widen out, I have to dolly out. But, in order to save more money, I don't have the special rig that would allow me to dolly with the camera an inch off the ground. The key grip suggests we put the camera on a blanket and, when I want to widen out, he'll just slide me back slowly. Another film-school solution. It works perfectly.

By 8:45, we're ready to do the first shot. Exciting. A movie. Real movie actors. Saying words I wrote. I work hard not to start strutting around like an even bigger asshole than I already am.

We slate the first take. Blanche starts her lines. She's in a bedroom down the hall, so she has to yell to be heard. Griffin yells back or whispers, depending on whether he wants her to hear what he's saying. He's great. Sometimes he speaks normally; sometimes he buries his face in his pillow; sometimes he rolls on his back and covers his face with his hands in frustration. Near the end of the scene, he grabs a pack of Marlboros and lights one. Blanche keeps talking as he lies on his back and blows angry smoke rings. I think everything he does is wonderful. It probably is, but my judgment stinks.

After three takes, I'm done. I overcome the instinct to look around and see what the agency has to say. There's nobody here today but me. The script supervisor tells me how long the scene ran. Which doesn't matter because it's a movie. My producer's going over the next day's call sheet. He doesn't care about this scene. He's just hoping we'll finish in a ten-hour day, so there's no overtime. Whether the scene works or not is entirely up to me.

I say I'm good. Let's move on. So far, the transition from commercials to movies is going great.

Day Fifteen.

THE CAMERA'S ON FIRST AVENUE, ACROSS FROM THE ENTRANCE TO BEL-levue. It's looking west through the cluster of apartment buildings where NYU houses nursing students. It's freezing this afternoon. Not unexpected because it's February. But really, really cold. We've spent the morning shooting inside a laboratory in the New York City Medical Examiner's building one block south. The main female character in the movie is a researcher studying how animals seek to replenish the chemicals in their brains that trigger pleasure. I thought the idea of a woman doing this experiment while toying with starting a new relationship after the end of a horrible one was interesting. It may turn out to be a subplot that's only clear to me. What the audience will understand is that she works in a room with a lot of mice.

I have two days of shooting left on the movie. We're ahead of schedule by four days. I think this is a major accomplishment. But, seriously, who cares except me and the producers? It has no bearing on whether I've made a good movie. None. I have a reputation in commercials for being fast. I would prefer to be known instead as efficient. Better yet, good. Crews say it's because I'm decisive. I know what I want and, when I get it, I move on. Maybe that's it. Anyway, everything's gone quickly. Whether I've made a good film or not is another matter.

The scene I'm doing has Marissa Chibas, the female lead, taking a long walk down the block. She's alone. In the prior scenes, she's had a rough morning, so she's a little at sea. I need her to walk in a straight line and cycle through a variety of facial expressions. In editing, I'll find something that fits the mood of what's happened before. Marissa and the AD are standing at the top of a set of cement steps a hundred yards away. I'm talking to the AD on the walkie-talkie while the camera guys finish setting the focus marks. When we're ready, I ask him to peel Marissa's oversize down coat off, so she does the walk in the light jacket she wore in the prior scene.

We do this because of continuity. But it's bitter cold, and Marissa's sick as a dog. She came down with the flu two days ago, but she's been a trooper ever since, never complained, continued doing perfect work. I want to get this done fast, so she doesn't freeze to death. The wardrobe girl takes Marissa's down coat off, so all she's wearing is the thin jacket over a cotton dress. She's surrounded by people in L.L.Bean Arctic Expedition parkas and snow boots. Hopefully they're acting as windbreaks.

We roll camera, and Marissa comes down the street. The focus doesn't hold. We put down new marks and shoot again. Same problem. This happens with extended walking shots and long lenses. Focusing a telephoto lens takes real skill. Some assistant camerapeople are spectacular at it and get everything on the first take. Others not so much. We do it again.

Between each take, they drape the enormous down parka around Marissa. Frustrated that we keep having to redo the shot, I suddenly bark into my walkie.

"Take the fucking jacket off. Now."

The AD reminds me she's sick.

"She's dying of cold. Let's leave it on her until you roll."

I'm only thinking about throttling the AC because he keeps messing the focus up. But I say something else.

"I don't care. I only need her to stay alive for one more day of shooting."

The joke I'm going for doesn't seem to land. Particularly with my leading lady.

Marissa Chibas has an interesting backstory. She is of Cuban ancestry. Her father was one of Castro's right-hand guys and then defected to the States. Her uncle led a political party that tried to defeat the Batista regime. He was a fiery orator with strongly held views. During his weekly radio show, he claimed to have proof of Batista's criminality. When the documents didn't show up, he blew his brains out. Unfortunately, they were on commercial break when he did it. And on radio. His niece, Marissa, is equally intense, a very focused, very talented twenty-two-year-old woman. Everything she's done in the movie is natural and authentic. She's made every word I've written sound far better than they have had any right to. I owe her and should treat her like royalty.

From a hundred yards away, Marissa's stare goes right through me. She doesn't threaten to shoot me. She doesn't give me the finger. She doesn't say a word. Just glares at me. And takes off her coat.

I can get very frustrated when I'm working. Nothing goes as fast as I want it to. Things don't happen perfectly the first time. Technicians constantly need to make adjustments. Takes are ruined because cars without mufflers go by. Actors flub lines. The boom man misjudges the frame and the mike drops into the shot. It's a constant barrage of obstacles that keep you from getting what you want. My response to these challenges is often to say something. And my filter doesn't always work great. Often, the moment words leave my mouth, I pray they'll be somehow trapped in little bubbles floating in front of my face, so I can quickly grab them and stuff them back in my piehole. But that never happens. They spill out, fully formed, in sentences. And I suffer the consequences.

A big gust of wind blows Marissa's dress hard against her body. It's this summery A-line number that she and the costume designer thought would add a little style to her role as a biology researcher. The stylist puts a purse over Marissa's shoulder and hands her her briefcase. The AD says she's ready. We slate and Marissa starts walking. She's perfect, going from distracted to confused to happy, not a glimmer of anger evident on her face. She walks up to the camera then right past it. When she stops, she keeps her back to me. The stylist runs over and puts the parka over her shoulders. The focus went soft for a moment midway through her walk. But, after what I said, I can't ask her to do it again. I'll deal with it in editorial. I walk over to Marissa and stand to her right.

"I'm sorry. I was trying to be funny."

Marissa keeps her eyes averted, her face angled to the sidewalk.

"Are we finished?"

When I say we are, she brushes past me and heads indoors.

I do this. More often than I care to admit. Frustrated, impatient, afraid, I come out with shitty comments that are mean and insult people. Often actors. Always people whom I need to like and help me. Stupid. Very stupid.

This Is
Not Brain
Surgery.

I'M DONE SHOOTING THE MOVIE. I DID MY BEST. WHICH I'M THINKING wasn't great. I'm waking up a lot in the middle of the night, replaying some scene in my dream, watching a mistake happen and being unable to fix it. Every night, another scene. Frustrating. Everything I learned on this job, I learned too late. That's the thing with learning by doing. You fuck up a lot.

I have a better understanding now of how directing a movie is different from directing a commercial. Film directors have complete control of their audience's attention. Commercial directors don't. Because a movie audience is sitting in a dark room with no distractions. Not in front of a television with nothing but distractions. Film directors control where the audience looks, how much they see, whether it's a detail or a wider frame, if it's a detail then which one, how long the viewer looks at a frame, and what they hear. You have all sorts of ways to control the time you spend with an audience when it's parked in a dark room. Still, you have to learn how to use it effectively. With commercials, your audience is actively trying to *not* look at what you've done. So you use tricks to make them stay put. All the tricks satisfy short-term problems. Short-term because it's all happening within thirty seconds. A movie's a long-term proposition so it requires entirely different architecture and solutions.

The material you gather is the same in both. You shoot multiple takes of the same action. Wide, medium, and close-up shots. What's called coverage. A wide shot allows the viewer to see the characters in context, in the world. A medium shot goes in closer, usually staying on one actor, sometimes including all of them. The world they are in becomes less important than their physical relation to each other. Then there are close-ups. These allow the viewer to see details, subtle movements, and expressions. Close-ups see much more intimately and intensely than the human eye ever does. In life, if you leaned over and stared at the weird mole on the face of a guy sitting across from you, people would think you were rude. Especially the guy with the mole. In a close-up in a movie, you're allowed.

The director tells a story by combining and interlacing the different takes. He uses them like a writer uses words, punctuation, structure, and rhythm. The director weaves the takes together, hoping he can make the audience experience the exact same things at the exact same moments. In some ways, it's relatively easy to have the audience stay with the program for thirty seconds. To hold their attention for ninety minutes, you have to think about those shots and scenes in an entirely different way.

That would have been good to know three weeks ago.

Film Editors.

EVERY TIME I WALK INTO AN EDITING SUITE, I PANIC. I TRY TO STEER MY thoughts in a positive direction. I tell myself it's going to be one of those days where I'll look at the cut the editor's done and be stunned by how awesome it is. Then my brain goes into abacus mode, tallies up past experiences, and goes dark. More than half the time, in spite of detailed conversations about how I think the spot should look and the hours and effort the editor has put into a rough cut, he or she will hit play and I'll watch something that's not good.

I am a prick about editing. No question. But I'm a prick for three reasons. First, I have a basic sense of how stuff should be put together. All those psychopath murder films at the pizzeria where I had to edit in the camera had some residual effect. Second, because my so-called professional beginnings were low budget and I often couldn't afford to hire an editor, I'd edit a lot of my jobs myself. Not necessarily well but I did it. So I have a sense of what's possible. The third reason is personal. If a spot looks bad, people will think it's because I fucked it up. No one blames the editor.

But I've also walked into edit rooms and been amazed. I've worked with editors who took my half-baked material and, through their skill, artistry, and effort, turned it into something really good. Way better than it had a right to be. These experiences helped me understand the basic framework of filmmaking. One component is writing. Another is casting. The third is staging the scenes. And the fourth is editing. Certain components matter more than others when you try and figure out why a film works. My experience is that great casting or remarkable editing, by itself, can salvage a film. Gifted actors can overcome a so-so script and a bad director and make them look good because of the performances they give. And a great editor can take boring performances, dumb words, and poorly staged scenes and make them seem to matter. But, unfortunately, even a great director cannot overcome bad casting and terrible cutting. Sad but true.

I hired a young woman to cut my first film. I'd never made a feature and she'd never cut one, so we were evenly matched. And she was cheap. Instead of having to rent space to edit in, she offered to cut the film in her loft on the Bowery. We had a Steenbeck editing table and a pile of editing supplies schlepped up the three rickety flights of stairs to her place.

In 1983, the Bowery below Canal Street was the Wild West. Chinese merchants had stores in the ground floor spaces but, in a lot of the buildings, the upper floors were unoccupied. I had the feeling that Sally and her husband were squatting in their place. If they had a landlord, he wasn't providing much. There was running water and electricity. But no heat, no kitchen, no walls, and no intercom. Whenever I came downtown to work with her, I'd have to call from a pay phone and she'd throw keys down, so I could let myself in. It was independent filmmaking.

Sally put together a very rough assembly of each day's scenes as I shot. Those rough assemblies use whatever master shot feels right, along with a few medium and close-ups cut in, so it feels like an actual scene. It's not finessed. But, when you're done shooting, within a week you can sit down and get a very quick, very raw look at the whole film. It's long. It's slow. But it's the movie as it's written.

When you watch that first assembly, it's usually just fucking terrible. I've sat through three of my own and been bummed out and panicked each time. I'm sure good directors must experience the same thing. The difference being that they *know* the rough cut will suck and don't sweat it. I'm dumb enough to think it might be great. An experienced director knows the editing process is where the film really gets made. Everything that's been shot is just raw material. Some scenes will be kept. Some will be tossed. Sequences will change, the script will eventually be forgotten. The only thing that will matter is creating an interesting film.

Ten days after I finished shooting, I went down to the loft to watch a first assembly. Steenbeck editing tables can only handle twenty-minute reels of film, so you don't see the movie in one uninterrupted sitting. You watch twenty minutes, then go have a smoke while the next reel gets loaded, watch another twenty minutes, and so on. We finished looking in the middle of the afternoon. I didn't know what to make of what I'd seen. Some parts were okay, some were awful. All my judgmental skills were still distorted because the actors were speaking my words. Maybe it was a little long. And repetitive. But overall…

…the film didn't work. Mainly because it was all talking. Ninety fucking minutes of talking. The characters go to work and they talk. They go to restaurants and they talk. They call each other and talk. They hang out with friends and talk. The arc of the film is supposed to be the slow-burning attraction between the guy and the girl. I thought it'd be interesting if they don't get in the sack until the end credits roll. The idea is right: two interesting people reluctantly fall for each other. It's nice and real and involving. But I hadn't created any momentum. The film would start and stop and start and stop. It needed to be reimagined and re-edited.

But I couldn't admit that. Yet. Instead, over the next three weeks, Sally basically just cut the film down into something easier to watch. But no big structural changes. We added some great music without any regard for whether we could afford it. That made so-so scenes seem better. Always a sign that the underlying scene sucks. By early May, we decided to show the rough cut to an audience. We rented a small screening room in the Movielab Building on West 54th Street, invited a mix of friends and film people. Sally and her husband sat over on one side. I was on the other side, all the way in the back.

The film didn't play very well. The funny scenes didn't get many laughs, which meant they weren't funny. The romantic scenes didn't have any heat. And the big narrative arc, two relationships coming apart, then two people, nervously single, reluctantly falling for each other, seemed stupid. As folks filed out, they'd offer some quick thoughts and ideas. The basic through line was they hoped we'd make it better.

Finally, it was just Sally, her husband, and I standing in the beat-up lobby. I asked her what she thought. Ever the diplomat, she said we had work to do. She had learned some stuff, watching with an audience really helps, fresh eyes, some things really surprised her, a lot to digest. She asked me what I thought.

I'd had an epiphany. By the end of the screening, I realized I was out of my depth. And I didn't know what to do next. I needed help.

What I actually said to Sally was that I thought some parts worked but a lot didn't. At which point, she interrupted me with a question. Would I give her a few weeks, by herself, to work on the film? She had some ideas. To her great surprise, I, the micromanaging, cocky, out-of-his-depth, first-time auteur who'd gotten his training making deodorant commercials, said without hesitation, "Do it."

I didn't see Sally for a month. We spoke on the phone once in a while, but that was it. I was aggressively jumping back into the world of commercials because I needed money. Sally called me one Thursday afternoon and said she was ready for me to take a look. She suggested we go to a screening room instead of the loft, so we wouldn't have to deal with all the reel changes. So, the following morning, I met her at that same Movielab screening room. She didn't offer up much in the way of a preamble. She'd rearranged things a bit. Used some alternate takes here and there. Let's take a look.

Ninety minutes later, I'd just seen a totally new movie. It was funny and charming and unexpected and romantic. Many of the dialogue-heavy scenes had been cut in half. Some had been omitted entirely. But I didn't miss any of it. For the prior ninety minutes, I'd watched something that was a complete surprise to me. It was now an okay movie. Certainly way, way better than what I'd written and shot. Sally had taken the raw material and made it entirely different and entirely better.

I'm someone who bristles at any suggestions from anyone about how to do my job better. I just get my back up. I figure I'm getting the criticism because it's apparent I don't know what I'm doing. I don't hear specific criticism. I hear someone saying, "You suck at your job." It makes for all sorts of conflicts when I'm shooting ads. But, this morning, I see how someone has taken raw material I generated and made it light years better. And I'm happy. Thrilled. I have a small fortune invested in this film. What I'd originally put together wasn't good. Meaning I was going to be out all that money. What Sally had done is taken the film, also known as my money, and given it a great shot of becoming a good investment. I wanted to make a commercial film. My original version wasn't. This recut one was.

Within two weeks, we were arranging screenings for potential distributors. After one in New York and another in Los Angeles, we got three offers. We made a deal. Prior to its theatrical release, the film was invited to Sundance, Toronto, and a few big festivals in Europe. We got a foreign sales agent who sold it across Europe, South America, and Asia. It was no blockbuster, but it did fine.

Whatever success *Cold Feet* had was pretty much due to Sally and the performances that Griffin and Marissa gave. That's two out of the three essentials. I was a barely competent director, definitely the weak link. My staging and shooting were too simple, and I didn't know yet how to show instead of tell. The actors and the editor had been able to overcome me.

Martin Scorsese came to a screening of *Cold Feet* in Los Angeles to see Griffin's performance. He then cast him in *After Hours*. Griffin's worked consistently as an actor and director for the last forty years. Sally and her husband, Dean Parisot, moved to Los Angeles. Dean was starting a directing career, and Los Angeles seemed a more promising place than New York. She worked on a Ninja Turtles movie and a Lily Tomlin project. Then she went to a job interview about editing another first-time director's film. He was an excitable guy with a weirdly encyclopedic knowledge of movies, fed by his years' working in a video store. In fact, during the interview, she was surprised to learn he'd seen *Cold Feet*. He hired her to cut his movie. *Reservoir Dogs*.

Sally Menke went on to edit every film Quentin Tarantino made and was nominated twice for the Academy Award for Best Editing on *Pulp Fiction* and *Inglourious Basterds*. She worked with Oliver Stone, Billy Bob Thornton, and a few others. But her permanent client was Tarantino.

Sally died a week before I started shooting my third film. She was hiking in the Hollywood Hills and tumbled off a trail. The last time I'd seen her was twenty years before when I went to the house she and Dean and their two kids shared in Hancock Park. When you walked in, you entered a center hall foyer then turned right into a large, open kitchen and family room. On the wall behind the big wooden dining table was a framed *Cold Feet* poster. I asked what the heck that was doing there. She said Quentin had bought it for her after *Reservoir Dogs* came out. At that moment, I was pretty sure Quentin had also found himself one discouraging afternoon in a screening room with Sally, freaked by the lack of reaction from a small audience of friends after they had watched his first cut. And that Sally had said, if it was all right with Quentin, maybe he would give her a few weeks to work on the film by herself. She had some ideas.

Dude, Where's My Car?

BEFORE I DECIDED TO HATE THE PEOPLE WHO DISTRIBUTED MY FILM, I liked them. They were operating from the premise that *Cold Feet* was a commercial movie, not some art house indie. That sounded great to me. Because commercial, in my mind, translated into millions of dollars at the box office. For a small film to have that kind of success, it would need great reviews, great word of mouth, and a great public relations campaign. You need a savvy distribution company to orchestrate all that. One that has relationships with theater owners, newspaper critics, college film departments, other actors and directors, foreign sales agents, television reps, all the people and players in this little universe that periodically turn a tiny film by an unknown director into a big hit. These guys seemed to fit the bill.

○ ○ ○

The company's first move is to get the movie into Sundance. Sundance in 1984 is still a small festival that's just relocated from Robert Redford's little ski resort to Park City, Utah. Festivals like Sundance are places you go to see movies that may or may not get commercial releases. It's for movie buffs. It's not yet about seeing movie stars. The people who make and star in independent films are unknown to most people. In fact, they're almost unknown to their agents. When they call me to let me know I'm going to Sundance, I play it very cool. I'm glad. It's also gotten into Toronto and a couple of festivals in Europe. I'm starting to think the movie doesn't suck.

In fact, *Cold Feet* is one of ten dramatic finalists in that year's Sundance competition. It's an interesting lineup. Of the ten directing finalists, five are first-timers. Jim Jarmusch, Bill Duke, Adam Brooks, Joel and Ethan Coen, and me. The second-timer is John Sayles.

Twelve months before, I'd started shooting what looked, to a lot of people working on it, like a little vanity project. In the intervening twelve months, I've gotten it edited, dealt with three distribution offers, and sold the foreign rights. I am still struggling in commercials, shooting low-budget, forgettable spots. I'm a C+-level guy scraping up work. But this plan, this hazy idea I had that I could use the commercial world as a stepping-stone to move into films, seems to be working out. I'm starting to think I know what I'm doing. What's become obvious to me is that, in the film business, you *have* to behave as if you know exactly what you're doing.

I'm out at the festival by myself. No one from the distributor has come with me to Park City to show me the ropes. I don't have an agent yet. I just wander around and join groups of people I don't know who seem interested in me when they find out I'm a director with a film in competition. Distributors, festival people, press, agents, theater owners, publicity people, everyone gets a fake version of me that sounds calm and cool.

The Sundance people decided they'd have the directing finalists share condominiums with established directors. The thinking must have been that some sort of informal mentoring would happen. My roommates are Paul Bartel and Jonathan Demme. Bartel's last film, *Eating Raoul,* was a dumb comedy about cannibalism. I idolize Demme. I've seen *Melvin and Howard* four or five times. He's made two other small films that were also good, but he's still operating in the minor leagues. It'll be nine years before he wins the Academy Award for *The Silence of the Lambs*. He sat in the row ahead of me on the flight out to Salt Lake City. The whole time, he made a big deal of reorganizing the piles of scripts he was reading. When, almost genuflecting, I introduced myself and told him how much I admired his work, he pretty much had me talk to the hand. This is consistent with his demeanor all weekend. He never speaks to me during our time in the apartment, so no mentoring comes to pass. He does ask if he can use the car I'd rented, but Bartel has already borrowed it. In the first of many come-to-Joseph-Smith realizations during this long weekend in Utah, I discover I am the only one of my roommates with enough money to rent a car. Lesson stored away.

When I get to Park City, I go to the festival headquarters and check in. As a directing finalist, I am invited to a lot of events and dinners. I've never been to a film festival before, so I'm curious about everything. Sundance is about generating interest in movies, either before their release or in order to get them sold. The film everyone is interested in is *Blood Simple*. That's all anyone's talking about. So, when I go to the box office to check on ticket sales for my film, I'm surprised to learn that the first showing of *Cold Feet* has been sold out for a week. I ask the ticket sellers if they have any idea why this happened. They say the film's getting good word of mouth. It has only been shown once in Boston at a screening thrown by my production company's office there. That screening hadn't caused any ripples in Boston, so it's a little weird to think it would cause a sellout in Park City, Utah. I don't overthink it.

I'm too nervous to go to the screening that night. Instead, I go to see Victor Nuñez's film, *A Piece of Green*, because it's being shown in the theater next to the one where *Cold Feet* is screening. About ten minutes into Nuñez's film, I start to hear steady, solid laughter coming through the wall. At exactly the right point for an audience to be laughing in *Cold Feet*. This continues for the next ninety-six minutes. The Nuñez film is slow and somber, so the audience is quiet throughout. They are not quiet next door. I'm thrilled. At the end, I can hear applause through the walls. I slip out of *A Piece of Green* and hang around the lobby listening to people talk. They like my movie. Nice.

Since Bartel still has my car, I take a shuttle bus into town and have dinner with a young agent my lawyer wanted me to meet. We talk about my film, the Coen brothers, the other films at the festival, specifically *Blood Simple*, what I want to do next, do I know the Coen brothers, and how much time am I willing to spend in Los Angeles. I feel like my life is about to change.

Or might. I've watched a few of the other finalists' movies. I haven't seen *Blood Simple* yet. My movie looks all right. In some ways, maybe because of shooting so many commercials, mine is slicker than some of the others. It may be my first feature film, but it doesn't look it. And my film is pretty different than the others. It's straightforward, more genuine, and makes no attempt to be arty. It's just a movie. A movie I hope will be appreciated by the widest possible audience. I didn't invest all this money to make something that would only appeal to critics or festival audiences. And that's where I feel like I'm standing at a distance from people like Sayles or Jarmusch or the Coens. My take is they want to be artists. I just want to be a working director. Granted, this is total speculation. I haven't discussed this with any of them. Once in a while, we're all in the same room, but we're not hanging out, doing shots, exchanging phone numbers. And the others have entourages of sorts. Agents, press people, lawyers. I'm here by myself.

This is what I'm chewing on at midnight as I take the shuttle bus back to the condo. Critical favorite director Paul Bartel still has my car.

The next day, I decide I'll man up and go to that night's *Cold Feet* screening. Tickets are sold out again. When I get to the theater, the person who's set to introduce the film asks if I'd speak for a moment.

What I say to the eager and predisposed-to-like-my-film-sold-out audience is ridiculous. Basically, I hold forth like an accountant. I tell them I'd made the film in seventeen days, finishing four days ahead of schedule, and that there'd been no overtime. Amazingly, no one in the audience cares about this. I then add some other equally stupid details for an audience that just likes watching movies. Nothing about casting the actors, the editorial process, the writing, the financing, the struggle to make the film, nothing creative or human. Just nuts and bolts, time and money. Massive buzzkill.

The audience sits politely through the screening. There are a few half-hearted laughs, uncomfortable squirming where, the night before, I'm sure there had been rapt attentiveness and, as Todd Rundgren's "We Gotta Get You a Woman" plays over the end credits, they exit quickly. No questions for the director. I go into town for another round of drinks with the agent. He asks how it went. Not as well as the night before. Way not better. I'd walked into this screening thinking I was going to finally get a little in-person recognition. Two days of hearing only about *Blood Simple* was annoying. Last night had been great. Tonight, another sold-out screening. This time, with me charming the audience. In reality, I buzz-killed the room. Brooks's easygoing nature, Jarmusch's hair and sunglasses, the Coen's nerdiness, how could these be more interesting than my talking about how I'd made the film without an hour of over-time? Man. They should *not* have sent me out to this thing alone. I am clueless.

On the final night of the festival, I go to a dinner party honoring the directing finalists. There are oversized, black-and-white photos of each of us suspended over the dining room, like the banners commemorat-ing retired Ranger and Knick jerseys in Madison Square Garden. It's a nice dinner. Redford speaks. So does the Mrs. Fields who makes cookies. Everyone knows the Coens will win the next day.

They do. Jarmusch gets a special jury award. So does Sayles. So does Brooks. I don't get anything. I think I've made an all right movie, but it is scorned as being commercial. But that's what I was trying to make. And I'm a commercial director. Which seems to have a terrible stink attached to it among these serious filmmakers. I wish I had made something that had registered more dramatically on the festival's radar. I didn't. *Cold Feet* got in, it sold tickets, but it didn't seem to matter. I'm a little frightened that this also means the film's going to bomb at the box office and I'll be broke, but I compartmentalize that and sneer at these fucking artists. I am good at that. Especially good at sneering at my two artist roommates and their precarious financial situations.

On Monday morning, I get my car keys back from Bartel and drive to the Salt Lake airport. I'm in line to check in for the flight to New York and find myself behind one of the festival judges. A journalist/movie critic. One I'd never heard of before the festival. I introduce myself. He gives me a distracted nod and says, "I didn't like your film."

Thank you. And fuck you.

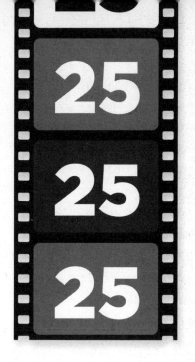

Double-Entry Bookkeeping.

COLD FEET WAS NOT A GREAT MOVIE. BUT IT HAD ENOUGH POTENTIAL TO attract offers from three distribution companies. I picked the guys who seemed the most committed.

Well, they certainly were. They decided the little film I'd made for less than two hundred thousand dollars was going to be their entrée into mainstream film distribution. And they marketed it that way. As a real commercial film. No mention that it was made for peanuts. No hints that it was a first effort by a twenty-something director. No attempt to play up the labor of love, diamond-in-the-rough thing. Instead, they opened the film on the third weekend in May. Only one other film opened that day. *Raiders of the Lost Ark*.

Cold Feet opened on a Friday in five theaters in New York City. A normal art film would open in one. Okay. The distributors were thinking big. Unfortunately, it got mostly mediocre reviews from the big critics. Some were worse than mediocre. One said during her television review, "Bruce Van Dusen, if you're watching, please do not make another film."

The picture hobbled through a few weeks in big cities. For some reason, in certain secondary markets, it became a minor hit. In Portland, Seattle, Toronto, and Vancouver, it played for months. This can happen with small films. Given enough time, they find their audiences. You just have to be lucky enough to hold on to the screens so that people can discover it.

Because this was before the internet, I had no idea this was happening. The distribution company said the New York, Los Angeles, and Chicago runs had been bad, they hadn't recovered their marketing and distribution costs, and no new markets were anticipated. So I was surprised when a guy I knew in Portland called saying the film was in its second month playing there and then when a magazine in Toronto called to interview me and then again when an acquaintance in Vancouver called to tell me he'd loved the movie. I started to have some questions. If they hadn't mentioned these cities, these successful, on-going runs, what else were they not telling me?

I called the distributors and set up a meeting. I asked that they send over their revenue and expense spreadsheets beforehand. Oddly enough, they did. As I went through the paperwork, I discovered a document that listed their actual expenditures. As opposed to the ones on the other spreadsheets they'd meant for me to see. Long story short, they'd kind of double-billed me for their marketing expenses. The picture had made a profit, albeit a minuscule one. And those continuing runs in the Pacific Northwest and Canada were only adding to the plus side.

Even an Amish egg farmer knows that Hollywood bookkeeping is criminal. I thought I had entered into all the business aspects of this with my eyes wide open. I had a good lawyer, I had many face-to-face meetings with the distribution people, I had a real sense of what I was dealing with. The only questionable link was the main guy, but he seemed to be the least involved in the artistic side. Because I'm simple, I didn't realize that the main guy would pay the most attention to the money while he let the underlings do the creative stuff. When I'd asked them to send over the records, my motive was just to prove that the film was still doing well in certain markets, so they'd keep supporting it. I was only going to make my money back if the film kept running. When I stumbled onto the scam, it just seemed stupid. Even these fucking art film guys were thieves.

Three people from the distribution company arrived at my office for the meeting. They walked me through the fake spreadsheet. I listened politely then handed Xeroxed copies of the real one to everyone at the table. There was a brief silence. The chief financial officer reached into his inside jacket pocket and took out a check. It was already made out to me.

"This should make us even."

This was almost worse than having them feign shock when they learned the jig was up. These asshats came to the meeting knowing they'd robbed me, prepared to hand over hush money but only if I'd discovered their theft. Clearly, they were such scumbags it would now be necessary to go through the annoyance and cost of auditing everything related to the film. Which we did. Which resulted in more bad bookkeeping being discovered. Which resulted in me looking at these three young guys who'd claimed to be totally devoted to the art of film, to the director's vision, to bringing small films to wider audiences, and realizing they were lying shits. Oh, wait. That's how the film business has always operated. Got it.

I was very happy to be back shooting commercials. You got paid 30 percent up front and the balance when the commercial was edited. Even if the spot sucked.

Dumbo
Tokyo.

IT'S THURSDAY, SEPTEMBER 27, A LITTLE AFTER FIVE IN THE MORNING. Blanche and I are driving into Manhattan. She'd started feeling contractions last night while we were watching *St. Elsewhere*. By 4:00 a.m. it's clear what's happening. Baby.

We called the obstetrician and woke him up. I had no qualms about getting the guy out of bed at this hour. He told us to head into the city and he'd meet us at the hospital.

We drive down the Saw Mill River Parkway, on to the Deegan, and then over to FDR Drive on our way to New York Hospital. It's nice at this hour. The sun coming up. Empty highways. Deserted sidewalks. Blanche is calm and cool. I'm trying to be calm and cool.

I offer to drop her at the entrance to the emergency room, but she wants to come with me while I park the car. Taking a little walk, getting some exercise before everything goes kerflooey, seems like a good idea.

I pull into a garage a block from the hospital. The attendant asks how long we're going to be. I point to Blanche's full-term pregnancy-filled T-shirt and say I have no idea. We walk down 70th Street and into the entrance to the emergency room. The place is quiet. We fill out the admission papers, and a nurse walks us back to where the beds are. It dawns on me that pregnant women and their husbands are probably the only people who are happy to be coming into emergency rooms. Blanche hops up on a bed, the nurse takes her vitals, and we wait. Five minutes later, the obstetrician appears. Joe does a quick exam and then announces we're going to have a baby later today.

I was afraid of that.

I give Blanche a concerned, guilty look then focus on Joe.

"When, exactly, later today do you think?"

"I can't say exactly when…why?"

I can barely utter this next sentence.

"Because I'm supposed shoot a commercial today. Can I do that?"

Joe doesn't know what that means.

"Depends."

"On?"

"How long does it take to shoot a commercial?"

Just his asking makes me think he doesn't think it's a terrible idea.

"This one…maybe four hours."

He shrugs and glances at Blanche.

"Shouldn't be a problem. Put it this way. I'm leaving in fifteen minutes and going to services."

"What?"

"Yeah, it's Rosh Hashanah."

No wonder those roads were really, really empty.

Reading this thirty-five years later, I don't think it gives the reader an entirely accurate description of what's going on. A husband leaving his wife alone to go through labor with their first baby is something only a real dick would do. I didn't think I was being a dick. I still don't. I think I was a responsible husband, a nervous-about-to-be-first-time-father and small business owner who'd put himself in a bad jam. As the due date had gotten closer, I'd had two choices: one, not take any work for the two-or-three-week window around when the baby was due or, two, bet that if I got a job, it wouldn't happen on the day Blanche went into labor. I lost the bet. Now, if I called off the shoot and postponed it for a day or two, I would have been on the hook for tens of thousands of dollars in cancellation fees. I didn't have tens of thousands of dollars. Add to this the fact that Blanche is an actress and, therefore, understands the weirdness of what work as a director entails. Sudden departures, abrupt changes of plans, unexpected twists and turns. She and I had talked about whether this might happen and what we'd do. We figured we'd navigate it. Neither of us bet on landing in the perfect storm.

So here we are. I'm thinking I've got permission to go shoot a commercial. Partially because our obstetrician is going to Rosh Hashanah services. At his temple in Westchester County. Twenty miles away. And his rabbi is very old and speaks slowly, so he doesn't think he's going to be back to the hospital before 3:00 p.m., which is fine because he's 100 percent certain this baby won't be born before early tonight. At the earliest. In fact, he tells us to leave the hospital. Blanche should go to the movies or something. And I should go shoot my commercial. He's got his beeper in case something crazy happens. And, with that, Joe waves goodbye and splits.

Blanche and I walk out of the hospital and over to York Avenue. She's feeling contractions, but they're random and very far apart. I ask her what we should do. Like if she doesn't want me to go to the stage, I'll listen. We go over it. The doctor's said the birth isn't imminent, I've got fifty people waiting for me, Blanche is healthy and chill…we should do what we have to do. I'll go shoot the commercial; she'll hang out with a friend. That's what we decide. To my dying day, I'll remember it like that.

Blanche calls one of her friends who lives a few blocks away. She's thrilled to skip work and hang out with Blanche instead. So we have a plan. I walk Blanche over to her friend's building and then hop in a cab to the stage.

I'd tried to anticipate something like this could happen. We'd booked a stage fifteen blocks north of the hospital so, if, by some weird chance, the baby was born during production of a job I didn't yet have, I could get back down to the hospital in ten minutes. That's like the blink of an eye. I am known for being an efficient director. Today, I am going to be so fucking efficient it will make everyone's heads spin. This is not a great situation. At all. But it's what I have to deal with.

The spot is for Japan Airlines. It's very simple. A Japanese American woman, dressed as a stewardess, delivers thirty seconds of copy. The spot is supposed to be shot in a single take. We've got a teleprompter for her, so she just has to read the lines, no memorizing required. And the lighting will take no time. I walk onto the stage a little after 7:00. I'm pretty sure we can be shooting by 8:00. If the actress is any good, we'll be done by 11:00.

I sneak my producer into an empty production office and close the door behind us. I explain what's happening and, in a panicky voice, shout that I need to stay in constant touch with Blanche throughout the morning. He has a great solution. There are five separate phone lines that feed onto the stage. He'll commandeer one, give that number to Blanche and Blanche only, and hide the phone itself in a desk drawer, so no one else will use it. Okay. We have some control here.

The agency for JAL is the New York office of Tokyo-headquartered Dentsu, the biggest agency in the world. All the JAL people are Japanese. All the Dentsu New York people except one account person are American. A Japanese agency runs differently than an American one. Consensus is everything. Total, 100 percent agreement on every single thing that happens. Which results in a number of bad things. First, everything goes super slowly. Consensus takes for-fucking-ever. Second, arriving at consensus is a weirdly passive process, so no one's willing to lead. Third, with no one leading, consensus often results in choosing the worst available option. Which is how we've come to hire an actress who can't act. She's a model. Everyone liked how she looked and convinced themselves her looks would somehow translate into her being able to deliver thirty seconds of copy. On a good day, this would be a challenge. On a day when your wife's in labor, it's nuts.

I decide not to include everyone on the set in what's going on in my private life. If they know, it'll make anything I say or do suspect. I will compartmentalize the baby stuff and focus on making the commercial.

I walk into the makeup room to see how things are going. The model's in the chair. We booked a hair and makeup team that specializes in Asian women. Black makeup people do black people. Whites do whites. Asians do Asians. Very specialized field for a reason that completely eludes me. As I walk in, the makeup guy's almost finished. The hairdresser is pulling the actress's hair back and fitting it under the stewardess cap she'll wear. I talk to the actress while the hairdresser uses a mouthful of pins to shape the hair into a bun. Looking at the actress's face in the mirror, it strikes me that something's wrong. Something's different. She doesn't look like the woman at the casting session.

It's her ears. Her ears are sticking out. Like Dumbo. This petite Japanese woman has ears the size of cut-in-half DVDs. And they really stick out. How did I not see this before? How was this not so obvious that it knocked her out of the running? I'm trying to figure out how to deal with this when it's all preempted. The makeup guy notices me staring. He takes my arm, pulls me out of the room, and says, once the hat goes on, he'll put some glue behind her ears and stick them to her head. That's what she did for her audition. They'll stay that way all day. Promise.

This is a first. For me, anyway. Actors put in fake teeth; they change the color of their eyes with contact lenses; they put lifts in their shoes; they wear wigs and dye their hair. But gluing your ears back, this is new. But I'm fucking glad it's happening. No one would want Dumbo as the face of JAL.

Makeup says it'll be ten more minutes. I go into the office with the hot phone and make a quick call to Blanche at her friend's apartment. The contractions are still happening but not getting any closer together. She and her friend are following Joe's advice and going to a movie. All's well.

Ten minutes later, the actress comes out to the stage and sits in front of the camera. I frame a closeup of her face then go over to video village. There are seven agency people and five JAL people. A lot of consensus needed here. The JAL folks don't speak much English. The agency producer translates what I say. I give a quick explanation of what we'll do this morning. Basically, shoot until we get a take we like. She's using a teleprompter, so her delivery will be pretty consistent. Should be a simple job.

Why did I say that?

I start shooting. The woman is terrible. Nervous, fumbling, embarrassed. She can't get through more than five words without blowing a line. The teleprompter is not helping at all. I seriously wonder whether she can read. Suddenly I'm scared. The compartmentalizing goes to shit. This could be really bad. I speak with her. Try to be supportive. I ask whether I can do anything to help. Maybe make the font size on the teleprompter bigger? Change the color? This is not the day I want to run an acting class.

I go over to the agency and client. They stare at me hopefully, which is weird because, based on what they've just seen, I can only be bringing bad news. But I am going to be upbeat, goddammit.

"First takes are always a little wobbly. She'll get more confident. We'll be fine here. She looks good, right?"

All bullshit. I don't know whether they're buying my optimism. The Americans are nervous. Averting their eyes, furrowing brows, wringing hands. The Japanese look right at me while I speak and, when I finish… keep looking at me the same way. Just staring. Maybe they're not getting any of this.

I go back to the camera. Just before I sit down, my producer comes and stands next to me.

"Phone."

I hustle over to the office with the hot line and pull the phone out of the drawer. I note that the phone is actually red. Blanche sounds a little less confident.

"The contractions are coming quicker. Like, a lot quicker."

"Two minutes, five minutes…?"

Like the exact spacing will help me understand what's going on.

"Less than a minute."

"How much less than a minute? Ten seconds? Five seconds?"

She and Lianne now don't think going to a movie is such a good idea.

"How's it going on the set?"

"Fine," I lie.

I don't know what to do. So I keep talking.

"Look, Blanche, do what you think is right. If you think you should go back to the hospital, do it. If the contractions really are coming fast, you have to call Joe. Him disappearing to services is total bullshit. I mean…"

Blanche doesn't hear all the last part. A contraction interrupts things, and she asks me to hold on while she groans and swears. When it passes, she sounds completely calm again.

"I just wanted to check in. I'll let you know if things change."

Amazingly calm. Amazingly solid. I have permission to keep going.

I go back to the camera and start again. The girl phumphers the lines, I keep the camera rolling, she starts again, messes up again, starts again, does a little better, then messes up completely. I stop. In my head, I am screaming obscenities. In one of my little mental compartments furnished with rope and towels, I am gagging and strangling her. I berate myself for not refusing to cast her. Then I switch lanes and start mentally berating the clients because I now have to solve a problem they've forced on me. And I can't even bill them extra for fixing their self-inflicted idiocy. In fact, this might just cost me money.

I start shooting again. More mistakes. I stop. I go over to the girl and ask her to take a breath.

"Next time, just see the words and speak them. Don't think, just chat with me, like we're on the phone."

We try another take. Disaster. I have to change the plan.

The agency and client see what's happening too. Something's got to give. I suggest, trying to make it sound like a burst of inspiration instead of the desperation move it actually is, that we give up on the idea of a single take. Let's break the script down into five short pieces, she'll read those short pieces, I'll change the framing for each one and then, in editing, you'll cut together the best takes. It's a great way to solve the problem and come away with a good-looking final product. In fact, it's the only way.

The Americans shuffle their feet and say nothing. They remind me of dogs distractedly digging for bones they remember burying a few weeks back. The JAL folks stare at me, simultaneously blank and intent. How do they do that?

It feels like I've been dropped into *The Taking of Pelham One Two Three*. The scene where Walter Matthau thinks none of the Japanese subway executives he's hosting understand English and he starts making nasty comments about them. It turns out their silence isn't lack of language comprehension but a cultural difference. Their English is perfect. I will not do that.

In my movie, this morning, as far as I can tell, the JAL folks' silence means they're agreeing with my new tact. At least, that's how I'm going to read it. I hustle back to the camera and explain to the model we'll do some shorter takes and see what happens.

It works. She can handle two sentences at a time. Maybe she was just scared about the idea of doing the whole script in one chunk. I shoot a few takes. Change the framing and shoot the next line. Progress. I run back and forth between the camera and video village. I look like I'm on amphetamines.

I finish two more lines then change the framing again. The girl has almost developed a rhythm. On to the last two lines. Home stretch. Then, during the next take, something looks wrong. I ask her to adjust the tilt of her head. She does. But the image looks even weirder. I zoom in. Fuck. One of her ears has come unglued and is sticking out at a forty-five-degree angle. She's half Dumbo.

I hadn't mentioned anything about the girl's ears to the agency. Now they know. The makeup guy hustles into frame, does some quick swabbing with a Q-tip and glue and, using his hands as a vise clamp, presses her ears flat against her skull. Presto, no mo' Dumbo. I shoot again.

I get four more takes before the other ear pops out. Glue, vise clamp hands, voilà, we start again. During the gluing, my producer appears next to me. Phone.

Blanche isn't speaking in complete sentences at this point.

"Going back. Hospital, Contractions. Painful."

Loud guttural noise. Unpleasant to hear.

"How close to done?"

"Soon. Almost done."

Weird new noise. Drowning person trying to hail a taxi.

"Hurry."

Oh, do I want to hurry.

I keep shooting. Every few takes, I speed walk over to video village and remark on how well she's doing. I don't even acknowledge the ears nightmare. I shoot for another twenty minutes. I have covered everything. It's noon.

I have been moving frantically, speaking loudly, basically acting completely nuts ever since the last phone call. I now stand in front of the clients, put on a car-dealer smile, exhale like I'm winded, and shove my hands in my pockets. I'm trying to give the impression that I've got all the time in the world.

"So?"

The Japanese give me blank stares that I choose to interpret as a mildly enthusiastic yes. The Americans say nothing. I turn to the agency producer, trying on a smile of pleasantly surprised shock.

"She did great. And I think we've covered everything. Amazing. Right?"

He looks at his watch, and his eyes widen when he sees that it's only noon. I can tell he's going to ask my producer for a refund because we've finished early. Whatever.

He says, very reluctantly, "Yeah, I guess we are."

I turn to my producer, tell him that's a wrap, shake the agency people's hands, shake the client's hands, then run down two flights of stairs, sprint out the front doors of the building, and step into Second Avenue with my hand already up to hail a cab.

When I get to the hospital, Blanche is on the delivery floor. She is propped up on a bed, wearing a sky blue, cloud-patterned smock, red in the face, and looking justifiably bewildered. Tiny electric wires disappear inside her, monitoring our soon-to-be-born child's vitals. Our obstetrician isn't here yet. Fucking asshole. I can shoot a spot faster than he can do Rosh Hashanah. It feels good to blame someone. The attending and the two nurses are a little nervous. The attending says the baby is in some distress. No shit. I'd be distressed too if my mother was literally crossing her legs to keep me from coming out until the OB shows up to deliver me. A few minutes later, Joe walks in. He has his hands in rubber gloves and inside Blanche in less than fifteen seconds, announces we're moving to the delivery room and, boom, we're moving. Ten minutes and no more than ten pushes later, Zane is born. He is scowling. His mother is smiling. So am I.

I will never again try to shoot a commercial and have a kid on the same day.

I hope.

Bronson and Eastwood.

As a rule, real stars aren't assholes. But you have to be talking about legitimate, big-deal, world-famous stars. Not a Rob Kardashian.

Most of the famous actors and athletes I've worked with have been great. Michael Schumacher, Arnold Palmer, Andre Agassi, Mia Hamm, Martin Short, Phil Jackson, Geena Davis, Alan Jackson, Nolan Ryan, Christian Vieri, Billy Dee Williams, Annie Potts, Kareem Abdul-Jabbar, Jane Seymour, Vanessa Williams, Lou Rawls, Steve Young. All really nice. There've been a few exceptions, but not many.

I'm standing next to fifty feet of dolly track by a lake in Calabasas, waiting for Charles Bronson to show up. I'm shooting spots for the US Department of the Interior. The campaign is about protecting the environment. The agency's convinced three movie stars known as macho tough guys to say poetic things about trees, flowers, and otters. Lou Gossett Jr., Charles Bronson, and Clint Eastwood will star in the spots.

I really wanted this job. I wanted to work with three super stars. I wanted it so badly that I pretty much offered to do it for free. But I got it. I've worked with a lot of celebrities, but these three are a step up. Most of what I do on this job won't be about directing. It'll be about managing the personalities. I'm planning to stick to my tried-and-true method of dealing with famous folks: Treat them like normal people. It works every time. I have theories about why, but they involve my completely bizarre theories on psychiatry, parenting, and toilet training, so I'll spare you. Suffice it to say, I don't kiss the ring. Especially if someone's being a dick. If I encounter one of those, I don't waste a nanosecond genuflecting because they're going to behave like assholes no matter how I treat them.

Bronson should be easy. There's a teleprompter, so he doesn't have to memorize any lines. He just has to do the character he did in *Death Wish* but with a little twist. Today, he's a crazed vigilante rhapsodizing about bunnies and pine trees. The one I did yesterday with Lou Gossett Jr. worked pretty well. He riffed on the sergeant character he played in *An Officer and a Gentleman*. We were done in three hours. Solid.

We're shooting the spots outdoors. With exteriors, you do a fair amount of waiting for the sun to get into the right position. It's a little after 1:00 in the afternoon and the sun's too high to provide flattering light, so I'm killing time, waiting for it to drop a little. A black stretch limo pulls into the lot and parks over by the equipment trucks and motor homes. The driver scrambles around and opens the back door. Bronson gets out and looks around. He's dressed all in black and wears wrap-around sunglasses and high-heeled boots. Even from fifty yards away, I can tell he's pissed about something. I hop off the dolly and head over to introduce myself.

The AD approaches Bronson and says hello. Bronson ignores him. The limo driver nervously rubs his hands together and shuffles his feet. It's all bad vibes. My turn.

"Hi. I'm Bruce Van Dusen."

"What d'you do here?"

"I'm the director."

"So maybe you can tell me why this idiot drove me around in circles?"

"Well, I don't know."

I scope the driver. He wears a pained grimace. Like something happened involving tainted pork. Bronson keeps bitching.

"We could have been here an hour ago."

"I'm sorry. He knew where…"

I'm supposed to be thinking about the route they took, but the only thing I can really focus on is that Charles Bronson is way shorter than I expected. And he has done a terrible job of coloring his hair. Especially the mustache. It looks like he dyes everything with shoe polish. And the leather jacket seems to actually be pleather. And the boots with big heels look like they're from Florsheim. Mother of God.

I try to put myself in his place. He's just gotten to location, half an hour late, driven by a guy who he thinks intentionally took him the wrong way. And he's now meeting the director, who looks to be thirty. He's thinking he's about to spend four hours working with a fucking child. He took this no-money job because his agent said it would raise his profile. Maybe it'll show he has a sense of humor about his persona. But, to do this, to get that little publicity bump, he's going to be working with a director who just graduated from first grade, and get driven to and from work by a half-wit. Fuck.

"I'll find out what happened. Let's get you in makeup."

Walking to the trailer, I explain the script. He's seen it.

"Not very well written," he tells me.

"Yeah, well, there's a lot of lawyers involved in advertising."

"I'm going to rewrite it."

"Sure. Okay. Let's get a few takes of what's written and then you can do it anyway you want."

"Where are we shooting?"

"Over there by the water. A dolly shot. Pretty simple."

"We'll see."

Bronson climbs the steps into the trailer. As the door bangs shut behind him, I walk back to where the AD and the driver are standing. I want to get to the bottom of this limo fiasco, so I turn to the driver.

"What the fuck happened?"

"That's bullshit, what he told you."

The driver is pissed. It's clear he thinks of himself as a professional Hollywood limo driver. He deals with movie stars all the time. He didn't fuck this up.

"We came a different way because he made me take him to a specific Rite Aid, so he could buy some mascara. He sent me in to buy it. The store was on the other side of the Valley, so I had to take a weird route back because of traffic. The 101 was stopped dead."

"Fine. Was he that nasty the whole ride?"

"Yeah. Bastard didn't even thank me for getting the mascara. Which *I* paid for."

I know enough now. I'm guessing Bronson's one of those guys who likes to get everyone walking on eggshells around him just to make sure they know who's the boss. I walk back to the camera. The limo guy runs over.

"Somebody owes me twelve bucks for the Maybelline."

Bronson spends the next hour in the trailer. I stay away. I figure a guy who uses a specific brand of mascara will have no problem communicating his needs to a makeup person.

An hour later, we're shooting. Bronson instantly becomes that guy, the *Death Wish* guy. You point the camera at him, it all comes together. He's great.

After five takes, he tells me he's going to change the script around. He adds a few words, drops others. After five takes of that, he tells me he made it a lot better. I go over to talk to the agency guys.

"I don't think he's going to give us too many more takes."

The creatives don't care.

"He's great. That fucking *Death Wish* squint is awesome."

"So you guys are good?"

"Yeah. All good."

I walk over to Bronson.

"You did great. We're done."

"They liked those changes I made, right?

"Loved them."

"What'd I tell you? Definitely made it better."

What am I going to say? He's working for free, I got what I needed, he did what he was hired to do.

"I agree. Much better. Thanks."

The AD calls a wrap.

"Thanks, Charles. I appreciate your helping out. It was a lot of fun."

"Yeah, good. One thing. Tell the goddam driver to follow my directions this time. No more bullshit."

"I'll do that."

I consider asking him to reimburse us for the mascara. Instead, I just try not to stare at the clumps of black Colossal Volume Express caked in his eyelashes.

The next morning I'm sipping coffee in a fogged-in parking lot at the Huntington Botanical Gardens. I'm waiting for Clint Eastwood. I'm figuring that because Bronson was prickly, Eastwood is going to be an even more enormous challenge. After all, he's by far the biggest star of the three. Biggest movie star in the world, actually. I'm ready.

The production manager comes out of the motor home on her way to grab breakfast at craft service. I buzz her.

"Which one is Eastwood's trailer?"

"He said he didn't want one. He'd use production's."

"Are you fucking kidding me?"

"That's what he said. I talked to him myself."

"Did we hire a different driver than the guy who picked up *Death Wish*?"

"We didn't hire a driver. Said he'd drive himself."

"What?"

"Yeah."

"What about food or clothes or whatever special stuff he might want?"

"Nothing. He's in what you said you'd like him to wear, and he'll have a few other options with him and…"

A late-model Buick station wagon pulls into a space next to the motor home. The driver kills the engine and gets out. It's Clint Eastwood. Wow. I walk over and extend my hand.

"Good morning, Mr. Eastwood. I'm Bruce Van Dusen. The director."

"Hey, Bruce. Nice to meet you. I'm good with Clint."

Not that I don't trust my production people, but I just want to make sure of a few things.

"They told me you didn't need a trailer? You're good?"

"I'm fine. I wouldn't mind a cup of coffee."

"We can have someone…"

"Just point me to craft service."

We walk over to get a coffee. I explain what I'd like him to do, which is basically walk a few steps and deliver the copy into the lens. I'm thinking that, because Clint Eastwood has never done a commercial before, maybe I should explain how it works. Then I think better of that.

"We'll be ready in about ten minutes."

"Just let me know when you need me."

"If you want to hang out in the trailer, I can have the AD come over and get…"

"You know what? Why don't I walk over with you and see where we're shooting."

So Clint Eastwood and I walk into the part of the botanical gardens that has dense, fifteen-foot-high rhododendron bushes. I think they'll look cool as a background, like something in a jungle. And it'll contrast with MacArthur Park, where I filmed Gossett, and the lake where I filmed Bronson. We get to the camera. I behave like Clint and I are old friends and introduce him to people very casually. And, because I am an idiot, I tell them his name.

"Clint, this is my AD, Malcolm. Malcolm, Clint."

"Nice to meet you, Mr. Eastwood."

"Clint. Nice to meet you, Malcolm."

"And this is my camera assistant, Todd—"

"Hey, man!"

Clint and Todd do a soul brother handshake and laugh. Clint claps him on the back and asks about his kids by name. Turns out they've done a few movies together. We've got the family vibe happening now. Nice.

I give Clint the basics. I do it all shorthand. I don't even know why I'm telling him anything.

"You start here, take a few steps as we dolly and deliver most of it from the mark. I'm using a thirty-five-millimeter lens, so I see you from the waist up. If you use your hands a little, gesture or something, I'll see that."

I hope it sounds like I know what I'm doing. Maybe this'll spark a little director-to-director discussion, some talk about lenses or film stock.

"Can you make the font a little bigger on the teleprompter?"

"Yes, sir."

Not exactly director-to-director banter, but technical anyway.

He takes his place, asks the teleprompter guy to run the script once or twice, then nods at me.

"Let's try one."

"Let's do it."

The camera rolls and the camera assistant slates the first take. Just before Eastwood speaks, something happens. His smile disappears. His eyes deaden. And his voice drops half an octave. He now looks and sounds just like…Dirty Harry.

I shoot ten takes. I have nothing to say. Seriously, what kind of direction am I going to give Clint Eastwood about playing Dirty Harry? As I work with more movie stars and celebrities, I'm learning that, once they start doing their thing in front of the camera, it's kind of magical and weird and spellbinding. You can't take your eyes off them. They emanate this kinetic energy. Because they're movie stars. They are this persona you've only ever seen on a screen but now they're there, right in front of you. There's also a downside to it—you love anything they do, so you're kind of useless as a director.

A good director gets a range of performances. Out of any actor. You might suggest a different shading of the voice. Or that they move the beats in the sentences around. You give the actor something new to play with. Dirty Harry doesn't need any help from me. When the camera turns off, he immediately reverts to being the guy driving the Buick.

Less than an hour later, we're done. I could stretch it out and do a few more takes, but I don't want to. It'll only make me look stupid and make Eastwood lose interest. The agency agrees that it's all great, so we call a wrap, even though it's not yet 10:00 in the morning. I walk over to where Clint's standing with his friend, the AC.

"We're done. Thanks."

"You're even faster than I am."

"It was all you this morning."

"It was fun. I'm glad I could help."

"It was amazing. Your voice, how it…"

Clint's smile disappears, his eyes tighten and deaden a little, he turns his face a bit to me. It's that Dirty Harry thing again. Damn. Cool trick.

We walk back to the parking lot, he signs some autographs for the crew, and then he climbs into the Buick. As he's heading down the single-lane road out of the lot, he drives by some folks who are walking up the road into the gardens. The first couple doesn't notice him. The man in the second couple does. He stops, stares, processes, and points. He calls out to the others behind him.

"That's Clint Eastwood!"

That gets everyone's attention. The visitors stop and stare and partially block the road and start waving as the Buick approaches. Clint has to stop, so he doesn't run anyone over. A guy leans in close to the driver's window. His wife screams giddily and waves. Clint throws the car into park. He rolls down his window, a tiny piece of his profile visible as he smiles at the visitors. The guy shoves a piece of paper at him for an autograph. His wife finds some crumpled paper and a pen in her purse and hands them over. Clint signs both, waves, and rolls away toward the 210 Freeway.

That was a lot different than what happened yesterday. No one asked Bronson for an autograph when he was leaving. No one was hooting and hollering when they saw him in the back of the limo. And I'm guessing the only person shoving things in Bronson's face was the limo driver handing him the mascara receipts, asking to be paid back. Actually, I'm not guessing. That's exactly what happened. Bronson handed the driver a twenty. Then asked for change.

Rocket Fuel.

BY THE LATE '80S, I'M STARTING TO CLIMB INTO THE MIDDLE LEVEL OF work. Kellogg's, Proctor & Gamble, McDonald's, Lever Brothers, regional banks, cruise lines, state lotteries, hospital chains. I thought, by now, I might be palling around with other people who do what I do. But commercial directors rarely socialize with other commercial directors. There just aren't any clubs for douchebags who wear Australian fireman boots, clunky eyewear, and backwards baseball caps. And, frankly, you're not all that hot on meeting each other. For two simple reasons: you look alike, and you look stupid. And, if they're working, it's probably on a job you lost.

Most of what you know about other directors you learn through the grapevine. It's always the salacious stuff. Who's a drug addict. Who's a drunk. Who's a pedophile. You assume they're divorced. If they're even marginally successful, they're divorced. If they're really successful, they've been divorced twice.

Here's why commercial directors are a generally miserable lot: com-mercial directors suck up to people they don't respect all that much in order to get a job they don't think is very good and, if the sucking up works and they get the job, then they shit on everyone around them because they hate themselves for having to suck up to people so they can get a job that's really bad. Makes perfect sense. When you lose a job, it's a different form of self-loathing. You cannot believe these people didn't hire you. And that they hired Your Nemesis, who, you know for a fact, can't direct, gobbles Vicodin, and has hair implants and an eye job.

For me, these grudges are like rocket fuel. They give me a lot of the energy I need to chase success. To bounce back from frequent failure. And to explain why shit hasn't gone my way. Anytime I lose a job, I curse and spit and chalk it up to the other director having friends in the agency. Never crosses my mind that he might have had better ideas than mine. Never. Then I start looking for someone to blame. My producer must have bid the job too high. Has to be. The sales rep was asleep at the wheel, not staying in touch with the producer to find out if there was something else we needed to do. The treatment should have been splashier. After a certain number of hours, I start to blame myself. My big ideas weren't any good. This loud, negative noise overcomes everything in my head for a few days. Even if I'm shooting another job, half of my thoughts are focused on how the fuck I lost the other one. Impossible. Then it spins. The brain does a great thing. It rationalizes. I now start thinking it's wonderful I lost the job. Maybe it's an exterior and it looks like it'll rain. Maybe it's with kids and dogs and I think life is too fucking short to do more of those. Pretty soon, I'm telling the same people I'd been yelling at that it's a blessing we lost it.

This rationalizing goes to shit when you lose five or six jobs in a row. Work begets work. Losing work begets losing more work. You start getting superstitious. You start counting money all the time. You start counting the weeks you can survive before everything's gone. That's a terrible place to be mentally. Better to stay arrogant and dumb and blame people and assume the next agency will be smart enough to hire you.

Underneath it all, though, I am really thinking something different. I work harder than the next guy to get a job. I make all that effort for a good reason. I don't think I'm as good as most of the people I compete against.

Effort and elbow grease can count for a lot. When I get on a phone call with the creatives for the first time, I do okay. I'm prepared. I'm clear and concise. I don't say "like" or "you know" or "that being said" every five words. I have ideas for enhancing the story. What can be done in casting. I'm quick to point out where the problems are in the spot. Things that need to be fixed. It took me a while to learn to start my spiel with some generic platitude about how good the spot could be before I start in on what's wrong with it. Creatives are open to suggestions. Especially if the suggestions might make them look good. When a director tells them the spot's not a total loss and could even be great, they're willing to listen.

When I really, really want a job, and I know I'm competing against people with far better reels and reputations than mine, I go full Sammy. I wangle an in-person meeting with the creatives. Maybe I say I'll be in the agency on other business. Maybe I'll say I'll be at an editor's across the street. Whatever it takes. I want to explain what I'll do, face to face. It really works when the agency is in Chicago and you're in New York and you fly out for a one-hour meeting. This pretty solidly telegraphs that you give a shit about the job. The creatives often think you're nuts. Why are you spending all this money for a one-hour meeting? They don't get the economics of it. I spend a grand on a plane ticket and lunch to get a job where I'll make thirty grand and come away with something good enough that I'll put it on my reel and it'll feed me for a year or two.

In the '80s and '90s, directors aren't thinking like this. They aren't thinking like businesspeople. Like it's beneath them to put themselves out there to get a job. Others should do that for them. They think they've achieved something just because they can call themselves directors. They don't seem to have a clue how quickly many guys say they used to be directors.

Actors Are Not Like You and Me.

FILM PRODUCTION IS A BLUE-COLLAR BUSINESS. WE GO TO WORK EARLY. Take the gaffer. The guy who lays out the electric cable and moves the lights around. He leaves his house in Sayville at 4:30 a.m. He loves commuting at this time of day because the LIE is empty. He grabs a coffee at Dunkin' Donuts, listens to some sports show on ESPN, spaces out, and smokes a couple of cigarettes. When he gets to work, he's still half awake. The coffee won't really kick in until nine. Doesn't matter. He just needs to be able to set up some lights and run cable.

The actor's a whole other story. He gets up at 4:30 too, not because he has to but because he works so rarely he's nervous as shit. He tiptoes out of his mortgaged-up-the-ass house in Maplewood but, even with leaving early, gets trapped in I'm-going-to-be-really-late-panic-attack-triggering traffic at the George Washington Bridge, forks over sixteen bucks for the toll, arrives at the set two minutes before his 8:00 a.m. call, and races into the house, guts in dysenteric knots, desperate for a shitter. Ninety minutes later, the actor is going to walk on the set made up, costumed, lines memorized, and looking good. People will spend the day staring at him, listening to him speak.

I have to tell both these guys what to do. It requires different languages.

The gaffer didn't think about much of anything on the way to work. Maybe why the Rangers continue to suck. The actor thought about a lot. Like why didn't he make himself a fresh pot of coffee for the drive instead of microwaving what was left from the day before? And why didn't he drink it black instead of using that funky-smelling two-percent, which must be what's making him feel like he's going to shit himself while he's trapped in the bridge traffic? And why, during last night's dinner, didn't his wife and kids feign some fucking interest in his life and ask him about this job, especially considering he doesn't work all that often? And, come to think of it, that dinner where they ignored him might be the reason why he didn't look at his script before going to bed, because the moment the kids got up from the table his goddam wife laid into him about booking so little work this year, adding, for good measure, that she's done borrowing money from her folks, which he knows would mean they'd have to sell the house, so, understandably, that whole crazy shit stew got him sweaty and anxious and he didn't close his eyes until Corden was over and then, next thing he knew, the alarm went off.

I have to convince this guy he's a genius, that he can do no wrong, that he's hilarious, charming, and as charismatic as George Clooney.

A gaffer's commute would involve calling in to *Boomer & Gio* to vent about the Rangers, illegally driving solo in the HOV lane and, after arriving at work and having a breakfast burrito, commandeering the downstairs john to take a dump. Whatever the gaffer might have fucked up the day before is water under the bridge. And fuck his family. They should pipe down during dinner, so he can watch the game. I don't worry too much about the gaffer's state of mind when I tell him the 12k is in the shot and he's got to go out in the rain and move it. It won't break him.

But the actor is fragile, obsessive, in therapy, and has trouble just moving on. And, if he's distracted, unable to mentally erase everything that's happened in the prior twelve hours, it will be clear to the camera. He won't be able to repeat the same words and actions over and over and make it feel as if he's saying them for the first time. Which is his job.

Mine is to help him come off like he doesn't have a care in the world, that acting is as simple as breathing and that he is amazing at it.

It took me a while to figure out how to deal with actors. First, I had to learn that they can only do what they can do. Before that, I'd think that, if someone looked the part, I could force some kind of performance out of them. You can't. During auditions, you see clearly what they're capable of. I finally learned to hire actors based on what they do and not what I hope they can do. (A very small number of actors are capable of anything. They are usually not doing commercials.) So I hire people who do a pretty good version of what I want in casting. And then, on the day, I direct as little as possible. Because I don't have to. I've cast properly. It's all easy now. I make a few comments. I try to be clear, concise, and simple. I make light of everything.

I've heard of directors trying to behave like therapists with actors. Trying to behave like lovers. Trying to behave like parents. One had the AD speak for him. He was too important to actually engage with the actors himself. Dumb.

I just behave like myself. I go down to see them first thing in the morning in makeup. I ask whether they've got everything they want: food, drink, power for their phones. Which surprises them because actors spend so much time being treated like shit. Today, to me, they're import-ant. The whole show depends on them. I describe the job, whatever it is, as the simplest thing they'll ever do. And I tell them that, today, it'll be impossible for them to make a mistake. Whatever they do will be good. If they flub a line, doesn't matter. If they miss a mark, doesn't matter. I want them totally confident and stupidly relaxed. And trusting. Of me. Because I want them willing to do whatever I ask them to do for the next eight hours. If I've told them they can't make a mistake, then they feel safe. Who doesn't want to feel safe in their job?

It's a little bit of a game because both of us know it's bullshit. They'll make mistakes. I just won't point them out. They'll miss marks. I just won't mention it. I'll say lots of things, usually a word or two after a take, and they'll adjust. I'll guide them to do what I want. I will direct.

It's not a lot. But it's something. A lot of directors' entire approach to directing is to say, "Again," after a take. Again? Really? What the fuck is that? Tell the poor guy what to do and how to do it differently. At least try to make it look like you know what *you're* doing.

That's the whole basis of directing. If the actors and crew think you know what you're doing, they'll do whatever you ask them to. If they think you're clueless, they won't trust anything you say.

My Girlfriend Took Some Film Classes.

I HATE PREPRODUCTION MEETINGS. YOU HOLD ONE THE DAY BEFORE A JOB shoots. They're soul-killing exercises in asphyxia. Twenty or so people, agency creatives, account people, clients, people you've never seen before but who must be connected to the job somehow and who are now first in line for the catered lunch, sitting around a conference table, reading documents out loud. Documents that everyone's staring at in the binders in front of them. It's like kindergarten. My goal is to get them over and done with quick. I frequently fail.

I'm in one for a luggage manufacturer. Trying to manage the unique aspects of this particular job. This one has three. One, the new president of the company is also the temporary marketing manager. Apparently, when he came in, he fired most of prior management, so he could bring in his own people. His new marketing manager can't start for another month, so, in the meantime, this guy's doing both jobs. Two, he has brought his girlfriend to the prepro meeting. Three, he didn't want to look at the casting tapes. He wants to approve the actors looking at their headshots instead. So he's eating an overstuffed turkey sandwich from

Nate 'n Al's while he arranges the photos of the cast into prospective pairings. Russian dressing and greasy fingerprints are getting all over the pictures. I'm praying the girlfriend will get him a fucking napkin.

In each form of filmmaking, a director has taskmasters. Feature directors deal with producers and studios and their stars. Television directors have stars, show runners, and network executives. Commercial directors' primary bosses are agency creative people. The ones who came up with the idea for the spot. There's an art director whose focus is visual stuff. A copywriter who's written the words. An agency producer who acts as the liaison between the agency and production company.

Then there's the secondary boss, the agency's client. The person who oversees the day-to-day advertising on AT&T, New York Life, Cheerios, or, in this case, a luggage manufacturer. His job involves a lot more than making spots. He worries about distribution, pricing, promotions, competitors' strategies, quarterly profits, revenue streams, vendors, higher-ups, and a million other things. They're often the kind of people who wear a polo shirt with the company's logo embroidered on it to a neighborhood barbecue. In one of the bizarre twists of process unique to commercials, the ad managers are given the final say on casting, locations, and, during the shoot itself, on whether scenes are good enough. It's kind of like forcing a 747 pilot to leave the cockpit and go ask the guy sitting in 3F whether he thinks the southerly route over the Atlantic is a better option that evening. The fact that the passenger doesn't know anything about flying doesn't mean he's stupid. It just means he shouldn't be consulted about what's happening in the cockpit. But, in advertising, because the brand guy has bought a seat, a very expensive seat, he gets approval.

Which is nuts. But that's the process. At this moment, I'm trying to figure out how to mind-force the luggage guy and his girlfriend into approving the cast. The agency people think he'll listen to me. Maybe if I let him keep dripping enough Russian dressing on the head shots he'll get a good feeling about them.

He looks at the girlfriend, giving her an expression that indicates a moment of truth is about to happen, and then at me.

"Do you like these actors, Bruce?"

"Yeah. I do. That's why I'm recommending them."

"No, I mean as people."

"I don't know them as people."

"I want people in these spots who you really like."

"Well, I'm recommending them because I respond positively to them."

"Great. That's what I want to hear. Book 'em."

Kooky. But he's on a roll now.

"You know the greatest thing about our new suitcases, don't you?"

"Uh. There's a lot of good things. The size. The weight. The…"

"No, no, no. The greatest thing is tilt, push, and roll."

What the fuck is he talking about?

"Our competition's commercials show people pulling their suitcases through airports. Rolling. All the same. We have to be different. Different and better. Look."

He goes over to a cluster of suitcases we've brought into the meeting, takes one, extends the handle then pushes the bottom of the suitcase away with his foot, pivots, then starts walking it around the conference table. He looks like a five-year-old in a pin-striped suit and a rep tie pulling around a little red wagon.

"We own that."

What "that" is is not clear to me. The suitcase he's dragging around the conference room looks exactly like any other suitcase with wheels. Maybe the zippers are in different places than American Tourister zippers. Whatever. I don't want this guy to start lecturing me on the differences between his luggage and all the other brands so I let this comment go.

"Well, right, so that's a part of the action in almost every scene. We're trying to choreograph it, so no one seems to be struggling."

He takes his hand off the suitcase handle and punches the air with his fist. Like he's won a race. He has very white capped teeth. And I'm not sure how much of the hair is real.

"Perfect. You get us."

Okay. Now we have a relationship, this nut and me.

After more reading aloud of the documents and a few questions about what time we need the agency and client on the set in the morning, the meeting ends. I beg out of dinner with the client, his girlfriend, and the agency. Call time is 6:00 a.m. tomorrow at LAX, so I'm hitting the sack early. Still the agency's mad. They're weirded out by the client as much as I am and want someone, anyone, else there to buffer things. Not me. Not tonight.

The next morning, we're lit and ready in just over an hour. The scene is a short one of a businesswoman running for her plane. She's hauling the suitcase behind her. Effortlessly. After I shoot a few takes, I wander over to video village. I ask the playback guy to show us the last three takes. I point out where I want to change the action, how I'd like to adjust the performance, where I'll move the camera to, and then ask what they're thinking.

The luggage guy is confused. Is this the opening scene in the commercial? Isn't it supposed to be a scene of a guy leaving his hotel? Luggage guy wasn't listening an hour ago when I explained we'd often be shooting scenes out of sequence today. I show him the takes again. He sits silently. This is normal. First thing in the morning, no one thinks anything sounds or looks right.

"Can we get the push, tilt, and roll to be bigger?"

"Sure. I'll ask her to do that."

"I know you get us. You get the brand."

I'll take any fucking acquiescence I can get. Just let me keep shooting.

By the third setup, one where a guy races through the terminal and effortlessly sidesteps a young mom pushing a kid in a stroller, everybody in video village is checking email, shopping online, or texting. This is also normal. Filmmaking to the people not actually doing the filming is exciting for about fifteen minutes. I still go over to check in, but now, before I even get over to them, they give me the thumbs-up thing. We fly along, everyone happy as clams, and we call lunch.

I like to sit with the clients during lunch. You talk about the job, what they're thinking about everything. But, hopefully, you also talk about other things, normal things. I grab a seat next to luggage guy and his girlfriend.

"How do you think it's going, Bruce?"

All business for this guy.

"Great. Actors are wonderful. The pictures are pretty. The luggage looks good."

"Completely agree. You know, I had a good feeling about this. After the meeting. Everything was clicking."

"I think so too."

"Paula also thinks the film looks great. Right, babe?"

"Very pretty. And everything looks so real!"

"She took some film courses in college."

"Nice. I'm glad you're both happy."

He's not a bad guy. He's probably a good dad. Maybe his marriage fell apart because his ex-wife joined a Pentecostal church, is handling snakes, and he's raising their kids single-handedly. Or she died in a train accident. Or he's always been single and adopted them from a Romanian orphanage and Paula was the adoption wrangler and they commiserated a lot and that's how they hooked up. It's all possible. He's a nice enough guy, and he's paying for an awesome lunch. Thank you.

I do the last two setups on the ground floor of LAX, one in baggage claim and the other outside by passenger pickup. I load up the scene with tons of extras moving this way and that to make things seem messy. Mess tends to make things look real. Then, eight hours and fifteen minutes after we got here, we're done. Everyone says they're happy. What they mean is they're relieved it's all over and nothing terrible happened. Weird. Agency people always act like they dodged a bullet when a shoot's over.

The client and Paula come over to say goodbye. We have a car waiting to take them back to the Bel-Air.

"Great day. Wonderful job."

"That's very nice of you to say. I'm incredibly lucky to have such a remarkable crew. They make it all happen. And you guys were great. Supportive and focused."

"Acting was top-notch."

"I thought so too."

"Are you going to join us for dinner tonight?"

"You know, I've got to go back to the production office to look at some stuff for tomorrow, so I can't. Maybe if I get done early I can try and join you. Where're you going?"

"Michael's. Paula's never been there."

"You'll love it. Sit outside. I'll try and join you. Thanks again for a great day."

I only have about an hour of work to do to make sure tomorrow's in place. But I'm also fried and tired of talking and just want to get back to the hotel and go for a run. And I already have tentative dinner plans with friends. When they pick me up, I ask where we're going.

"Michael's. It's a nice night so we can sit outside."

"No. Let's go somewhere else."

Grad
School.

I CAN COME OFF AS A SARCASTIC WISEASS, BUT I'M NOT. I DON'T FIND GAGS
that hinge on guys getting kicked in the balls, farts, or dim-witted fathers
backing their cars into garage doors to be hilarious. I'm no good at staging those kinds of things anyway. For some reason, I am good with dramatic, emotional stuff. Stories about loss or love or longing. Those ideas
might sound ridiculous in the context of commercials, but they're not.
Good stories need to hook a viewer *and* move them. I aim even higher.
I want to make you cry. Getting people to tear up watching a movie is
hard. Making it happen in a thirty or sixty second commercial is really
hard. But, when it happens, it's powerful. And kind of inexplicable. Why
an image or scene can trigger that reaction is hard to figure out. I'm
always trying to learn why.

All the spots I've done that succeed like this came from a great script.
They're based on words, not sight gags. And a very simple story. All I had
to do was cast properly, put the actors in the right location, make pretty
pictures, and edit it properly. Sounds like a lot but, basically, my goal is
just to not fuck it up.

As I did more of these spots and learned how to make them better and better, I fell into using a specific structure. One rule seemed to be that you needed to slowly get closer and closer to the performers as the drama intensified. During the big moments, you were in tight, seeing every little thing in an actor's face and eyes. Closer than humans can see with their own eyes. It works. Audiences like getting voyeuristically close during uncomfortable moments.

In January 1985, I went to see a movie called *My Life as a Dog*. On paper, it's a simple story about two young brothers managing life as their mother is dying of cancer. Very sad, very moving, and oddly funny. The director, Lasse Hallström, got amazing performances from the kid actors. He also managed to mix humor with heartbreaking sadness. One particular scene killed me. Whenever the mom takes a turn for the worse, the boys are sent away to a relative who lives in a tiny town in the middle of nowhere. The kids go by train. The first time they go, we see them arrive in a medium shot getting off the train and being greeted by an uncle. After ten minutes of movie time and a month of story time, they go back to live with their mom. But she gets sick again, so they go back to the country. Same kinds of shots when they get off the train. And, again, after a while, they go back to Mom. But she gets sick again and dies. This time, the brothers are split up and sent to different places. The younger brother is sent back to stay with the relative who first took them in. This time, when he arrives alone, Hallström puts the camera what feels like five miles away from the train station, so that, when the boy gets off, he's the size of an ant and the train looks like a tiny toy. You can't see his face, an expression, nothing. And it made me and everyone else in the theater start sobbing uncontrollably. An epidemic of weeping. And all we're seeing are tiny specks on the screen. WTF?

Two years later, I'm having lunch on the set of a Lasse Hallström movie. He's directing *Once Around*, his first American film. It's about a big, dysfunctional family coming together for a holiday. Three friends of mine are in the crew, and I thought it'd be fun to watch another director work, so I flew to North Carolina to spend a day or two on the set.

Lasse is a very nice, easygoing guy. When we're introduced, I tell him what a fan I am then quickly steer the conversation around to that scene. Why, at what was one of the most emotional moments in that film, had he used a wide, wide, wide shot and not something close? I tell him how the audience I was with reacted, me included. Why did he do that?

Lasse says he'd also shot a close-up of the boy getting off the train. And something a little wider. The normal choices. But something had told him to also shoot that wide shot. And, when they put it in during editing, it worked best of all. Initially, it made no sense to him either.

Does he know now why it worked? He thinks he does. In a close-up, the boy's face would communicate one specific thing and the audience would have just that one specific thing to react to. There would be no question as to how the boy felt about his arrival. But, when he used the wide shot, where the audience couldn't see facial expressions, each audience member filled in the emotional blank themselves. They all knew the mother had died. Yet they all had different feelings about how the boy was dealing with it. By using a shot where the kid's face couldn't be seen, everyone answered the question differently, the way they thought made sense. And everyone bawled their eyes out. The most emotionally effective shot was the least intimate. Weird.

I don't know if what I learned that day qualified as a rule. What I did learn was that a good director would admit he wasn't always sure what would work, during both shooting and editing, and would try something different, at the risk of being wrong, just as an experiment. Sometimes you never know.

A year later, I made a spot for a Michigan hospital network. One simple scene. A woman and her adult daughter are sitting in a crowded hospital waiting room waiting to see if the husband/father has made it through a risky heart surgery. The first twenty seconds focus on the two women nervously killing time. They're on pins and needles, distracted, tense. When the surgeon enters the waiting room and approaches them, the daughter doesn't see him. She's looking in another direction. The mother does see him and panics. Stands. Sits. Grabs the daughter's arm and points over her shoulder. The surgeon comes close. The mother and daughter slowly stand, silent, scared. His first words, "Mrs. Oliver..." really just his tone, let us know the father's pulled through the operation fine. The mother breaks down crying, and the daughter smiles and holds her mom by the arm. I did all the normal coverage. Opening shot to see the whole waiting room. Close-ups of the mom and daughter as they waited. Close on the doctor as he came in. And I remembered to shoot a very wide shot of the three of them at the big moment. But it felt wrong. Too far away. Too much other stuff going on in the frame. Just too damn busy. Viewers would want to be close-up then. When we cut the spot, the close-ups worked well in the beginning of the story, but the most effective, gut-wrenching takes of the surgeon giving them the good news were the wide ones. Who knew?

The script was great. The cast was great. The location was right. The film looked real. And I remembered to do the wide shot as coverage of the key moment. And endured my DP and AD telling me the shot was useless and that we didn't have time to get it. It might not have been essential. Who knows. But I got it. And I started getting it more and more. The spot won some awards. I think, I hope, I gave credit for that counterintuitive wide shot to Lasse Hallström.

Speed.

PART OF MY STYLE, PART OF WHAT'S HELPED ME HAVE A CAREER, IS THAT I work very fast. I can get done in eight hours what a normal director needs fourteen to do. I've only seen a few directors work, but they are often kind of slow and indecisive. They don't act with a lot of confidence. And, when they start filming, they don't seem to have a very clear sense of what they want. They just shoot and shoot. They don't direct. They'll often just say, "Again."

That's demoralizing for everyone. Crew, actors, production, clients. You want to give the impression you've got a map and have flown a plane before.

Anyway, I go fast. I get my first shot of the day within ninety minutes of the call time, when the crew gets to the set. I'm usually happy after seven or eight takes. I keep moving. I never sit down in my chair and start mumbling or looking glassy-eyed at the AD with an expression of being lost.

This works. Crews stay alert. Actors shine because they stop thinking and just do. It also helps them sound and look very natural because

I never give them time to practice. Clients like it because they get to see all the money they're spending result in something happening quickly. I like it because everyone does their best work, I look like a genius because everything's going so well, and, dirty secret, I make more money because I finish quicker. Whatever overtime we've bid, we won't spend.

Setting up video village the right way is important. Video village is where we put a giant video monitor, so the agency and client can watch what I'm shooting. I have my production staff make it as comfortable and distracting as it can be. We fill the area with magazines and bottled water and snacks and assign someone to constantly get them coffee and lay out multiple chargers, so they can stay on their phones and laptops all day. Wi-Fi is essential, so we install portable units. You give these people a solid Wi-Fi connection and, within two hours, they can't be bothered with what you're shooting. That's ideal for me. I want them focused on whether they want a chai latte or a flat white and clicking on a Zappos pop-up. That way they leave me alone.

In the beginning of the day, just before I roll for the first time, I go over to video village and tell everyone what I'm going to do. How the day will unfold. I tell them I'll keep coming over to see what they're thinking. I don't use the word "collaborate," but I hope they interpret what I say as being a feint in that direction. I remind them that they can tell my producer anything and he'll pass it along to me. And then I start shooting. It's usually before 9:00 a.m. It takes me five or six takes to figure out what I want and then get it. Once I do, I go back to video village and tell them I'm pretty happy. There's lots of feedback. Lots of ideas. I shoot some variations to accommodate this. After twenty minutes, I'm ready to move on to the next scene. The crowd at video village is nervous. How could we have gotten this scene so fast? But we did, so we move to the next setup. We start shooting again, I go over to check in after a few takes, and there are fewer comments. So now I move faster. Fifteen minutes later, I'm happy. Done. Ready to move on. By 10:30, we're on the fourth setup. Everyone in video village is focused on their computers and phones. They look up, once in a while, when I come over and give me a thumbs-up or a smile. They've lost interest and just let me do my job.

When I want to wrap, meaning call it a day, usually in the middle of the afternoon, I go over and ask if they're all comfortable. They look at their watches, gulp because it's kind of early, hesitantly agree that we're done, and sign off. Sometimes the client will ask if I've ever been able to go this fast before. I lie and say today went exceptionally well, actors were wonderful, good location, they paid close attention.

People who've never worked with me before—crews, actors, clients—think I'm a little manic. I'm always yelling that I'm ready to go, what the fuck is the problem, why can't we roll. I'm not really pissed. It's just that, if I'm not going fast, yammering all the time, I lose interest. I hear stories about commercial shoots that go on until midnight. Just the thought of being that slow pains me. I grimace. Plus, I think of all that extra money they gave away because they couldn't figure out what the fuck they wanted.

Little People.

WE'RE SHOOTING IN A MALL JUST OFF THE 405 IN THE SAN FERNANDO Valley. It's a weeknight, so the place is quiet. I can't remember which restaurant chain the spot is for. The story's about two couples trying to figure out where to eat dinner. In the background is a huge food court that we've filled up with a ton of extras. We have fifty. Thirty-five adults. And fifteen little people.

Ever since Vic Morrow and three families of Vietnamese extras were killed during the making of *The Twilight Zone*, California law has prohibited using children under the age of seven on a set after 8:00 p.m. But, Los Angeles being a can-do town, someone had the bright idea that, if you dressed little people up to look like kids, bingo, you *could* be shooting kids after 8:00 p.m. Someone tells you this and it sounds ridiculous and impossible. But it's not. Not impossible. As long as you put all those extras in the background and use a telephoto lens, so things go very out of focus back there, it works. Like a charm. So here we are.

Because I want to stare at something I shouldn't, and because I'm the director and I can, I go over to makeup and wardrobe to check out the little people. When they show up, they're dressed like everyone else. T-shirts, jeans, Nikes, wraparound sunglasses, team hats. Some of the women wear dresses or skirts. All of them have brought suitcases stuffed with children's clothing. T-shirts decorated with balloons and clowns and footballs and kittens and planets. Sneakers with those soles that light up when you step on them. Most of the women put their hair in pigtails. They change into shorts and jumpers and other age-appropriate stuff. A lot of the guys have little cowboy hats. It's weird.

My AD has done the little people thing before, so he's rolling with it. He blocks the scene, assigns little people to parents, tells some to hold hands with their "parents," and has others run around like kids on a sugar high. We have a little carousel in the shot, so he puts a few little people on that. With no instruction whatsoever, on the first take, a little person riding one of the wooden horses takes off his cowboy hat and starts yelling, "Giddyup!" and "Look, Mommy! I'm widing a bucking bwonco!" I ask him to pipe down a little on the next take because he's too damn enthusiastic.

On a night shoot, there's always a lot of coffee and sweet stuff on the craft service table to keep people wired. And craft service is one odd place tonight. I go over between takes to grab a tea, and there's a couple of little people, dressed as five-year-olds, drinking coffee, checking their phones, talking about callbacks and agents with their little people actor friends.

I spend fifteen minutes standing next to one of the LAPD movie cops who's been assigned to our job. He's seen it all, but he hasn't seen this. We both watch, silent, once in a while sharing a glance. Not a knowing glance. Just a who'd-have-ever-thought-it glance.

Simba.

CAMERA MAKERS WANT YOU TO THINK IT'S EASY TO TAKE GREAT PICTURES. That's the basis of all their commercials. They're often set in exotic locations where everything is so stupidly photogenic Stevie Wonder could take a few good shots.

The vignettes in this Canon spot show one couple rock climbing, another couple mountain biking, and a third couple in the Serengeti taking pictures of wild animals. These kinds of vignettes often feel pretty bogus because the people in the scenes are actors and the locations are all in Southern California. Adding to the feeling of bogusity is the fact that the vignettes have been thought up by people who've never done the things featured in the commercial. Nobody's climbed a rock, mountain biked, or safaried in Africa. It's Google search creativity. I saw a picture of it once. It happened. When we make these kinds of spots, we try to cast people who actually do this stuff and hope a little authenticity rubs off on the project.

We did the rock-climbing sequence yesterday on a cliff that dropped two hundred feet into the Pacific. I put the camera on a crane and hung it over the edge of the cliff, tracking with a pair of excellent climbers who clambered up toward us, smiling, sweaty, and gorgeous. It was very important to the agency and client that the girl not only be a world-class technical climber but also look like Gisele Bündchen. This being California, we found five women who fit the bill. Sabine, originally from Belgium, not a country known for vertical drops, scampered up the face, smiling her perfect smile on cue. The guy did the same, but no one looked at him.

On the second day, we're at Ahmanson Ranch. The place is gigantic: twenty-five hundred acres of undeveloped land. The rolling hills, uncut grass, and hundred-year-old trees make it a good stand-in for lots of exotic places. Pretty much wherever you point the camera, it looks like you are somewhere other than Los Angeles. Maybe Australia. Maybe Argentina. Easily the Serengeti. In reality, you're a ten-minute drive from Ventura Boulevard.

The Africa vignette is about a couple driving around in a Range Rover then stopping to take a picture of a leopard. The location scout found a perfect place for this shot centered around a large tree that sits by itself in an enormous meadow. If you frame it in a wide shot, all you see is the tree, a horizon line and infinite sky. Just stunning. We've done some driving shots on the dirt roads. The couple look all *Out of Africa*-y in their khakis and safari jackets. It's fake as shit but it works. Now we're setting up near the tree to do the leopard shot.

The animal wrangler we've hired to supply the leopard is a big, taciturn guy with a handlebar mustache and a cowboy hat. An old school Hollywood film guy. He doesn't carry himself like some kind of rarefied genius, acting like what he does is magic. His job is simply to make animals do what you want them to do. Done and done. He walks the leopard out of the trailer on a leash. Instant, massive letdown. Turns out leopards are not very big. In fact, they're the size of bobcats or really big coyotes. Not the wrangler's fault. We, me especially, had assumed a leopard would be bigger because we did our research on Google.

The wrangler places the leopard in the deep grass, I look through the camera, and it's obvious this is not an amazing frame. And advertising images, especially for a camera company, need to be amazing, somehow, some way. Looking over my shoulder at the agency and client standing around the video monitors, I can tell they're bummed too. The wrangler comes over to me at the camera. His assistant keeps the leopard on the leash over by the tree. I ask the wrangler if we can put the leopard up on a platform, so we can see it better. He says yeah. Then, he asks, "What's your concern?"

"The thing's way smaller than I thought it would be."

I try not to sound like a whiny bitch.

He nods, stares off in the distance for a moment, then asks, "You want to look at a lion?"

"You have a lion with you?

"Yeah. In the trailer. A lot of times, people see these leopards and are surprised by how small they are. I always bring a lion with me too."

I go over to the agency and recap the conversation I just had with the wrangler. They start laughing and say, "Shit, yeah, let's look at a lion!" Much as I want to, I can't take credit for this animal upgrade.

Lions are fucking huge. We place this one in the same spot over by the tree, and it looks majestic and cool and perfect. Once we get that shot, the wrangler asks if maybe I want to look at the lion perched in the tree. Continuing the theme from earlier, I say, "Hell yeah. He'll do that?"

"Should. And it's a she." So then we do another version of the shot with the lioness draped across the tree branches. Great.

Done. That's a wrap. As we're loading up to leave, the wrangler's hanging around chatting with everybody, and the lioness is next to him on the leash. Being up close to an animal like that turns everyone into children. Everybody wants to pet the lioness. Even the three-hundred-pound Samoan Teamsters. Pretty soon, there is a line of grown men waiting patiently to take their turn. As the line gets longer and wraps around behind the animal, the wrangler says, quietly but clearly, "You don't want to stand behind her." The message doesn't quite get through.

Two or three guys are still standing behind the lioness. Not close, maybe five yards away, but directly behind her.

Suddenly, a thick jet of dark yellow urine begins shooting straight backwards from between the lioness's hind legs. It's like a tiny fireman has hooked up a piss hose and aimed it right at the guys. It soaks a gaffer, a prop guy, and one of the Teamsters. If you think cat piss smells terrible, think again. Lioness piss smells a million times worse. And spews backwards in a stream so powerful it travels horizontal to the earth. That is amazing.

I Think She's Got Something.

I'M IN THE SECOND HOUR OF A CALLBACK SESSION IN NEW YORK. I'M WITH five people from the agency. We need three actors for this spot. All have to be able to deliver lines. Which is sort of a requirement of acting. The young woman we're watching is struggling. Because she's not an actress. She's a model but her agent sends her out once in a while for parts where speaking is required. She's extremely pretty. But can't speak more than four words in a row without messing up. But the extremely pretty part often is enough to have male creatives put her on their callback list.

I made this mistake a lot when I was starting. I somehow believed that physical beauty was going to morph into acting ability once I personally spoke with the woman in question. Didn't happen. Ever. Now I try to just bring good actors back for a second look. But, because commercial production has a lot of committee decision-making built in to it, I can't just bring back my people. Whoever the agency likes comes too.

The copywriter next to me thinks this young woman is going to get better. He just knows it. I try to get her out of the room quickly, so we can move on.

"Okay. Thanks for coming in."

She heads for the door, and the casting director follows to bring in the next person.

"Wait. Wait. Wait. Can we have her read it again?"

She hesitates, looks over her shoulder in my direction, but I signal it's all right for her to go. Once the door closes behind her, I speak.

"She can't act."

"I don't know. I saw something…"

Yeah. A gorgeous face.

"She's not good. And we have a lot more people to see, so…"

The copywriter gives me a goofy smile. Then pleads with me.

"…one more time, okay?"

Ugh. The casting director brings her back in again and, again, she delivers the lines poorly.

After she leaves, I put her headshot on the growing reject pile. The writer is playing with his coffee cup.

"Sometimes they surprise you."

"Sometimes."

What I do is not brain surgery. It is, however, kind of, sort of a craft. You learn it by doing it hundreds and—if you're lucky like I've been— thousands of times. You get better at it, the more you do it. Strangely, a lot of people think that law doesn't apply to them when it comes to creative endeavors. They think that, just because they want to be a director or a writer or a painter, by saying it, they are one. It is fortunate that simply believing you can do something is not all that's required to actually be a colorectal surgeon.

By the time I'm casting this job, I've been directing for twenty years. I've done hundreds of spots and a movie. I don't know everything, by a long shot, but I know a little. And I'm good enough and, probably more important, reliable enough now to take on almost any project and improve it. To use whatever skill I've got to make something better. In most cases, I know what to do.

I'm slightly more secure in my place. I'm better behaved. I'm no longer running from something; I'm running toward something. I just want to do my job as well as I can. And agencies are now paying me so much, there's an unspoken guarantee that the result will be really good. It will be, *if* they let me do it properly. A big if. I can't deliver if I have to engage in the charade of collaborating on essential stuff like casting. I've lost patience at trying to explain why I think we should do what we need to do. I can come off in casting sessions like this one sounding like an exasperated parent. We're doing it because I said so. There must be a way to say it differently.

Bigger.
Better.
Worse.

SOME DIRECTORS ARE AMAZING WITH MUSIC VIDEOS. BUT I SUCK AT THEM. When I realized this, I started adding other directors to my little company's roster who might be good at this stuff. At this point, record companies are starting to pay serious money to get these things done. And a couple of companies have appeared that just do music videos and are making fortunes. Propaganda. Vivid. Limelight and Partisan in London. There's a lot of money floating around, and it all looks a lot more exciting than doing toothpaste commercials. My three forays into this market, Cameo, Shooting Star, and Freddie Salem, had been a bust. I decided some of this work might come to my company if I brought in a director who had some serious cachet. A friend of mine knew a guy who knew a guy who knew Wayne Maser.

Wayne is a fashion photographer. His work for jeans and cosmetic companies is scandalous. Since I'm doing pretty boring work, adding a guy with some real controversy attached to his name seems like a good idea. The controversy was late-'80s predictable: drugs, romances with models, public spectacles, blowing assignments, palling around with wasted European royalty, especially if they have yachts and summer places on Pantelleria. I arranged to meet him one afternoon up at Sant Ambroeus on Madison Avenue. It's full of the above-mentioned Europeans. Wayne's in a dirty T-shirt, dirty jeans, no socks, and Gucci loafers. We have a coffee, he seems interested in making some extra money, and commercials and music videos pay a lot more than shooting stills. He tells me that, the weekend before, he'd been flown to Paris by some baron to take naked Polaroids of the baron's fiancée. Interesting way to spend your weekend. We work out a deal. I spend some money on ads in *Backstage* that play up his scandalous reputation. His manager warns us that Wayne can be unpredictable. That's okay. He might make me some money.

Rick Rubin, the guy who owns the Black Crowes' label and is sort of producing their new record, thought it'd be a good idea if Wayne shot the video for the single. So Wayne, Rick, my producer, and I are sitting around the pool at the Sunset Marquis, discussing what the video would be about. Normally, I'm the director, so the pressure's on me to run meetings like this and fill in all the creative blanks. Now I'm just here as a chaperone and to make sure Wayne doesn't go psychotic like he did on the first job we got him.

That was a commercial for a Midwestern department store. During two days of shooting in the abandoned Michigan Central Station in Detroit, he terrorized four young models, berated them for wearing what he thought were cheap thongs, threw cameras from the tops of ladders when he couldn't figure out how to turn them on, and referred to the agency creative director as a cocksucker. In Wayne's defense, the guy was weird. You didn't know who he was one day to the next. He'd wear a complex toupee Monday and then show up bald Tuesday.

Anyway, I'm only there to listen. Which is really worth it because Wayne constantly uses film terms I've never heard before, which he feels the need to physically illustrate. For "smash cut," he'll suddenly stand and smash his palms together or pound his fist on the table, upsetting the cocktail glasses and fruit platters. When he talks about "wave dissolves," a new term to me, he does something with his hands that reminds me of the Itsy-Bitsy Spider going up the water spout. Rubin never flinches. He deals with musicians, so this must be right up his alley. He asks two or three questions and gives us the go-ahead to shoot.

When Rick leaves, Wayne, my producer, and I stay at the table to figure out what to do next. Wayne proceeds to lay out all sorts of insane demands involving the crew he wants for the job. His stylist has to be flown in from Milan. He's got some cinematographer from Paris who's exactly right for the job. He also wants five nights in a suite at the Bel-Air, so he can get some more ideas. Some of his demands involve locations that were never mentioned in the meeting, like the Chateau Marmont lobby or Sunset Boulevard outside the Roxy or the Santa Monica Pier. None of which is doable for the money. Wayne pouts and we come to an impasse. Everyone agrees to sleep on it and have another look at things in the morning.

Wayne lives on a different circadian clock than most humans. He's up all night and very, very late to start the day. Our meeting the next morning convenes at four o'clock the next afternoon. Now he's even more bombastic. He's also come up with some new film terms. Smoke dissolve. Bleach cut. Hyper motion. He illustrates these with moves that remind me of stuff the dancers on *Hullabaloo* did. A scene with candles has grown to epic proportions. Chris Robinson, the Black Crowes' lead singer, is now going to be in the Rose Bowl, surrounded by giant candles, singing the song. He'll be wearing some kind of custom-made outfit that the stylist is going to have Giorgio Armani design.

I realize not only is this guy *not* going to make me money, he's probably going to make me go broke. He doesn't have a fucking clue how budgets work. I don't think he even has a clue how gravity works; otherwise, he wouldn't have thrown the cameras off the ladders. I push back a little, suggesting how we might be able to do the job with an American stylist or a DP from LA. Nah. Wayne wants what he wants. And I want to stay in business.

I call Rubin. I tell him we're pulling out of the project. I'm honest with him. I'm too nervous about Wayne's ability to do the job for the number we've agreed to. If he'd like, I'll be happy to find another production company that will work with Wayne. But, personally, if I were Rick, I'd start over. Rubin is surprisingly chill. I sever our relationship with Wayne. I never shoot another music video. I wasn't good at it. And my taste in others who might be was shitty too.

Actually, it was shitty in all sorts of directions. As music videos became such a jammed-up silo, overflowing with people trying to do it, I started looking for directors who did less trendy, more dependable things. I found a guy who did car commercials. This is as bread-and-butter as you can get. Every year, all the car companies shoot tons of these. And they believe that there are only a few guys who can do it properly. Car guys who've done it before. I hired one. We immediately got him work. Shooting cars. After two jobs, he called me and started in on a combination whine-irate rant. The crux of it was that, while his reel was made up of car commercials and that's what he'd done for fifteen years, he was expecting me to get him work as a comedy director. This guy's fifty years old, with no sense of humor, the demeanor of a Xanax addict, and braces on his teeth. The only thing funny about this nut was the comment he'd just made to me. Six months later, we let him go.

It was terribly frustrating. I looked at so many companies where multiple directors pulled the weight. Each one had a different specialty. Each one went hot and cold, but at different times, so there was a flow to it. I couldn't figure out how to hire the right guys and put this together. So I went back to doing what I'd always done. Be the only director on my roster. And solely responsible for covering all the bills. Sink or swim based on just what I did. It's exhausting. On the other hand, it tightens the circle when you're trying to play the blame game. If you fuck up, it's on you. It's not because some meathead throws a camera off a ladder or another one refuses to take a job because he wants to do something funny.

Job Security.

WE LIVE IN HASTINGS-ON-HUDSON. IN A WHITE CLAPBOARD HOUSE BUILT in the '20s. My architect neighbor says it's from a design kit Sears used to sell in their catalogue. It has a living room and dining room, a kitchen, a family room, two fireplaces, four bedrooms, a porch that looks out over the Hudson River, and is just fine for the five of us. My neighbors are pretty chill. The architect's on one side. A guy who runs a nonprofit's on another. The guitarist for *The Late Show* is two houses down. A medical researcher is across the street. The newest neighbor, and the only dick, is a dentist who spends all his time outdoors in a sleeveless T-shirt looking for proof that my dog is shitting in his pachysandra. Everyone has kids. We're a little ostracized because ours go to Fieldston, a private school in the Bronx. Some folks assume we think we're too good for the local public school. We're not. It just seemed like Fieldston was a better place for them. Fieldston's fine. The downside is the trust fund Bolsheviks. Parents who forget *their* rich parents are paying the grandkids' tuition and still loudly claim to be "of the people." Parents' Day can be annoying.

I do simple, dumb stuff with my kids. Take them to the grocery store with me if I do the big shop on Saturday. Hang out in the dining room with them before they get on the bus in the morning, trying to pry a few words out of their zipped shut, sleepy mouths. Walk with them and the dog on the aqueduct trail that runs through town. Get ice cream. Go to bookstores. See movies. We go out to eat as a family on Saturday nights. I let them pick the place. The kids are funny, smart, normal. Each is good at their own thing. We're lucky as shit.

My six-year-old daughter likes to sit on the radiator while she's waiting for the bus to come. She treats it like a test of her tomboy toughness. If she's wearing thick pants, she can last a minute or so before feeling like her butt's on fire. Today, she's picked out the yellow overalls she's been partial to lately and they're thinner than her jeans. She only lasts thirty seconds before she hops off and swears. Where she got this mouth is unknown.

The bus pulls up. My son comes running downstairs with the largest backpack a third grader has ever worn. The two of them crash through the door.

"Have a good day. See you this afternoon, guys."

My son stops at the bottom of the steps.

"Can you take me to the library later?"

"Sure. When you get home, we'll go."

I hope I'm not lying.

My working life is normal. At least, to me, it is. I have an office in New York City. On 23rd Street across from the Empire Diner. I'm in the office a couple days a week making phone calls, working on bids, prepping jobs. On the days I scout or shoot, I go to sound stages in Queens or houses in New Jersey or Westchester. Some days I fly to Los Angeles or Miami or Italy. I have clients who come back over and over. I am very lucky. There is something seemingly predictable about the whole thing. But that's an illusion. Because, on any given day, when I roll out of bed, chances are I am unemployed. Meaning, on that day, I don't have a job. Or one on the books. I still go to the office. It gives me a sense of routine and structure. I'm shooting about thirty jobs a year. That's an okay number. I'm trying to double it. But, this morning, as I climb in the shower, I'm out of work. In a week or two, owing to a combination of luck, perseverance, and a little skill, I'll be back at it. Employed for a few weeks. At the end of which I'll be out of work again. I never describe it this way to my kids because I think it will freak them out. If Dad is out of work on Monday, how is it possible that we are going to school on Tuesday and to the dentist on Wednesday and then off to camp when school ends? They wouldn't get it.

They're also little kids, so their memories are short and faulty. Which works in my favor. Because plenty of times when I say I'll be home to take one of them to the library or swim practice or a friend's house, I'm not. So far, ages eight and six, they're not keeping score.

But Blanche is. My absences for work are getting longer and more frequent. Life in the suburbs is just not so interesting for her. She's started auditioning again and getting very close to being cast in big television shows. It's confidence-boosting and infuriating for her. Being back in it seems really close, really possible, and just out of reach. I am of no help. I can't understand why, when I'm doing fine and keeping us safe and sound, she feels the need to go back hard and heavy into acting. Especially if it would mean she'd be in LA for months at a time. If it works for her, it'll mean both of us will be gone. That's not what I pictured. I don't think it's what she pictured. But where she's at is not what she pictured either. I get it. Now.

What Happens in Vegas.

CNN IS ON IN THE LOUNGE AREA AT THE INTERNATIONAL TENNIS CEN-tre in Las Vegas. It's a little before 7:00 a.m. Wolf Blitzer is announcing repeatedly that the US Air Force is bombing Baghdad. Saddam Hus-sein's invasion of Kuwait was exceptionally stupid, and he's now experi-encing, in military parlance, the kinetic consequences. They cut to that idiot press officer, Baghdad Bob, who loudly announces that there are no bombs falling anywhere near Baghdad, as black plumes of smoke rise a hundred yards behind him.

My producer taps me on the shoulder and points toward the front doors. Andre Agassi and a small entourage are coming in. I'm doing a commercial with him for Donnay, the racquet he plays with. We'll shoot one day with Agassi here in Las Vegas then go to Los Angeles for the rest of the filming. Today is pretty simple. Agassi has to say two lines, and then I'll shoot a variety of shots of him playing. Normal sports commer-cial template.

I love tennis. I play tennis. So I'm looking forward to today. The variable is Agassi. He's in the tabloids. He's supposed to be a bit prickly.

Journalists complain about dealing with him. He's not warmly embraced by the tennis establishment. Even with his massive talent, he seems to have a bit of a chip on his shoulder. To me, completely understandable. He's twenty and has become an international rock star. That'll make anyone nuts.

Agassi and his group hesitate by the door. My producer hustles over and introduces himself. Agassi's brought along his brother, Phil, his girlfriend, a hitting partner, and his trainer, a big hulking guy named Gil Reyes. Agassi grew up in Vegas and still lives here. Because he's a star, we've come to him. Mountain to Mohammed. I've never been to Vegas before. It's entertaining. In a horrifying kind of way.

I go over and introduce myself. Agassi's a combination of wary and jumpy. He's got a shag haircut with the ends dyed blonde. He seems younger than twenty. His girlfriend is even younger. I keep everything short and simple.

"I'll be ready in an hour, we'll only need to shoot for a few hours, it'll be easy, and you'll be done before lunch."

Agassi doesn't really engage. I get distracted eye contact, often focused on someone else. I'm used to people who aren't actors getting schizo when they're going to have to be in front of a camera. I ignore it and tell them this will be just another normal day. But with some cameras.

"Anything special you guys want this morning? We can have someone grab you some breakfast from craft service."

Agassi's brother shows me a bag from McDonald's he's carrying.

"We're good. You guys got any Mountain Dew?"

An athlete's training diet.

As my producer leads them toward the makeup room, the group straggles to a stop as they get near the television. The news about Iraq continues in a loud, endless loop. I walk behind them on my way out to the courts and say I'll see them shortly, hoping this will dislodge them from staring at the tube. It doesn't.

Lighting an indoor tennis court is a pain in the ass. It's a big space, and there are rarely any windows to use as a source. You can't use the lights they use to film with because they make everything go green and red and look like shit. So you have to start from scratch. Lots of cables, lots of instruments, lots of stands, lots of flags. Time spent lighting makes me crazy. I decide to let it happen without me.

I go back inside and head down to makeup. Agassi's in a chair getting worked on. I try to start a conversation about clothes. I always feel weird telling men what I want them to wear. With a famous athlete, you always have to navigate sponsorship stuff. Agassi isn't interested in anything I have to say and ignores me. I steer my conversation to his brother, explain I understand the Nike thing, and ask that they just try to pick stuff that's informal, so it looks like Andre's practicing, not playing a match. Phil nods. I decide to make him the point man for all the details today and keep my interaction with Andre to a minimum.

Before I head back to the courts, I ask Andre again if he's got everything he needs. Any special requests? No. He's happy with the Egg McMuffin and Mountain Dew he's devouring.

We're ready at 8:30 a.m. Andre walks on the court encircled by his entourage, like a long-haired boxer on his way to the ring. He is still very gun-shy. Too many bad media experiences, I guess. I walk him over to the bench we've set up and ask him to take a seat.

"I thought we'd start with the lines. Get them out of the way. Then do the action stuff."

A tiny nod.

"I like to roll the camera and have you say the line a few times in a row. Easier to get comfortable that way. Cool?"

Nod.

I walk over to the camera, which is set up about fifty feet away because I'm using a long lens. As I sit down behind it, I make a few other comments. I'm a little wired this morning, what with a bad night's sleep, too much coffee, and the bombing, so I'm speaking kind of loud. And, because I'm going deaf, I talk really loudly to start with. It must sound like I'm yelling. Agassi cringes, gives me this "come over here" gesture, and I do.

"Don't scream at me. If you want to say something, come over."

"Okay. Sorry. I always talk too loud."

His lines are really short so he can remember them easily. I have him say each one ten, twelve times in a row, not stopping to re-slate. Instead of just saying the always-unhelpful "again," I give him a quick suggestion each time just before he speaks: quicker, add a smile at the end, rearrange the words, start the line looking away then find me as you speak, hands on your knees, lean forward, laugh on the last word, cross your arms, bounce the ball while you speak. It helps him forget he's in front of a camera. When anyone forgets they're being filmed, everything they say and do starts to sound more natural. It works well with Agassi.

After three takes, I walk over to the bench.

"That was great. Let's move on to the next line."

I say this so fucking quietly, he kind of leans forward to hear me.

"Really?"

"Yeah. Let's do the next one."

We slate, and he does the next line ten times in a row. It's even better than the first one. I walk over again.

"I'm happy. So we're good with the lines. Give me half an hour to get set up for the next stuff, okay?"

"We're done?"

"Yup. You did good."

"Wow. Great. I'm gonna go watch TV."

When we give Andre a five-minute warning, he goes on the adjacent court and warms up with his hitting partner. It's fascinating. They start standing way behind the baseline and hit the ball back and forth, aiming as high as the ceiling will allow, hitting with hyper-exaggerated topspin. The ball goes way, way, way up in the air then drops just inside the baseline. Over the course of five minutes, they bring the trajectory of the ball down to a few feet over the net. By this time, they're both crushing it.

I go over to Andre. He's back to being a little eyes-averted and wary. I give him the basics of what I need him to do: move left to right on the baseline, hit backhands and forehands, maybe a few overheads. I'm using enough proper terminology so that I don't sound like a total newb.

"You play tennis?"

"Yeah."

"Okay." Some small reassurance is evident in his voice.

I always assume that famous actors and athletes have a basic understanding of filmmaking. They've all been in front of cameras before and kind of know the drill. So I treat them accordingly. I tell Andre which scenes I'll do in slow motion and which will be normal. That I'll use long lenses for most everything. He's interested now and not annoyed with me.

I shoot a couple of takes. Everything's great. He's amazing. I just have to fill the time now, so the clients don't think they're getting ripped off. I walk over and join him on the opposite baseline.

"Can you hit the ball right at the camera?"

"Sure."

"I'm going to shoot in super slow motion, so it should look cool."

"Put something on the front of the camera."

"Why?"

"Protect it."

I ask the grips to rig a small piece of plexiglass in front of the lens, thinking this is unnecessary.

We call action, the rally partner feeds him a ball, and, after one warm-up shot, he begins crushing balls that slam into the plexiglass almost every time. It's a twelve-inch square target he's nailing from seventy-eight feet away. When the ball hits the glass, it violently shakes the camera. Five takes is plenty. I get a few more shots of him playing, hitting an overhead, another of him stretching way out to reach a ball, and we're done.

I don't like to have the AD announce that it's a wrap until I've thanked the performers. They're the reason we've been able to get done so quickly, so they deserve my personal and private thanks. I go over to the baseline.

Andre's expecting me to explain the next shot when, instead, I tell him we're done and shake his hand. "You're kidding?"

"Nope. You did everything perfectly. Unless there's something else you want to do? We've got time."

For the first time today, he smiles.

"No. Hey, this was way easier than I expected. Shoots are usually a pain in the ass."

"You made it easy."

"Look, if I can ever do anything for you, tennis stuff, any time, get in touch with Phil. Be happy to help out."

I nod, squint, and say something completely out of character.

"There is something."

"Yeah?"

"Hit with me for five minutes."

He scopes me standing there in khakis and a button-down shirt.

"Okay. Five minutes."

I grab one of the Donnay racquets. We go out onto a court, and I hit a ball across the net. I am praying to God I don't totally clutch and begin dumping all the balls into the net. But it's okay. He hits, I hit it back, we start to rally. Thank Christ I am keeping cool here. I hit a few out, but most stay in play. Then he catches a ball and holds it toward me.

"Ready?"

For what?

He hits me a ball, I return it, and then the next one's moving way faster. Faster than I've ever dealt with. Four, five, six times it goes back and forth. By the sixth, it's not like any version of tennis I've ever played. I see his racquet go back, preparing to hit the ball, I see him swing, there's a loud crack and then a blur as the ball goes by me. I miss or, at best, whack it off the frame.

Then, instead of hitting to my forehand, Agassi starts putting all the balls to my backhand. I hit a slice backhand. I can control the ball, but it doesn't have anywhere near the power of the two-hand backhand he hits. And he hits everything with enormous topspin, so not only is the ball coming at me at a hundred miles an hour, it's hitting and then bouncing up over my head. I'm trying to see the ball, get my racquet up high, swing down, and get it back. It's a disaster. I shank some. Frame a few. Then out and out whiff a few. He gives me one or two more forehands, and I raise my hand like I'm surrendering and walk to the net.

I offer gracious thanks. Then I ask how come he hit all those balls so high to my backhand.

"So you'd miss. You slice, so you can't hit a high-bouncing ball to your backhand."

I'm absorbing the fact that, even just fucking around, Andre's brain is processing the whole thing as a match he has to win.

We walk off the court. My producer's been watching from a viewing stand above the court. She's kind of amazed I did it. I am too. Agassi joins his group, who are all watching CNN. More bombs are falling. A CNN correspondent who's stayed in Baghdad after every other journalist fled is reporting live from his hotel balcony with the air raid sirens blaring and searchlights slicing through the darkness. I look at the four of them from behind. The balding brother. The girlfriend with long, curly brown hair. The close-cropped crew cut of the trainer. And the long, blond-tipped mullet of the world-famous tennis phenom.

My producer, DP, sound guy, and I go out for lunch. We find some place just off the Strip. It's gaudy and the food's pretty bad. A lot of theme. It's a midwinter weekday, so the place is deserted. The only other people in the restaurant, besides us, are locals. And Vegas locals are one skeevy bunch. Our group stands out because we have our own teeth. I think out loud about why Agassi's group was so caught up with the Iraq stuff. They're kids. Doesn't seem like world events would be that big a deal to them. The sound guy had spent some time on set hanging with the trainer. Turns out Agassi's dad was born in Iran. Like most Iranians, the dad loathed Saddam and his boys did too. Andre and Phil were happy watching all that ordnance dropping on Hussein's palaces.

I Fucking Hate Steve.

I BID AGAINST ONE PARTICULAR DIRECTOR ALL THE TIME. MEANING, AGEN-cies talk to both of us about a job and then decide he's their guy. I lose out 70 percent of the time. I hate this guy. As busy as I am, as consistently employed as I am, I'm still working on a lower rung. At first, getting paid so well made me forget that part. But now losing the better work all the time is driving me crazy.

I came into the business with certain disadvantages. Not like a limp or impaired eyesight or something that lets me park in a good spot near the front of a building. The main one was I didn't know anybody. I had never met a director. I'd only seen one shoot for a single day. I had never worked in an agency. It's a real disadvantage. My nemesis used to work in agencies. He gave lots of directors work, watched them in action. He's still buddies with half the agency people he bids with. It helps. A lot.I feel like he's personally blocking my progress. It makes my climb a fucking slog. As he pulls further and further ahead, I pray that he gets hit by a bus.

Remember the Alamo.

We're in Del Rio, Texas. I'm finishing a campaign for Houston Power & Light. We started a week ago in Houston and arrived by chartered plane in Del Rio this morning. We were getting sick of the eight-hour drives back and forth between locations so we splurged for this last company move. We have a day to kill, so we drive over the Rio Grande into Ciudad Acuña, Mexico. It is one fucking depressing town. We go because everyone wants to see a bullfight. I'm not an animal rights person. I eat meat. Wear leather. PETA protestors annoy me. But watching some fat guy squeezed into a pair of satin clam diggers and a sequined toreador jacket do theatrical lunges as a sedated and severely malnourished bull stumbles by him makes me want to root for the bull. There are eight of us, and we make up half the audience. The rest seem to be relatives or girlfriends of the toreadors. The original plan was to hang around and have dinner in Mexico, but I pull the plug on that. We go back to Del Rio and grab some Tex-Mex and a few beers.

I have been nervous all week about shooting tomorrow's job. It's fucking enormous. A reenactment of the Battle of the Alamo. Well, the part before the battle actually starts. But we're dealing with two hundred extras, tons of horses, wagons, livestock, pyrotechnics, and lots of weapons. We're also dealing with an approaching category 5 hurricane. Gilbert is inching west across the Gulf of Mexico, heading right at us. Everyone's fleeing the coast and driving inland. This part of Texas is a mess.

The biggest variable of the job, other than the weather, is the two hundred extras. My producer made a deal with a guy who represents historical reenactors. These people dress up in period costumes then stage elaborate, historically accurate re-creations of famous events. Each reenactor specializes in one or two events and one or two characters in those events. One guy might be an expert at performing as a Union medic at Antietam. He also might do a bitching job as an infantryman in the 20th Maine Volunteers at Gettysburg. Other people deal with Shiloh and Manassas. The organization we've made a deal with does Alamo reenactments. Like many elements of enormous importance on a film shoot, we've never met any of the people involved. We've taken them at their word that they'll show up. Normal film production business practice.

The next morning, a little after 6:00, we drive into Brackettville, Texas. It's a tiny town in the middle of nowhere. We go through two blocks of identical one-story houses on postage stamp–size lots. I make out a sign that says they're part of a retirement community for Army personnel.

Just past this neighborhood of homes is the turnoff onto the road leading to the location. A car's parked there with its headlights on, facing the street. The taillights illuminate a large weathered sign that reads: Happy Shahan's Alamo Village. Open June 15th. Two production people working for us are directing cars up the road, telling crew and cast where to park.

We're in this godforsaken part of Texas for one reason. John Wayne and some nut named Happy Shahan built a replica of the Alamo when Wayne was shooting his movie of the same name in 1958. When the picture was done, everyone forgot about the place. But, in the '70s, Happy thought maybe he could turn it into a tourist attraction. Not a bad idea, except a tourist attraction requires tourists. No tourists come through Brackettville, Texas. Maybe with the hurricane some will, but they'll be fleeing, so probably not looking for a fun family distraction. Anyway, we've rented the place. Because it's perfect.

As we get halfway up the road, the sun's breaking the horizon, so I can see some of the landscape that surrounds the faux fort. It's rough and rugged and harsh. And I can see shapes, clusters of people here and there. As we continue driving, I see more and more people scattered over the landscape. When we pull up to the fort, we're on a small hill, so I can see out in every direction. Now I see people everywhere. Groups in tents, groups with horses, groups around campfires, groups in sleeping bags, groups in covered wagons. Everywhere. There're at least three hundred people, probably closer to four hundred, scattered over the fields surrounding the Alamo structure.

I exhale. My whole idea for telling the story is based on starting with the camera looking out over the exterior wall of the Alamo and seeing a shit ton of heavily armed Mexicans getting ready to attack. I knew the fort was there, but I wasn't sure hundreds of historically attired attackers would actually show up.

I move on to the potentially bigger problem: the hurricane. It's just before 7:00. Normally, we'd have a good amount of light once the sun cracked the horizon. With the socked-in cloud cover, we've got pretty much none. Gilbert has created an enormous low ceiling that's crawling west at a snail's pace. You can't see where the sun is. The light is weirdly ambient. And it'll probably start pouring at any moment. You deal with unexpected shit a lot. Weather is unpredictable. Trucks break down. Props get lost. People get lost. Equipment breaks. I walk onto a set every morning, assuming the wheels will fall off something. This is not my first rodeo, but it's my first hurricane. When the agency producer comes up to me in a panic, unsure whether we can work because it's so damn dark, I just tell him the clouds'll make it even more dramatic.

Everything comes together very quickly. Production, props, and wardrobe organize the covered wagons, horses, open fires, fake rifles and muskets, extras dressed as soldiers, extras dressed as civilians, extras dressed as Mexicans. Every time I look up, the sky's more threatening. According to the radio, the hurricane is going to destroy everything in its path. Hopefully that path is a little to one side of us.

When you're dealing with a rapidly worsening weather situation and you're shooting outside, you get the wide shots first. You can always hide the fact that it's raining when you do close-ups by building small covers. Basically, clear umbrellas you place over whatever you're filming. But there's no way to put an umbrella up over a hundred acres of Texas scrubland, so you have to get those shots before it pours. The crew works fast. They want to get done quickly and get to somewhere safe. According to the radio, the roads heading inland are bumper to bumper for fifty miles. There's a lot of panic out there. I remind whoever will listen that the storm will have blown itself out a little by the time it gets to us. No one asks where I studied meteorology.

As soon as the camera is mounted on the crane, I climb on to see the shot looking out across the scrubland. There's a problem: The reenactors blend in too well with the landscape. Their clothes are the same palette as the dirt and brush and the light is flat from the cloud cover, so there's no contrast. I'm not sure how to solve this. Maybe they need to all be walking around? Maybe we need to move them closer to the fort? The production designer solves it. He sends some of his guys out with old tires and kerosene to create some "campfires." As soon as they light the first one, it acts like a visual beacon. Your eyes focus on the smoke and, once the reenactors start moving around in it, you start seeing them really well. Perfect.

We block the shot. Start up high on the crane, look out over the scrubland filled with smoke and soldiers, boom down into the fort, and discover all the people running around like chickens with their heads cut off, trying to figure out whether to stay or go before they're attacked. On the first take, we almost have a bad accident. One of the female extras who's supposed to hustle into the frame as the camera descends stands too close to a big open fire we've got going in the fort. Her dress catches on fire. She screams, a prop guy has a bucket of water at his feet and puts her out in the nick of time. I start thinking we're going too fast. The storm is making people buggy. If we aren't more careful, other bad shit will happen. I should slow down, but I can't slow down. If I don't get this done quick, we'll have a hurricane on top of us by noon. We go forward.

The rain holds off. I get the wide shot. I get the medium shots. Still no rain. I block the action inside the fort where the defenders start to form a rough circle around William "Buck" Travis. This is the big moment. In the spot and in Texas history. Travis is in charge of the regulars who will make what turns out to be their last stand defending the Alamo. Legend has it that he draws a line in the sand, asking those who are staying to walk across the line. Apparently, it didn't matter what choice you made. Santa Anna overran the fort and killed everyone. Anyway, the speech makes for a good scene.

It keeps getting darker and darker. Challenging. But dramatic looking. And no rain. After some pickup shots of the defenders, I do the scene with Travis.

The guy playing Travis is an actor we've brought in from Los Angeles. He's great. He looks like an old Indian fighter and sounds like one. And, because he's so good, I get what I need in two or three takes and keep us flying along. When I'm about three shots away from being done, my producer appears next to me. Technically, it's time to call lunch. The crew's been working for six hours. Union rules say you feed everyone after six hours or pay a penalty. We have to get this done. And then get everyone out of here. No way we can stop for lunch. My producer and I decide it's worth paying the penalty today.

Two more scenes and I finish. My hustling back and forth all morning between the camera and the agency has been frantic. This time, when I go over and tell them I'm good and I think we're done, everything goes weird. Granted, it's an odd situation. They've hired me to shoot for at least ten hours. I've only shot for six. Now that doesn't really matter because I've done more in six hours than I'd promised I would in ten. But, when you do an enormous job with a big budget, clients always feel ripped off when it's all been accomplished in half a day. Yeah, Hurricane Gilbert is coming; yeah, it all went really well; yeah, we were efficient; but can we really, truly be done, have everything we need for whatever comes up in editing with only six hours of shooting?

Yes. We can. And we are. We call a wrap. Let's get everyone out of here.

The reenactors pack up and hit the road. It looks like a wagon train. The crew does the fastest wrap I've ever seen and is gone in an hour. Seeing this weather report two days ago, my producer had booked us on a 4:30 p.m. flight out of San Antonio. We figure, if we haul ass out of Brackettville immediately, we can catch it. We pile into a station wagon and speed down the dusty driveway. I wave to Happy as we go by. He looks like he's having a fine old time.

When the nose of the plane lifts up, I breathe out again. Almost every other flight out of San Antonio had been cancelled. Who knows why they let this one go. As we climb in a northeasterly direction, the scale of the hurricane is more clear. That wall of gray goes on for fucking ever. No rain. No lightning. Nothing. Just something that clearly is going to do big damage. The pilot says we'll have a lot of bumps as we fly around it, so fasten your seatbelts. Gladly.

We land at Kennedy around midnight. I walk into the house in Hastings around 1:30 a.m. I'm filthy and smell like shit. I climb into bed with my clothes still on and fall fast asleep.

Used Up and Spat Out.

I'VE GOT ONE SOLID PIECE OF BUSINESS ADVICE FOR ANY YOUNG ENTREPRE-
neur. Don't sue your best client. It does not build good feeling, engender
trust, or add years to your relationship. If you get so angry with a client
that you see yourself edging toward this kind of move, talk to someone
who has long experience in business and thinks rationally. Avoid lawyers,
many of whom will happily get you into a mess like this. You're better off
discussing it with a real small business expert, like an Uber driver or the
guy who delivers your Chinese food.

I opened my production company when I was twenty-two. I didn't
know any rules. I'd watched a guy do it for a year or so, and it didn't
look complicated. I boiled things down to two laws. You set up something
that costs as little as possible to run on a day-to-day basis and then take
in more money than you spend. To keep costs down, for the first three
years, I ran my company from my apartment. I kept my payroll to one
person: someone to answer the phones. I only paid the guy who was selling me if he got me a job. And I only paid myself if there was anything left

after paying the rent, the sales commission, and the person who handled the phone. And I didn't actually pay myself. I just left anything that was left over after paying the bills in the business account.

I didn't know what other production companies charged to make a commercial. So, when I started bidding on jobs, my estimates were low. Like, insanely low. The formula for estimating costs in my industry was you totaled up your costs, added a director's fee, and then marked it all up 30 percent. My method was to take my costs, add them up, then add five thousand dollars on top. No director's fee, no overall markup. It meant I was charging a lot less than everyone else. Once I could convince agency producers that I'd done it before, that it's not a too good to be true offer, I started to get work.

Five years in, I knew more. And I charged more. But I was still a lot less expensive than anyone I bid against. This resulted in other companies hating me. Rightly so. I was upsetting the model they'd worked for years to convince the agencies and clients was the only way to go. I was oblivious. I just focused on the simple fact that I had a better chance of getting a job if I was the lowest bid.

By ten years in, I was a better director, bidding against better directors. But I brought a version of my pricing model with me. I was now charging a director's fee but a lower markup than everybody else. So I continued to make enemies. I didn't care. I was working steadily for big agencies and clients. I'd moved my office out of my apartment. I had a tiny satellite office in Hollywood. I had four full-time employees and four sales reps scattered across the country working on commission. I was pushing and shoving and fighting for gigs every day, but the trend was up. And I'd become a big supplier to a large Detroit agency, W. B. Doner. They made lots of spots for retailers in secondary markets. A lot of the work was cheesy: ten seconds of entertainment, twenty seconds of selling the car, the stereo, the clothes. I became a favorite of theirs. If you asked me why, I'd tell you it was because I was smart and efficient and a good director, who, once in a while, won them an award for something

I'd directed. If you asked them, they probably would have said, "He's cheap as shit."

One summer, they hired me to do a flashy campaign for the Detroit NBC affiliate. It was an opportunity to make something sexy and fast-paced and gritty. Crime scenes, smoky bars, reporters in empty break-fast joints, Little League games, the Lions taking the field, Martha and the Vandellas rehearsing, Elmore Leonard watching a Tigers game, fire-fighters responding, amusement parks, helicopter shots of the city center at night. I spent a week shooting. When we finished, Doner refused to pay my final bill. A little less than twenty-five grand. They had approved a variety of cost overruns during the shoot but were now saying they hadn't. Cost overruns are normal and negotiable. Sometimes you lower them after the job's done, but you never get stiffed. That's what they were threatening, and it was a lot of money. To me.

But twenty-five grand was bupkis in the big picture of how much Doner was paying me every year. I kept shooting for them as we fought over that bill, but, when the spot started winning awards, I lost my shit. Unfortunately, I lost it while being out of range of a food delivery guy from Xi'an. So I sued my biggest client.

The results were predictable. Doner stopped hiring me. Almost half my billings disappeared. Instantly. The suit went nowhere because they could run the clock forever with their lawyers. I was standing on a god-dam soapbox arguing that I was right and they were wrong. I didn't get that, when money's changing hands, right and wrong are sort of irrelevant. And it never crossed my mind that this move of mine might be wrong. Because, if I'd done something wrong, that meant I'd done something stupid. And I couldn't admit I was stupid. But I was. Stupid and wrong.

○ ○ ○

Three years later, I'm waiting for my rental car in front of the Westwood Marquis hotel and I see one of the Doner producers I worked for. He's on his way to some function at the Playboy Mansion.

"That sounds weird."

"It'll be great. Hef throws a good party."

Why or how this pudgy schmuck in an ill-fitting suit and scuffed Florsheims with no heels had gotten himself on the guest list at the Playboy Mansion was beyond me.

"You working?"

I was that week.

"Yeah. I'm out here for a month. In the Hollywood office. Three jobs. Busy."

The Hollywood office was a ten-by-eight room on the Sony Lot. I was out here for two weeks. One job.

"Do you miss us?"

"I liked working for you guys. Just at the end there, I thought you weren't being fair."

He started laughing.

"Fair? Are you kidding? We fuck everyone over. Use them up and spit them out. What happened to you is normal for us."

"The lawsuit probably didn't help."

"You sued us?"

"Yeah. That seemed to be the straw that broke the camel's back."

"I didn't know."

"Seriously?"

"Seriously. But you'd had a big run with us. No one goes longer than three years. Something happens, we find someone new to start fucking over. Kind of funny that you sued. That takes balls."

A limo pulls up.

"This is me. Nice to see you. Don't make yourself nuts. My guess is the lawsuit didn't matter. You were already toast."

He climbed into the back of the car and pulled away. I felt vaguely better. It was just business as usual. Everyone fucking everyone over. Bullshitting. Lying.

Lying?

That fat fuck wasn't going to the Mansion. He was probably going to some whorehouse. That's the only way he was ever going to come in contact with a woman. With my lies about three jobs and spending the month in LA, we were even.

Change Partners.

I'VE HAD MY OWN COMPANY FOR SEVENTEEN YEARS. IT STARTED SMALL AND got bigger. At the ten-year point, I had offices in New York, Boston, and Los Angeles. I've tried adding other directors, hoping they'd make it grow. That part of the plan never worked out. Fine. I made a mistake. Onward. But, by the fifteen-year mark, something's changed. Making a go of it as a single-director company isn't working anymore. My work has suddenly dried up. And I'm plowing lots of my own money back into the company to keep it going.

Most commercial production companies are owned by a producer. The producer worries about getting the work, maintaining the clients, paying the bills, hiring and firing. The directors are just hired guns. A director-owned company is rare. But the guys who own their own companies are my idols, and I've tried to follow in their footsteps. The thing is my idols are much better directors than me with lots more business. After seventeen years, I know my company cannot keep going. I have a wife and two kids and a limited set of options. I have to do something.

Every five years or so, once I began working steadily and exaggerating my success in the press, I'd get an offer to join another production company. Flattering. But I wasn't interested. I could do it myself. Plus, I was afraid. I didn't think I was very good at my job yet. If I'd moved into a big, serious place, surrounded by experienced directors, I was sure I'd be found out. I was successful mainly because I'd built my business slowly, in my own part of the pasture. I was working on a smaller scale, with smaller budgets and smaller clients, with lower risks and expectations. I didn't need someone else's help. I was convinced I'd get there on my own. So, as appealing as the idea of joining the big time and the big boys was, I knew I wasn't ready yet.

I am now. Not because I'm suddenly in the mood to learn something. I just want to be a director and not hassle with running a business. The costs are killing me, the industry is going through one of its periodic contractions, and I don't think I can make it. I've never felt that before. I've saved a lot of money, but having to put big chunks back into the business is terrifying. And I am slashing my prices in order to get work. This makes sense if you're doing it to get great jobs. The theory being that doing good work will create more demand for your services. It makes no sense when you are selling yourself cheap to do dog food commercials. I let the word get out that I'm interested in talking.

I have a reputation as a little engine that could, which makes me an appealing item. I am a commodity. A director with a following, someone who'll generate a few million dollars a year in billings. Which means sizable profits to a production company. That part of being a commodity is okay. The bad part is that the people who work with me—a producer, a production manager, an office manager, and a receptionist—are of no value to someone else. Another company already has those people. As I start negotiating with the companies that are offering me a slot, I ask about whom I can bring along with me. While they all phrase the answer differently, each of the executive producers makes it clear that they are interested in me. That's it.

I make a deal. It's a good one. For me. It's bad for my staff. I'm joining a new company, but they're out on the street. I put myself through contortions of rationalizing. I have a wife and kids. All three of my key employees are young and single. I have a large financial risk. They have none. I have to do what is best for me.

It isn't a great feeling.

Page Six.

I start working at the new company immediately. The first gig I get is a Jif commercial. Three yuppie couples talking about peanut butter. An hour before lunch, my producer tells me the company's owner needs to talk to me.

"How's it going?"

"Fine. Everyone's happy."

"Listen...you got a minute?"

Sounds like this'll take more than a minute.

"I'm getting sued."

"By who?"

"An ex-producer."

"That sucks. What's the issue?"

"He claims he was my partner."

"Was he?"

"Fuck, no. Guy's an asshole. Never."

"So fuck him. It'll go away."

"Thing is, he's putting shit in the papers. Page Six."

"About?"

"Ridiculous shit. Like RICO statutes."

RICO statutes are what the feds use to charge Mafia types.

"Look. All I'm saying is it might get bad. You have a good reputation. I wouldn't want you to get caught up in this. If you want to bail and leave, I get it."

My company's gone, and I'm in a terrible place financially.

"Is the guy lying?"

"Yeah. Mostly."

Mostly?

Fuck.

I'm in. Signed on. Committed. I can't undo this. Maybe my producer seemed a little rough around the edges when we were negotiating, maybe he had surprisingly long and strong relationships with certain agencies, but I'm sure he's not a thief. And I'm also sure that the guy who got pushed out is pissed because he's out of a very good thing. It's just business. Somebody's day in the sun just ended. Not mine.

Shooting in Shitholes.

MANILA IS A VERY BIG, VERY POOR CITY. SIGNIFICANTLY MORE THIRD world than first. Police behavior usually determines that for me. If the local cops operate brazenly as shakedown artists, you're in the third world. In Manila, every time one of the drivers taking us to location changes lanes without using his flicker or goes through an amber light, we get pulled over. The cop takes the driver's papers, threatens him, makes as if to rip them up, which causes the driver to whimper and beg, which then devolves into my producer handing the cop ten US dollars, which makes everything go away. Hateful. A city I will never return to.

I'm doing commercials for AT&T. They feature Lea Salonga, the star of *Miss Saigon*, and, since she's living here temporarily doing a show, we've come to her. Because we're shooting so many spots, we've pre-ordered sixty thousand feet of film. That's like ten American Tourister suitcases worth of film. During a shoot, you don't carry all that film with you all the time. You take what you think you'll need for the day and park the rest at the production office.

Today, we're shooting in the presidential suite at the Mandarin Oriental hotel. It's the only location I'd seen that could be re-dressed to look like a fancy New York apartment where, in the commercial, Lea supposedly lives. The art department has changed out all the furniture, a fake kitchen has been installed, and the window treatments are different. It now looks like we're in a building on the Upper East Side. We'll spend the morning here and then move to another location on the other side of Manila.

The first scene is all dialogue. Lea's on the phone in the New York apartment talking to musicians in a recording studio in Manila. I have her mainly adlibbing lines about instruments and rhythms. She's a seasoned performer, so it all comes naturally to her. Everything's going fine. Especially considering it's the first day of shooting and we're working with a Hong Kong–based production team we met five days ago and fifty Filipino laborers who speak no English. Everything's good.

But the Hong Kong–based production manager keeps coming up to me every five minutes looking more and more unhappy. For some reason, he's obsessed with how much film I'm shooting.

"You shoot a lot of film."

"It's the first scene. It'll slow down once we get going."

"I hope so."

This isn't the kind of conversation you normally have with a production manager. I ask my producer to find out what's going on. They go off to the hallway and have a chat as I keep shooting. My producer comes over when I cut.

"He's just nervous about how much film you're using."

"I know that. But who cares? We have sixty thousand feet for this job, right?"

"Right."

Makes no sense to me. I wave the production manager over.

"I'm a little confused here. You seem very concerned about how much film I'm shooting. We have sixty thousand feet, right?"

"Yes."

"So what's the problem? I've barely made a dent."

"I don't know if we'll have enough film."

"Seriously? We have sixty thousand feet. Don't you think that's way more than enough?"

"Yes."

I suddenly start to wonder if I'm in a *Twilight Zone* episode where I think I'm speaking English but what's really coming out of my mouth is Urdu.

"So, again, why are you so nervous?"

"Because we only have four thousand here."

"But that's okay. If we need more, you'll send someone to the office and get more."

"Yes."

But now he's ashen. There's something missing in the conversation. Mentally, I default into an ethnic generalization where Asians do anything to avoid conflict and embarrassment. Maybe I've said something insulting and he's ashamed to call me on it? It wouldn't be the first time.

"We bought sixty thousand feet, right?"

"Yes."

"And it's at the office?"

"Yes."

Wait. Flickering lightbulb.

"The office here in Manila?"

"No."

Bingo.

"Which office has the film?"

"The Kodak office. In Singapore."

"How long will it take the film to get from Singapore to Manila?"

"One day. Normally. But now three because tomorrow's Valentine's Day."

"So we have enough film. But the film is not in Manila, where we're shooting. It's in Singapore, and it'll take three days to get here because of a holiday I didn't know they even celebrate in this country?"

"Very big holiday here."

"I think it would be good if you call Singapore immediately and have them FedEx all the film here now. Like this minute."

"Yes."

We never figure out why all the film hadn't been delivered to Manila originally. But the producer and I do realize that, for the rest of this job, we need to ask every question in multiple ways, each time framing it from a different angle. We even do this when it comes to what's for lunch. They think we're dumb as rocks.

In hindsight, I'd say this was all our fault. We didn't ask the right questions. Well, we sort of did, but we just didn't know the right way to pose them. There's a lesson in this. I think it's that people who speak different languages don't understand each other very well.

Getting Better All the Time (Not).

MY WORK LIFE IS NOW NUTS. WONDERFUL, BUT NUTS. MOVING INTO THE new company has proved to be smart. I do a lot better just being a director instead of also trying to run a business. A whole lot better. But everything comes with a price. I work all the time. I'm always on calls, watching casting tapes, scouting locations, always in motion. When I'm shooting in New York, I'm out the door on the way to location by 6:00 a.m. I shoot fast so I'm home early, but I have to go upstairs when I get there and watch casting tapes for the next job. And I'm traveling a lot. Work has me out of town and away from home two, sometimes three weeks a month. So there are a ton of those *Lost in Translation*–type phone calls where Bill Murray's in Japan trying to stay connected with his wife and kids back in New York by calling them every day. But, because of the time difference, he's going to bed as his wife is trying to get the kids on the school bus. These kinds of calls are exercises in omission. I don't go into any detail about what I'm doing because I'm sure it'll sound exciting and fun and drive Blanche crazy. We are talking but not saying much. Going through the motions. Out of sync. Big time.

I try really hard to be a solid husband and father. I make the nightly calls, fly home on the first flight I can get after a job wraps, jump in and try to become the primary parent when I'm home, hire plenty of housekeepers and babysitters, get us away on vacations whenever there's a break. But it isn't enough. Blanche is on a constant, low-level angry boil. She thinks she dumped her career in the trash when we had kids. I don't think that's true, but she does, so it is.

The fact that our life is going along fine on the comfort, health, and financial security front doesn't matter. I get it. Sometimes. But I keep playing back all the early conversations about stability. How hard it is, and essential it is, to create. How hard it is, and essential it is, to keep it going. How each of us has to sacrifice different things to make it work. When I lose my temper, I lose it because I think everything she's furious at is just me honoring my side of the bargain. This is what I said I'd do, and I'm doing it. Isn't that the normal we'd talked about? Apparently not.

I was leaving one morning in a raging blizzard to fly to LA. We were renting a six-bedroom Tudor monstrosity while our house was being remodeled. We'd fought the night before about something and then, around 3:00 in the morning, discovered the youngest kid had gotten out of her crib and covered herself, the walls, and all the furniture in her room with Vaseline. Funny, but not that night. After two hours of cleaning up, we're downstairs waiting for the car. Blanche is on the other side of the stone-floored entrance hall staring daggers at me.

"I'm sorry about us being in this house. It's a pain."

"Right."

"And I'm sorry that I keep leaving you to deal with all this."

"Right."

"This'll all end. Soon. I have to do it while I can. When it's over, we'll live a nice life."

"Right."

"I just need a little more time."

"How long?"

She'd never asked that before.

"I don't know. Maybe two years?"

"Two years? Two more years of this insanity?"

"So maybe less."

"This isn't going to work for two years."

The car pulled into the driveway, the headlights panned across the entranceway walls, each of us momentarily bleached and strafed.

"I'm sorry. I know what you're feeling."

"I don't think you do."

"It'll get better."

She turned her back and went into the kitchen.

"Blanche...?"

"When are you coming back?"

"Friday. I think. There may be a..."

She kept walking into the kitchen and let the door close behind her. Honestly, everything couldn't have been worse.

Rocky and Bullwinkle.

NOVA SCOTIA LOOKS LIKE AN EDWARD HOPPER PAINTING. SIMPLE WHITE clapboard homes. Empty two-lane roads. Wheat fields framed by weather-beaten wooden fences. But there are none of those cool-looking guys in fedoras and ladies with great gams sipping java in a diner. Just a lot of drunks and junkies sleepwalking down the streets. I'm here with sixty technicians; four actors; three semis of grip, lighting, and camera equipment; and one custom-designed tractor-trailer carrying four picture vehicles. We dragged all this crap here because of a moose.

The commercial's for Ford Explorer. It's not a bad idea. A mom and dad think their kids are watching too much television. Specifically, too many cartoons. So the parents hustle the kids out of the house and into their Explorer. And they go exploring. In the magic place that is advertising's Nirvana, this twenty-second car ride takes them past rivers, over mountains, along beaches, through Times Square, and, eventually, to Nova Scotia where, to sew it all up, the car comes upon a giant moose standing by the side of the road. The kids point and the parents beam, and the announcer talks about rebates. It has an actual narrative, good visuals, and a little twist at the end. I can do something with this.

We spent a couple weeks scouting locations for the rivers, mountains, beaches, and Times Square. Those were easy to find. Finding a moose was not. The production people finally located one. It had been in a lot of movies. In Canada. Where else? The trainer guaranteed the animal would do whatever he told it to. Come. Stay. Look left. Look right. All on cue. Because this moose had been "imprinted."

That sounds vaguely scientific, right? All it means is that the moose grew up around people. The result is a moose that thinks all humans are bringing it lunch. I'm calling him Bullwinkle before the plane lands.

The night before the shoot, we take the J. Walter Thompson clients out to dinner in downtown Halifax. It's a sketchy town. The biggest thing that ever happened here was an accident. In 1917, a French frigate loaded with a world war's supply of dynamite blew up in the mouth of the harbor when it collided with a Norwegian freighter. The force was comparable to a three-kiloton nuclear explosion. Two thousand people died, thousands more were injured, most of the buildings in town were destroyed, and, to throw salt in the wound, the explosion triggered a tsunami that swooped in ten minutes later and drowned half the people who survived the blast. Every historical marker you see tells you how many people died on the spot where you're standing. Not that fun a place.

We go to a steakhouse, drink expensive, shitty red wine, and smoke excellent Cuban cigars. When we stumble out of the restaurant around 10:00, it's raining. It's also still kind of light because we're so far north and it's July. Weird.

In the hotel lobby, as we're going our separate ways, my line producer reminds the Thompson guys that a production assistant will pick them up at 5:00 a.m.

"Even if it's raining?"

"It won't be raining."

"What if it is?"

"It won't be. Five. Lobby."

I lag behind and start a fake conversation with my producer, so I don't have to ride up in the elevator with the agency. These days I'm trying to avoid unnecessary interaction with talent, clients, crew, whomever. I'm burnt out. I just want to be left alone until I show up to do my work. When they're out of earshot, I get right to it, "What if it *is* raining?"

"Does it matter?"

"No," I lie.

"You'll figure something out."

"Hey, I thought of something during dinner. Can you get us some Cuban Montecristos we can send back to New York?"

"I'll send someone."

We walk across the lobby and wait for the elevator. My line producer stares at the closed reflective doors.

"I just want this fucking job to be over, so I can go home. My wife's about to divorce me."

My stomach goes into a knot. I say nothing. I will not let anyone know what's happening in my private life. I've found that having a distance from the people I work with every day helps. Mainly because I have to be a prick so much of the time. I don't want to be friends with the people I work with. I don't want to know about their problems. And I certainly don't want them knowing about mine. I want them to think I'm screaming because they've fucked up their job not because I feel like my life is collapsing around me. This is the third line producer I've had this year whose marital situation has gone to shit once they started working with me. I'm shooting so much that I need three of them to take turns running my jobs. They all look exhausted. I look even worse, but I think the weathered, craggy thing is cool. As he gets off the elevator and the doors close, I start wondering if it's too late to call home. Maybe. I then ask myself if anyone at home wants to talk to me. Maybe not. I'm pretty buzzed, so I let that synapse sequence fizzle out.

The alarm goes off at 4:30. I go to the window. It's pouring. In thirty years of shooting, I've only had one rain day. A rain day is where you're planning to shoot outdoors but it rains all day, you have no indoor location available as a backup, so you pay everyone to stay home. Paying seventy people to stay home and look at it rain will cost me somewhere between sixty and seventy-five thousand dollars. You can get insurance for this but, like all catastrophic insurance, it's exorbitantly expensive and the insurance company has thousands of ways to weasel out of paying the full bill. So, whatever happens, you're on the hook for a big sum. Even though I'm supposed to make a ton of money on this job, we didn't buy rain insurance, so a rain day would be painful. My phone rings.

"By the time we get to location, it'll be over."

"From your mouth to God's ear. How bad is it at location?"

"I haven't heard from production. The cell service in this place is fucked. Let's just stick to the plan."

I lie down on the flattened, unhealthy-looking brown shag carpet, do a little stretching, hop in the shower, then head downstairs. My line producer's already in the van. I climb in the front passenger seat, and we head off. Halfway to location, the rain stops and the sun peeks out. No rain day. In fact, all the leftover wetness on the trees and grass will vastly improve the shot.

On arrival, the assistant director introduces me to the moose trainer. He's what you'd expect: a barrel-chested guy in a flannel shirt, wide leather belt, floppy-brimmed canvas hat decorated with fishing flies, and a Ted Kaczynski-style beard. Also, since he's Canadian, he's wearing terrible shoes. I need to quickly figure out if this guy knows his shit.

"What's your take on how we should work today?"

"Tell me the shots you need."

"I need three. Moose in the woods. Moose walking over to the car. Moose really close to the car, looking at the kids. What's the best order?"

"Do the shot of him in the woods first, then I'll bring him over to the car, and you can do those."

"When you put him somewhere, how long will he stay put?"

"Long as I want him to."

"Can I get really close to him?"

"Yeah, yeah. No problem. He likes people. He's imprinted."

I've done enough stupid animal gags to know that sometimes animals don't do what they're told for very long. So I always try to do the absolutely essential shots first, just in case that "imprinting" wears off.

I climb into a production van and drive down a dirt road to the location where the moose gag will happen. A female production assistant is at the wheel. She's from Toronto, in Nova Scotia for the summer, in film school, wants to direct, something about a screenplay.

"How are you this morning?"

"Good. You?"

"Bet you're happy the sun came out."

"I am."

"You would've had to find a different camera position if it was still raining…"

"Yeah…"

But no. I would have gone back to bed. And bought a rain day.

"If you go down this road, past where we're set up, there's a nice rise. I thought it'd be a cool shot."

Jesus. It's 6:00 in the morning. I'm not interested in what the agency has to say, let alone what this PA's thinking.

We pull up at the location, I hop out and walk over to the picture car. A picture car is a brand-new, never-driven model of the Explorer. It's there just to look pretty for the camera and for the actors to sit inside. We've had four of these cars shipped from the factory in Detroit. We were supposed to have six, but the semi bringing the other two from a shoot in Los Angeles caught fire somewhere in Arizona and they melted. Really.

I say hello to the actors playing the family. The kids are out cold in the backseat, mouths wide open, bodies bent into strange shapes. Actor Dad is sipping coffee and smoking a cigarette. Actor Mom is making a big deal of waving her hand around to disperse the smoke.

The AD hustles over.

"Where's the moose?"

He points to a grove of birch trees across the way.

"Wow." That is a big fucking moose.

Moose Man appears. He must have walked too close to one of the trucks because he's all splattered with mud. He's even got some in his beard. But he's outdoorsy, so it works for him. I point toward Bullwinkle.

"Should we start over there?"

"I'm thinking maybe first we should do the stuff by the car instead. That possible?"

"Whatever works best."

"Okay. I'll bring him over."

Moose Man climbs through the fence and heads across the meadow. Because the field is an ocean of mud, he walks like he's on a planet with incredibly strong gravity. His boots disappear up to the ankles with each step. The farther he goes, the deeper his boots go in. There's no grace in this. Finally, Moose Man arrives next to Bullwinkle. He starts talking to him. He's moving his hands around, twirling them in our direction. He steps closer to the beast and gives it a tap on the rib cage. The moose takes a step back. Moose Man tries a solid whack. Another step back. The next whack has more effect. The moose starts moving at a trot. Coming right at us.

"Gimme the camera. Now!"

The camera assistant loads the Arri onto my shoulder. An Arriflex BL with a 25-250 Zeiss zoom lens is a sixty-pound hunk of metal and glass. I grab the handles and look through the viewfinder. Bullwinkle is coming right at me.

"Roll."

"Where do you want the focus…"

"Roll the fucking camera!"

I aim the camera through one of the backseat passenger windows. The little girl is in front of me, still a little sleepy and weirded out by the huge lens poking into the car. As a result, she's looking at me, not at the moose.

"Don't look at me. Look over there! The moose is coming!"

And, in a few seconds, the moose is there. The actors do naturally what I hoped they'd do: go nuts. The moose pushes up against the fence, five feet from the car. I take a few steps left or right, so I can keep his giant antlered head in the frame and still see both kids. Then I see something in the background. Fucking Moose Man. He's slogging across the field, those big, Roots-shod feet slurping through the mud. He's right in the center of the shot. I bark at the AD.

"Tell that fucking idiot to lie down."

The AD repeats my guidance. Verbatim. I hear Moose Man's voice on the walkie.

"It's all mud!"

I need this shot. The trainer is ruining it. But, if he gets down—okay, technically lies down—in the mud, he'll disappear and all will be forgiven.

"Tell him to lie down. Now!"

Again, instructions repeated verbatim. Moose Man takes a knee then lies down flat and disappears. All I see now are the kids, still amazed by the giant beast. Mom is amazed too. She's laughing and pointing and having a grand time. The boy picks up the disposable camera the prop department had put in the back seat and starts snapping pictures. Everything seems almost real. Then Bullwinkle disappears.

"Cut."

I hand the Arri back to the AC. I walk around the car to see where the moose went. There he is. Lying down. In the mud. Moose Man's voice comes over the walkie.

"Can I get up?"

"Yeah. And please come to camera."

The AD, Moose Man, and I stare at Bullwinkle, who's sprawled on his side in a giant puddle. I turn to Moose Man. He looks like a rabid fan for a team whose mascot is mud.

"I got an okay shot just now. But it'd be great if we can do it again."

Moose Man's looking down at Bullwinkle.

"Lemme see what I can do."

What he can do is bupkis. Fucking Bullwinkle loves mud. Loves it more than obeying his imprinting buddy's orders. Moose Man tries gentle prodding. Awkward noises. Bribing the beast with Reese's. Tries everything. An hour later, we're avoiding eye contact as the poor bastard pleads with Bullwinkle. He's anxious and crestfallen.

"I've never had this happen…"

All men say this a couple of times in their lives. All animal trainers say this when their high-priced animal behaves like a stupid animal. "When's he gonna get up?"

"I just don't know."

"How's he feel about not getting paid?"

I love this AD.

I decide to abandon the moose for the time being. Time to do some driving shots. Scenes you use to bail you out of problems in editorial. I get on the walkie, every once in a while, for a moose report. No movement.

We drive back to the staging area. The agency guys are hanging around the craft service table, stuffing their faces. They don't seem to care about the moose. I appreciate this vote of confidence, but I'm concerned that there really isn't enough footage to work with. Also, since we're on the sixth day of this job and they're hung over from last night's dinner, not to mention ready for a nap because we got up at 4:00 a.m., they just don't give a shit. But they will, believe me, when they get to editing and only have one moose shot to fuck around with.

"You got plenty of stuff."

"There's a couple good moments."

"We only need a second or two."

"I feel like we need to see the thing coming over to the car."

"We can work it out in editing."

Actually, you can't if there's no footage to work it out with. I'm always the first person on the set to think I'm done, but I don't feel that way this morning.

"Let me see what's going on."

So, once again, the AD, Moose Man, and I stare down Bullwinkle. I'm wondering whether a cattle prod might do the trick. We decide to wait it out.

Two hours later, the moose stirs. I ask the AC to bring the camera over. The moose lumbers crookedly to its feet.

"If I put the camera right in its face, will he attack me?"

"Might try and see if you taste good."

"Gimme the camera."

I stand as close to Bullwinkle as I can. If I get a few shots of his face, they'll address most of my editing worries. Bullwinkle cooperates, staring right into the lens. I think it'd be a good idea to have a wide shot of him by the fence, so we swap out lenses and grab that. Bullwinkle stands there, moving his head a little. It works. Then Bullwinkle lies down again.

I hand the camera to the AC. For the second time today, I'm standing over this goddam moose lying in the mud.

"What d'ya think now?"

I'm moving into the torture segment of my interaction with Moose Man.

"I can try and get him to stand up again."

"This fucking moose isn't getting up," says my AD.

My AD woke up at 3:30 this morning and was on set by 4:30. He's had a very long day. Which works like sodium pentothal on film crew members. At 10:00 in the morning, they're bright-eyed and bushy-tailed and will lie to you if you want to be lied to. By 5:00, they're exhausted and it's all brutal honesty. I agree with my AD. We're done with the moose.

"I have what I need. If he doesn't get up in ten minutes, let's wrap."

Ten minutes later, he hasn't moved. The AD calls a wrap, and the sixty technicians start packing the camera, grip, lighting, and prop equipment into the trucks. I ask the AC to leave the camera out, just in case Bullwinkle rallies.

Usually, when I call a wrap, I shake everyone's hand, tell the agency how happy I am with how the job went, and leave fast. The crew, the poor bastards who do the actual heavy lifting, have another hour or two of work ahead of them, packing everything up. This afternoon, I feel like I have to stay put. Because, if the moose stands up while people are still here, it'll look like I got lazy.

An hour and a half later, everything but the camera is packed. The prop trucks have left. The lighting and generator vehicle has gone. All the talent has been shuttled back to the hotel. The motor homes are on their way back to town. It's down to Bullwinkle, Moose Man, the AD, the AC, and me.

"What d'ya think now, captain?"

The AD's tone is facetious. But the trainer can't take offense because he's fucked up so badly.

"I just don't know. They're unpredic…"

"You think?"

"He just might get up again."

"How much you wanna bet?"

In situations like this, it's my call. I'm the Decider.

"Let's get the fuck out of here."

Moose Man is bummed.

"I'm sorry. I wish he'd done better."

"We'll talk about it later."

"I don't understand…"

"Dude, we traveled sixty people and a shit ton of equipment up here, spent a fortune doing it, all because you said your moose could do everything but speak Japanese. And, when his moment came, he didn't deliver."

"I couldn't know the…"

"You see what I'm saying, right? All the people, the money, the…"

"No, I get it, I see, but…"

"We're not going to deal with this now. You get him on your truck and out of here. We'll talk about it in a few days."

In the van on the way back to town, the agency producer offers to buy a wrap dinner. We wind up at an Italian joint. Me, my line producer, and five agency people. I grab a seat between my producer and the copywriter. I quickly down most of a bottle of red. The conversation begins to sound funny. Yeah, that stupid moose lying in the mud was hilarious. Fucking hilarious.

Three hours and many bottles of wine later, the seven of us climb into the van to take us back to the hotel. As I'm getting out, the production assistant who's driving hands me a thick manila envelope. Fuck. Her screenplay.

"Here."

The envelope feels like there are two hardback books inside.

"Your cigars."

Oh, right.

"Are you going into the production office tomorrow?" I ask.

"Yeah. Do my paperwork."

"Great. Take this with you. Have them FedEx it to me at the office in New York."

"Cool."

"You know how this goes, right?"

"I know how to FedEx…"

"Yeah, sorry, but it's that Cuban cigars are illegal in the States so…"

"I got it."

"Best thing to do is stuff some laundry in the package around them. When they x-ray, they won't see the cigars."

"I got it. You'll get your Montecristos."

Two days later, after flying from Halifax to Portland, Maine, to attend my kids' summer camp visiting days, during which I fell asleep during lunch, riflery practice, a swimming event, a tennis match, and some terrible musical number with kids dressed as ducks, I stride triumphantly into the office on Lafayette Street. My other line producer steers me into the small conference room, so I can start watching casting tapes for the next job. My executive producer plants himself in the doorway.

"You are a totally stupid fuck."

"Good morning. Nice to see you."

"You just pissed fifteen hundred bucks down the fucking toilet."

"What's that mean?"

"FedEx called. Customs seized that box you sent from Canada."

"Jesus."

"And, on top of that, they're going to fine us—you, actually—two grand. Don't you have any fucking idea how to send cigars across the border? You ever heard of dirty laundry?"

"I told her to do that."

"Who's her?"

"The PA."

"You had a PA take care of FedExing fifteen hundred bucks' worth of cigars? You're a fucking idiot."

"I told her to do the dirty laundry thing."

"She did that."

"So what went wrong?"

"On the waybill, where they ask what's in the box, she wrote, 'Polo shirt, gym shorts, socks and Cuban cigars.'"

"I guess she's very literal. She wants to be a director."

"Well, she's fucking dumb enough to be one."

I just made this fat fuck two hundred grand, and his thanks is to call me an idiot.

At the end of the quarter when I got paid, the comptroller made a special note on my statement. She docked me fifteen hundred bucks for the cigars I'd charged on the company card and another two grand for the US Customs fine. Usually, I split all expenses with the company. But that seems to exclude fines from the Treasury Department.

You're Not My First.

I'M LOCATION SCOUTING IN BOLOGNA, ITALY. IT'S THE SECOND WEEK IN A sweltering July. The spot I'm shooting is for Bertolli olive oil. It's about a woman driving all over Italy visiting the best purveyors of olive oils. I'm getting paid to meander through the most beautiful parts of Italy and periodically set up my camera and have a gorgeous woman examine a couple of olive trees. I'm trying to figure out a way to make the commercial feel like a series of chapters in a longer story. Each farm, each town, each city will have a different feel and look. I'm aiming for part pretty travelogue, part best business trip ever. She'll start in Rome, head to Florence, on to the outskirts of Turin, and, finally, end up in Bologna. I've never been to Bologna before, so I'm enjoying wandering around the city.

I work a lot in Italy. Mostly in Milan and Rome where the film business is centered. They're beautiful cities. But, to me, the whole country is amazing looking. Everywhere I go, I'm bowled over by what I see. I seem to be the only person alive who thinks Milan is one of the most beautiful places on earth. All the grays, the thousands of versions of that one color, amaze me. The Italians, at least Italian film people, are over it. But even they appreciate Bologna. Bologna has a unique palette. Not as red as Rome, but definitely red. Not sooty like Milan, but old. Not primary like Positano or filthy like Naples. And the city is a maze of covered walkways. Apparently, it was designed this way so that, on rainy days, you could go anywhere in the city without an umbrella. It is drop-dead gorgeous. And, for me, with my hyperactive enthusiasm gland firing constantly, every time I turn a corner, I find another fabulous place to put a camera.

We're scouting with a small crew. I want to do a shot where the woman walks down a narrow street, then, as we follow her, she suddenly enters a big square. Tight to wide. Dark to light. We wander around with the location scout looking for a place to do this.

Late in the afternoon, we find it. The perfect spot. The narrow street doesn't have any modern stores or signage on it, all the buildings are old, and the street ends at the top of three steps that go down into a gorgeous piazza. I stand in various places trying to figure out the best spot for the camera. Once I find it, I start explaining to the production people what we'll need for the shot. Midsentence, I glance down. Just to the side of my left foot are two thin pieces of gray tape that form an "X."

When film crews go scouting, they mark where they want to put the camera with a taped X. This is because the crew people who scout the job may not be the same ones who are there when you shoot. By marking the spot with two pieces of gaffer tape, if new guys show up first to prep the shot, they'll know exactly where the director wants the camera to go.

I am looking at an X that must have been placed there by a prior film crew. Someone else decided that this spot, my spot, was their spot, the perfect spot, for a shot. Someone else has already seen what I am just seeing now. Not only seen it but done a shot from here. I am no longer going to be doing something original. In fact, it seems I'm going to do exactly what someone has already done. Demoralizing.

I've found Xs in remote mountain ranges in Utah, on Madison Square Garden's loading dock, on runways at LAX, and all over the sidewalks of New York City. I've found them on boardwalks in Atlantic City, on the observation deck of the Empire State Building, and next to the S-curve on the Calgary Olympic bobsled track. When I see them, I get angry, then frustrated, and then force us to keep looking for something else.

But, sometimes, I wind up using the damn spot. Because it *is* perfect.

Second Exit.

My career is about to die.

No one looking at it from the outside would agree. Because I'm at a high point in the work arc. I shoot more than a hundred days a year. I finish a Ford commercial in Nova Scotia, get on a plane for Milan, shoot Fiat, fly from Milan to Toronto, shoot for TD Bank, then fly back to New York and shoot my twentieth Advil spot of the year. Advil's in a Tong War with Tylenol. One makes an ad criticizing the other, and the other responds. Nuts. And profitable. My commercials are all over. If I sit down and endure two hours of prime time, I'll see five spots I've directed. Most of them for stuff like Advil or Kellogg's or Crest or a yeast infection cream. I'm in the top ten, probably five, in terms of how much work I'm doing. But the majority of it is not very good. It'll definitely never win awards, never make people laugh, never even register when, if someone asks if they've seen anything I did, and I tell them. I'm doing great, the envy of many. That guy Steve who used to make me so crazy is barely on my radar. I lapped him two years ago. And I'm putting away all the money I'll ever need to take care of my family *when*, as opposed to *if*, the whole thing crashes and burns. Which is the issue.

I am absolutely certain everything is just about to stop. It has to. Because, for all the activity, I'm shooting crap. Now, crap is the lifeblood of commercials. All directors shoot a certain amount of crap. But people are now standing in line to have me do it. Which does weird things for my shaky self-image. I boil it down to this: I do all this bad work because I'm a hack. A getting-rich, slick, and efficient hack. And, pretty soon, everyone's finally going to figure this out. They haven't for twenty-five years, but Judgment Day is coming.

I am adept at doing certain tricks. Like a trained seal with a camera. My best one, how I get the actors to perform, makes any spot I do feel pretty real and unstaged. At least compared to most ads. But most of the ideas I deal with are weak, so, in order to be watchable, they require these tricks, which loops back on itself. My partner calls what I do polishing turds. He says it as a compliment.

He owns the place and has become a close friend of mine. We've even started going on vacation together with our families over the holidays. He and I grab lunch once in a while at Bowery Bar. Sometimes we talk about work. Sometimes we don't. Lately, I'm bringing up my fear that my career's about to plunge into a death spiral.

"We need to do this different."

"Different? What the fuck are you talking about? Everything's perfect. You're doing great."

"I'm shooting shit."

"Who fucking cares? They pay you the same to shoot shit as the good stuff."

This approach is not working. I try a different tact.

"Why don't we slow down a little?"

"I agree. You should spend more than five hours shooting a job. You're too fast. People get pissed."

"I mean maybe we shouldn't jam every job in the world into the schedule?"

"Why the fuck would we do that?"

"Because, if we don't, my career will be over. Soon. No one'll want to shoot with me."

"That's going to happen anyway..."

"Because I'll have shot too much for too many people, right?"

"No. Because you're an asshole."

This is where he's wrong. Not about the asshole part. I'm at the Everest summiting point of my assholery. Somehow most of my clients just find it quirky so I'm still working all the time. But he's wrong about shooting too much. I've built my business on having clients come back. Most directors shoot for a client once, maybe twice. Mine come back over and over and over. I have tons of loyal clients who shoot with me ten or fifteen times. But they'll get sick of me. They have to. So I'm concerned about new work. And I'm sure no one will want to give me any.

I try another angle.

"I believe, if we slow down and make a little less money in the short term, we'll make a lot more in the long run."

"You're crazy."

No, I'm not. I am at a fork in the road that inevitably faces a successful creative person and his business partner. His interests aren't mine. I am the commodity. That he controls access to. I have a lot of value. Now. When that value dries up, which it will, a new commodity will take my place. People get sick of a singer's voice. They stop going to a movie star's films. A comedian's schtick gets old. They don't want to read another mystery about that same old detective. Nothing lasts forever. Certainly nothing on the creative side of the ledger. I have to look after my time in the sun.

"I want to keep directing commercials. And I want to keep doing it with you. But we have to change how we do it."

I'm hoping we can discuss this. But my producer doesn't do discussion well.

"Here's my advice. Just take the money and shut up. Who cares when your fucking career ends? You'll have all the money you'll ever need."

"But maybe I want to keep making it. And directing is the only thing I know how to do. If this ever stops, the only job I'll be qualified for is toll collection. And with EZ Pass out there..."

"So quit. I don't give a fuck."

Amazingly, this is how we discussed the future of a thriving multimillion-dollar business. These are the same negotiating skills we're using in both our crumbling marriages. We're idiots.

We get through the meal, but nothing changes. There are a lot of uncomfortable silences. I start a few sentences then trail off midway. My producer just sits silent, looking past me onto West 4th Street.

I'd rehearsed my lines this morning as I was driving to work, but, when I quit over coffee, it sounds like it came out of nowhere. We walk back to the office, I clear out my desk, and drive home. I'm not exactly sure what I am going to do next. But I am certain that, whatever I do, I'll be able to add a year or two to my career.

Why, I have no idea.

Please Shut Up.

I START A NEW COMPANY. IT TOOK TWO WEEKS. I HAD PUT OUT FEELERS TO key people when I was thinking about this and, lucky for me, they all joined up. I'm smarter this time. Seven years at a big company is a great learning experience. You pick up lots of good things and lots of bad things. But one insight dominates: you will always be the best, and often only, advocate for yourself. You can go all Darwinian and Machiavellian, but it's simple. People look after themselves first. Maybe not Mother Teresa. But definitely commercial directors. The practical effect of this is I try not to listen when people blow smoke up my ass about what they can do for me. I used to fall for it hook, line, and sinker.

Splitting up with my old partner was simple. And bizarre. Simple because I showed up to shoot the three jobs that were booked before I left. Simple because he paid me what he owed me. Bizarre because we went on vacation together with our families five days after I resigned. Ridiculous. But we'd done it for years, the kids were all looking forward to it, the house and plane tickets were paid for, and we figured we could

211

behave like adults. When I add this detail to the story of my quitting, people tell me I should have my head examined.

Our relationship had always been fair. Everyone in my business has terrible business stories. All involve not getting paid. I don't have one story like that. Not one. I've never had anything but a handshake deal with anyone, and I've always been paid what I was owed. I always tried to act accordingly. For the first few months after leaving, when a few of our shared clients tried to get me to shoot for them, I told them I didn't think it was kosher. I took my clients and left my old producer his. Seemed fair.

I put together a small, really capable team of sales and production people. I'm not desperate to find work. It mostly finds me. We do not take every job. We work, but just enough. Lo and behold, I'm getting better, more interesting work and not spewing fire from my mouth all the time. One of the first jobs is that enormous campaign for TD Waterhouse.

This one came about because I'd worked with the creative director when he was running a small agency in Rochester, New York. Twenty years later, he's at a big place in the city. Twenty years ago, Rochester was the kind of place I could get work. Like Cleveland or Pittsburgh or Portland or Milwaukee. The big guys weren't bothering to go prospecting in the smaller markets. But there was plenty of work out there. Banks, hospitals, tourism, television stations. When an agency bid me, I'd get on the phone and usually have better ideas than the local guys they were used to shooting with. I was a problem solver. And I was enthusiastic as all get-out. Anyway, those bank jobs in Rochester paid off. Connecting dots never stops.

○ ○ ○

I'm in a production motor home in the employee parking lot at KTLA. Phil Jackson and Kareem Abdul-Jabbar sit across from me in swiveling captain's chairs upholstered in green velvet. Phil's knees are up around his armpits. He doesn't look comfortable. Phil's six-eight. Kareem Abdul-Jabbar is seven-two and looks even more uncomfortable. His knees are up to at least his ears and his fingers touch the carpet. Because

I can never not talk, I ask how they manage their height out in the real world.

I learn that Buicks are the best cars for giants to rent. For some quirky reason, the driver's seat in a Buick can be pushed back farther than any other car available in rental fleets. And one hotel chain has slightly bigger king-size beds. Other than that, they deal. Because I don't follow basketball, once I've asked the dumb questions about height, I'm out of topics. Doesn't matter. These guys are old pals, so I leave them alone while I go set up the next shot.

This TD Waterhouse job has been going on for four days. We're shooting all over Los Angeles in restaurants, homes, theaters, beaches, the Staples Center, LAX, and office buildings. It's a challenge and it's a blast. One spot is about Phil Jackson moving to LA to coach the Lakers. He's led the Chicago Bulls to five titles, and there's hope he'll revitalize the Lakers. The other is about Geena Davis acting in a period movie drama where one scene requires her to use a bow and arrow. The job has an interesting cast of characters.

The first scene I'm doing today has two morning drive-time disc jockeys riffing about Jackson's arrival in town. I decided to use a real radio studio. We'd never be able to build one that looks as good as the real thing. I also needed a television studio and the interior of a remote broadcasting truck, those big vans covered with satellite dishes that they send to breaking news sites. My genius producer cut a deal with KTLA, a station with television studios, radio studios, and remote trucks on their lot. I have the run of the place for six hours.

TD Waterhouse wants this campaign, their first big foray into American advertising, to look great. I am the lucky recipient of their spending madness. They've given me two commercials. The budget's more than a million dollars. Anything I ask for, I get. Even if I ask for it long after the budget's been approved. We have Jackson. Davis. Jabbar. Every great sitcom character actor in LA is doing a bit part. Kareem is here because, on a whim, the creative director thought it'd be cool to have him deliver a joke at the end of the Phil Jackson spot. Yeah.

That'd be really funny. Fast-forward to this morning. Kareem's out in the motor home with Phil.

Sometimes commercials are a great gig. Big budgets. Good ideas. And the ability to hire great people. You're working, and it doesn't suck.

I leave the trailer and walk across the parking lot to the television broadcast center. To my right, across Sunset and up the hill, is the Hollywood sign. It's falling apart. Has been for years. The broadcast center is a big, windowless cinder block box. A huge poster advertising the team that anchors KTLA's five o'clock news is on the wall. They're expertly blown dry and wear loud ties with knots the size of fists. A few palm trees have been planted along the perimeter of the building. Palm trees in Los Angeles always look like they're dying. A production assistant is at the door with a walkie-talkie. Production assistants out here all are young directors just finishing the final draft of the script they've been working on since dropping out of film school.

"Good morning, sir."

I'm forty-eight years old. Wearing a T-shirt, jeans, and skateboarding sneakers. Hair down to my shoulders. There's no fucking way I look like a "sir." Anyway.

"Morning. Have you seen my producer?"

"He went up ten minutes ago."

His walkie blares. He moves the mic fob close to his mouth.

"Copy that. Director's on his way up."

I head up the back stairs. Worn, scuffed linoleum steps, industrial iron bannister. It smells like cigarettes. I climb up to the third floor. There's another production assistant parked here.

"Good morning."

No "sir" this time. Good.

I point right.

"Down there?"

She nods then mumbles into her walkie. I head down the hallway. Activity. The corridor's jammed with equipment cases, monitors, a dolly, cameras, grip stands, lights, and the sound man's rig. This ton of crap goes wherever a film crew goes. It's like a tool kit that requires seventy people to move it around.

The walls are decorated with posters of the station's radio personalities. Seems like everyone who works at KTLA uses the same blow dryer. I navigate through all the crap and reach the door to the studio we're using. There are fifteen technicians inside this tiny room running electrical cable, positioning lights and grip stands, moving the real studio equipment around to accommodate our invasion. I go over to where the camera's being set up and join my assistant director and the director of photography.

Another benefit of bigger budgets is being able to use star technicians. Super stars. Award-winning costumers, production designers, and, particularly, directors of photography. I say good morning to my AD and then to Vilmos Zsigmond, the cinematographer. Zsigmond has shot more than fifty films, among them *Deliverance, The Deer Hunter, Heaven's Gate,* and *McCabe & Mrs. Miller.* He also won an Academy Award for *Close Encounters of the Third Kind.* I'm mildly confident this job will look fucking excellent.

Vilmos is one of the best in the world, as well as low key and funny. I've been teasing him about his Hungarian accent, asking whether he ever took an English-as-a-second-language class. He has not taken a swing at me and insults me back. The punch lines involve what it feels like to be a talentless hack. I think they're jokes.

When we scouted this location last week, we decided it should look dark. Radio studios usually don't have windows, and we want it to look real. So Vilmos is only using three small lights. The tiny bulbs built into the knobs and dials create a nice glowing ambience and fill everything in. It's beautiful. I go looking for the agency.

The creative director and the producer are having breakfast and reading the papers in video village. I really like this creative director. He went to Jesuit schools, still reads Latin, and has a sick sense of humor. I also like him because he's a writer. I've worked for the producer many times over the years. He's one of those guys who is the first to laugh—bray like a donkey, really—at his own jokes and thinks it's okay to comment on girls' asses when they're standing right next to him. For some reason, for the past four days, he's pretty much left me to my own devices.

The AD brings the actors in and places them at the console. I give them a short list of what I want them to touch on. Phil Jackson's name. Some traffic and weather. Maybe one of those stupid signature phrases DJs use, like nicknames for each other or ridiculously overenunciated adjectives. I walk back and sit behind the camera with the script supervisor. I ask Vilmos to constantly change focus during the take. Keep it messy. Like a bad documentary cameraman would do it. A camera assistant slates the take.

The comedians invent some terrible traffic jam and riff on that. The guy does something stupid with the pronunciation of the word "ridiculous." On the next take, I ask him to do that more. Everything's loose. The crew is smiling. The actors are showing off. One of those mornings you can't believe you're getting paid to do this. Always the thought you have just before a shit tsunami hits you.

As the assistant is about to slate the fourth take, the producer barges in. He gets a few feet inside the door but can't get any farther because of all the equipment. He barks at me.

"I gotta talk to you."

"Let me do one more take."

"No. Now."

I follow him out into the hall. He gets three steps from the door, pivots to me and starts in.

"What the fuck are you doing?"

"What?"

"Why are you rolling?"

"Because I was ready to start shooting."

"It's not lit."

"What're you talking about?"

"It's too fucking dark."

I try to change lanes and run this through the diplomacy chute. This is a very tiny chute for me.

"Well, that's how it should look. The room doesn't have windows. It should be moody and dramatic."

"Moody's fine. But it's pitch-black in there. You can't be getting an image."

"We're definitely getting an image."

"No way. Use more lights."

My interior monologue changes lanes from diplomacy to ad hominem attack on this putz. I excel at them.

"Look. This is how I want the scene to look. It looks great. Also, the guy lighting it has won an Academy Award. Which gives me a certain level of confidence that everything's lit properly. If you don't agree, why don't you go over and share your concerns as well as your technical recommendations with Mr. Zsigmond? I'm sure he'll be very interested in your thoughts."

What am I supposed to say? Really? He doesn't know what he's talking about. If I do what he says and add lights, it'll fuck things up. This is not me being insecure or threatened. This is me doing my job. Which, in this case, means telling this guy to sit down and shut up. Who doesn't love to be told that?

The producer gets red in the face, starts a few sentences, stops all of them, then turns on his Converse high-top clad foot and goes back to his chair in video village. Over his shoulder, he mumbles.

"Just shoot it."

I go back into the radio studio. I don't mention the conversation to Vilmos. I play around a little with the actors to get us back up to speed. We do two more takes, and I'm happy. I go out to video village and ask what they think. The creative director is thrilled. The producer is still red faced and pouting. He reluctantly says we can move on.

As we're moving to the next setup in the television studio two floors down, I do my best to avoid the producer. He's avoiding me too, so it's a symmetrical dance of loathing. Our paths cross an hour later at the craft service table. The craft service person is one of those gratingly happy New Age women with a sing-song voice who's always got some vile infusion she wants to put in your tea or a smelly emollient she wants to rub on some pressure point in your arm. People like this always look to me like they have terminal cancer or a contagious disease, so I never take their advice. The producer loves having women touch him, so he's got her rubbing crap all over his pressure points. Mid ooh and aah, he turns to me.

"Obviously, Vilmos knows what he's doing. Sorry."

In thirty-five years of directing, I have never had an agency person apologize to me. Never. Until today. So I accept in a big, effusive way. He then turns to the craft service woman and comments on her breasts while she's dabbing essence of echinacea on the insides of his wrists. Weirdly, she's flattered.

It all goes into the mental folder I keep labeled "Behavior triggered by embarrassment and self-loathing—self and others." I get self-loathing. But the embarrassment part confuses me. A lot of agency people I deal with seem to be embarrassed by themselves. By how their lives have turned out. They talk about where they went to college thirty years ago or where they got in but didn't go. Or that they once worked at Chiat or Goodby or Weiden or some agency cooler than the one they're in now. They seem to do it so they can imagine themselves higher up in some creative hierarchy than they really are. Agency people often tell me that their next job is with an "A-level director." I know I'm not the top of the heap. But if I told some creative guy that my next job was not a piece of shit like the one I'm doing with him, strictly for money, but an actually good job, I'd be out of business. I realize it probably isn't really said to shit on me. It's more that they need to tell themselves that their entire life isn't the Charmin spots we're shooting and, that once in a while, they get to wear the backwards baseball cap and the Oakleys on a Hollywood set and stand next to that year's star director. Unfortunately, that good feeling they're hoping for rarely happens. Because most A guys will have their AD tell them to get back over to video village while the A guy makes the commercial.

I'm still on a rising career track. I have a lot of experience and, for some weird jumble of reasons, I'm popular. To people I've never worked for, I'm an "A" guy. They defer, give me some freedom, and want to stand next to me in their backwards ball caps. It's nice. I wish could have figured out how to just start as an A guy. Would have made the job much easier. Especially when they start bothering you and you give them short shrift. Since you're an A guy, they don't get bent out of shape. So new clients are great. But I have a lot of old clients. People who kept me busy when I was a "B" or "C" guy. They serve a hugely important purpose. Any time my head gets swelled because I land a great job, the next day, I do another Advil commercial. It reminds me of where I came from and, most important, what I'll always be. A working guy. And I realize that, after thirty-five years, climbing and crawling up slowly, no matter what level you're at, the people who hire you are somehow, some way, gonna be in your face. That's the job. That seems to be why I get paid. But it gets really old.

Forty-Three.

I'M SURROUNDED BY SECRET SERVICE AGENTS, IT'S POURING RAIN, I'M frozen and pretty ill at ease. It's the first Wednesday in November 2001. Seven weeks after the 9/11 attacks. We're waiting to be cleared into President Bush's Crawford, Texas, ranch. Adding to the elevated level of tension is the fact that Vladimir Putin is also here. Security is unbelievable.

After 9/11, every American discovered their own version of patriotism. Me too. I live in New York. My office is on Broadway and 18th Street. I was driving to work on 9/11 and heard Howard Stern talk about what he was seeing on the television. A small plane, he thought. I kept listening as I drove south. Robin interrupted as the second plane hit. Instantly, I made a hard right onto 57th Street and started flying up the West Side Highway. Cop cars behind me, cop cars ahead of me, cop cars screaming downtown. I stopped at my kids' school in the Bronx to get them. The details were fuzzy at that point and the school hadn't been locked down yet, so I snuck them out. When we got home, we watched the buildings collapse. By noon, Air Force fighter planes were patrolling over the city, doing wide arcs over Hastings. I definitely was inclined to think that someone's ass needed to be kicked. And I was happy to help the president give a message to the American people.

A copywriter I know wrote a script about the meaning of Thanksgiving. He thought it would be cool if Bush delivered it. The White House said yes. The spot is a PSA, sponsored by the Ad Council, and it will only run once, on Thanksgiving Day. The American president, the American holiday, the first one after the attacks. Sounded worthwhile.

Four days after hearing about the job, my producer, a camera assistant, a gaffer from New York, ten crew people from Austin, and I are huddled under a tent watching a heavily armed team of security people and their bomb-sniffing dogs examine our stuff. What they're doing gives new meaning to "going through things with a fine-toothed comb."

The ranch is three miles outside the town of Crawford. Not really a town. More an intersection. It has one school that goes kindergarten through twelfth, a gas station, and what Texans call a café, a joint where you can get a sandwich, a Coke, newspapers, coffee, jerky, and beer. The café owner has gotten rich since Bush started using the ranch as the second White House. When we drove by it on our way here this morning, the parking lot was jammed. A ton of people who all looked like they worked for networks or newspapers scattered around the lot yammering on their phones.

Bush's property is a couple hundred acres of undeveloped land. Six months ago, you wouldn't notice it as you drove by. Now you can't miss it. At the head of the driveway, there's a massive security station. Two bomb-hardened booths manned 24/7 by Secret Service and Texas Rangers. A series of electronically operated gates you drive through, then a single lane framed on either side by oversized concrete blocks where the cars are held one at a time and searched. Across the street, there's a small city of mobile homes used by traveling White House personnel. I don't even think about setting foot outside the tent while our stuff's being examined. There are too many guys with machine guns. And some speak Russian. It all works perfectly with the pouring rain.

It takes just under two hours for Secret Service to go through everything. When they're done, our Secret Service contact instructs us to get back in the vans. He climbs in the first van with the producer and me and directs us to the location.

This kind of landscape must resonate emotionally with born-and-bred Texans, but it's boring as shit to me. There are some rolling hills, but the only vegetation is scrub brush and stunted trees. We head down a deeply rutted dirt road that's turned to mud during this morning's rain. A small fleet of SUVs and pickups are in motion around us going who knows where. Up ahead, I see a couple of barns. We pass a white, one-story clapboard house on our left. It's surrounded by a phalanx of black Suburbans. Six guys with submachine guns stand in the rain at the foot of the driveway. Others stand on the porch and still others at various points on the house's perimeter. A lot of these guys have enormous heads and flat faces. They look Russian. They are. Our Secret Service guy says that's where Putin and his wife are staying. It's also where we were supposed to shoot the spot. But the Putins got here first.

We pull up in front of a long, weathered barn. It was red once. On the end where we park, the sliding doors are open. Secret Service guys are visible inside. As I get out of the van, a young guy in a rep tie, white shirt, khakis, and a blue blazer runs over holding his clipboard over his head like it's an umbrella. He's a White House advance person. As soon as we're in the barn, he asks if I can shoot the spot here. He's being polite to ask because he and I both know I don't have a choice. I tell him sure, and he nods and smiles and starts working his Blackberry. I'm walking around looking for a place to set up the shot when he runs back and says there's been a schedule change.

"The president's gonna be ready early. Around eleven. Can you be ready?"

I was supposed to have the Bushes at noon for a total of forty-five minutes. But what am I going to say? I need more time for my art?

"No problem. I'll be ready at eleven."

There was no prep on this job. We didn't scout locations. I didn't see photos of anything on the ranch. All I'd been told on a quick call with the advance people was that we'd work in the backyard of the guesthouse. Which now we can't do because the Putins are there. You roll with stuff like this.

One end of the barn is full of stuff the Bushes have tossed out over the years. Baby furniture. Bed frames. Old lamps. Bookcases. Sports equipment. In the middle of the barn, there's a cluster of hay bales. Maybe this'd be a good place to shoot. A little trite but definitely casual. I ask the advance guy if it's a possibility. He tells me this is where Brokaw did his interview with Bush two weeks ago. Never mind.

At the other end of the barn, another set of sliding doors open out onto a corral. I slide them open further to see what kind of light comes in. It's still raining torrents, but I figure, if we place the Bushes far enough inside and use the open doors to frame them, it'll be pretty. The gaffer says he can light it with two instruments bounced into a show card. It'll take fifteen minutes. I tell the advance guy this is where we'll work. He runs off.

It's a little after 9:00 a.m. The crew starts bringing equipment in. We've brought the absolute bare minimum of stuff. No dolly, just a tripod. No big lights, just small ones we can run off house power. One zoom lens, so I'll never have to change lenses during the shoot. Once the camera is in position, two older ranch hands appear. Real, actual cowboys. Hats, boots, belt buckles, snap shirts, a thousand lines on their faces. They tell me they work at the ranch full time. They're curious about where I'll have Bush stand. I show them, and they start checking out the barn's rafters. Turns out Bush is allergic to bees. Really allergic. The cowboys see two nests and immediately start attacking them with high-powered streams of insecticide. They pretty much drown the bees. Then they knock the nests down with a broomstick and, for good measure, stomp on them. It stops us from working for a few minutes, but I'm okay with that. I don't want to be the guy filming some PSA with Bush when he goes into anaphylactic shock.

The advance guy's back. Agitated.

"Can you be ready at ten forty-five?"

I don't hesitate.

"Sure."

The guy is ecstatic. I'm his best friend.

It's a very simple job. Bush and his wife will stand in one place and read a script from a teleprompter. I'll shoot a wide shot of them doing the script a few times, then a close-up of each of them reading their lines. Because they're not moving around, all the angles will cut. Any editor will be able to put it together in fifteen minutes. I'm only worried about making sure the background is far enough out of focus, so you won't see an ark floating by in the background. That fucking rain is something.

A new advance person appears. A woman, older than the first guy, more harried, very brusque. She doesn't ask, she orders.

"You need to be ready by ten thirty. Putin's leaving, the president needs to meet with him before that, blah blah blah."

Her tone makes it seem like this is a challenge I can't handle. Fuck her.

"I'm good. Whenever he's ready, let's do it."

The advance lady walks away, barking into her phone.

Ten o'clock. We're ready. And waiting. The rain is fucking insane. I'm really concerned the thumping noise it's making on the barn's metal roof is going to ruin the sound takes. But the sound guy says he'll record everything on a boom mike, a very specific form of recording that minimizes extraneous sounds, and we'll be good. He's lying, but it is what it is.

Ten fifteen. Still hanging around. No sign of advance people. But I notice more Secret Service guys and some tough-looking plainclothes characters with machine guns have quietly entered the barn. This is definitely a unique work environment. Two agents come over to me.

"You the director?"

"Yup."

"We need all these people out of the barn. You and the sound guy can stay."

This won't work.

"I need the sound guy, the gaffer, and the assistant cameraman. Have to have them."

The lead agent stares at me and thinks.

"All right, those three and you, but everyone else goes."

My producer leads all the rest of our crew out the back door. I feel terrible because it doesn't look like there's anywhere out of the rain to put them. But the producer, ever resourceful, commandeers a van, so at least they're out of the storm.

Ten thirty. Still hanging around. Me, three crew guys, lots of security, many automatic weapons. The rain is, if anything, worse. I'm fidgety and want to do something.

Ten thirty-five. Fuck. The storm's worse than ever. The rain is we-in-terrupt-this-program torrential. And it's darker than ever. I should relight. The sound guy looks up at the roof, furrowing his brow. He won't make eye contact with me.

Ten forty. Why did I believe these advance people? I would have had plenty of time to move the camera and relight. Goddammit. Never let people who are panicking mess with your plan.

Something happens. The Secret Service guys raise their voices. Three of them, hands inside jackets, move from the middle of the barn down toward the entrance. Others hustle past where I'm standing and take up positions at the opposite end of the barn. There's yelling outside, like we're on the edge of a public disturbance.

"Step away."

"Keep back."

I just stand still, right by the camera. A late-model white Ford-150 drives into the barn. No vehicle in front of it, none behind. It stops twenty feet short of me. The wipers shut off, the driver's door opens, and Bush gets out. No one else in the car with him. He's wearing a sport jacket, a button-down shirt, and jeans. He looks around, sees me, and nods his head.

I guess I should walk over and say hello. Nobody gave me any specific rules of protocol, so I just go for polite.

"Morning, Mr. President. I'm Bruce Van Dusen, the director."

"Morning, Bruce. Crazy weather. Not ideal for filming, is it?"

"We're coping, sir."

I've met and worked with plenty of people who are famous, rich, beautiful, uniquely talented, brilliant, and revered. There's always something memorable about that first moment of contact. Meeting the leader of the free world while standing alone, but for the eight heavily armed Secret Service agents, in a dilapidated barn in Texas seven weeks after 9/11 with Putin fifty yards up the driveway takes the cake. This guy, who's a few years older than me, is relaxed, engaged, and doesn't show that he has what I think at that moment is the worst job in the world. I behave just like I would with anyone else. I give him a little shit.

"Mr. President, word is you're a very punctual guy. The advance people were rushing us like crazy, saying you were going to be here at ten..."

I glance at my watch.

"You're a little tardy, sir."

He smiles. Barely. Thank God.

"Lot going on this morning, Bruce."

I'll bet. I'm nervous, so I keep asking questions.

"How's your visit with Mr. Putin been?"

"Productive."

I tell him I know he needs to get our shoot done quickly.

"That's okay. Couple things came up so I got a little more time."

"Yeah?"

"I asked Putin this morning if he'd change his itinerary. Add a stop on the way home. I want him to go to New York and take a look at what happened. See it with his own eyes. They're delaying his departure for an hour or two, while they see if they can do that."

Good to know.

I explain things. Where he and his wife will stand. That the script's loaded on to the teleprompter. I'll shoot a few takes, and they'll be done. I ask if Mrs. Bush is on her way. Yeah, she's coming in a van.

"I was ready first, so I drove over without her. It's the only place I'm allowed to drive myself."

I hadn't ever thought of that.

"You ever been to this part of Texas before?"

"Yeah. Austin a few times. Waco, twice. I'm a big Texas fan."

"Where else you been?"

"Houston, Dallas, Amarillo, El Paso, Del Rio, Brackettville."

"Brackettville? What were you doing in Brackettville?"

"I shot a job at this place where John Wayne…"

Right then, two vans arrive and pull in behind the president's pickup truck. Security people in one; Mrs. Bush, a makeup lady, and more agents in the other.

The First Lady comes over, and I introduce myself. She is pretty, charming, and relaxed. Because I always assume people in exalted positions prefer being treated like normal folks, I keep chatting.

"You guys have dinner last night with the Putins?"

Mrs. Bush chimes right in.

"We did. A nice barbecue."

"What do you talk about at a dinner like that?"

The president takes this one.

"Teenage daughters. Theirs are about the same age as ours. We agreed they're pretty challenging."

I ask about the stuff in the barn, how long they've had the place, and what they've done to it. They're nice people. I explain to Mrs. Bush how I'm going to shoot the spot and suggest we start.

It takes about fifteen minutes. Bush flubs his lines a couple of times. Mrs. Bush never does. Whenever I speak to him, I call him Mr. President. Once, when I finish saying something like, "Let's try that a little faster, Mr. President," he looks back over his shoulder, then at Mrs. Bush, then at security, then back at me, makes a little light-bulb-going-off-in-his-head facial expression and says, "Oh, right. I'm the president." Even the guys with the machine guns crack a smile.

We finish. Bush is pleasantly surprised it all goes so fast. Mrs. Bush says she's freezing and is heading back to the house. I thank her and say goodbye. I figure the president will go with her.

"You want to take some pictures?"

He says it. Not me.

"Sure. That'd be nice."

"Who's got a camera?"

My producer runs to get his.

"Who're all the people in the van outside?"

"Local crew guys. Security wanted 'em out of here while we worked."

Bush looks toward the sliding doors.

"They wanna be in the picture?"

"Probably."

"Go get 'em."

Ten of us stand in two rows, Bush puts himself in the middle of the back row. We take a few shots. I ask if he'd mind taking a picture with just the four of us who've come down from New York. My gaffer and camera assistant—two wonderful, tough, third-generation Italian union guys—will shit themselves if they get a picture of just them and the president.

"All of you guys live in the city?"

We do a bad unison yes.

"How is it?"

"It's still a little weird, sir. People don't have their footing back yet."

"I can imagine…let's take that picture."

Once we've got the pictures, the crew starts breaking things down. Bush is standing next to me. No advance people around. The Secret Service guys stay at a distance, twenty feet away. I'm nervous. So I keep talking.

"What's Putin like?"

"Nice man. Takes a little while to warm up. Sees some things different than we do. Some things the same."

I ask if he learned anything that really surprised him.

"Yup. Putin wears a cross around his neck. I noticed it after dinner. I pointed to it and asked, 'What's that?' He said it was his grandmother's. She'd been Russian Orthodox. Just before she died, she gave it to him. He never wore it, just kept it in an old jewelry box he left at his dacha outside Moscow. A while back, the dacha burnt to the ground. Literally nothing left but the chimney. Putin went out to see the place. Just a pile of ashes and the chimney. Some old guy who looked after the property was hanging around. He signaled for Putin to follow him. They walked over behind a barn where no one could see them. The guy reached into his pocket, took something out, opened his clenched fist, and revealed the cross. He'd found it inside the ruins of the house. Now Putin wears it. Every day."

You learn all sorts of things if you just keep asking questions.

The president has to go. The advance people are on him. I thank him again for his help, say it was a pleasure meeting him, especially thank him for getting the guys out of the van and into the picture. And I wish him luck in the days ahead.

"You have the hardest damn job in the world."

He smiles.

"I feel honored to have it. Just gonna try my best. Helps that I have an amazing wife and children."

Leaving the ranch is a lot quicker than going in. Security does a cursory check of everything, signs us out, and we start the drive back to Houston. It will be tight, but it looks like we can catch a 4:00 p.m. flight to LaGuardia. In the single instance of annoying insanity on an otherwise remarkable day, the copywriter starts demanding that we stop at McDonald's. I try to talk him out of it but fail. Halfway to the airport, we see one and pull in. I ask him to hurry; we're tight for time. When he hasn't returned after fifteen minutes, I send the producer in to look for him. The fat fuck is sitting at a table, eating a goddam bacon cheese-burger. He says he doesn't like eating in cars.

The president of the United States drives himself. A cross-wearing Russian premier changes his itinerary to fly to New York. A copywriter causes us to miss our flight so he can eat a Quarter Pounder with cheese.

American Airlines Flights #1 and #32.

WE ARE AWARDED A JOB LATE ON A FRIDAY NIGHT. BUT THE CONTRACT won't be formally signed until Monday. This happens. We've worked for the agency a number of times, so we figure the signature is just a formality. This job's schedule is very tight, so I decide to get a jump on things and fly out to Los Angeles first thing Monday morning, so I could start scouting.

American flight #1 lands in Los Angeles just after 11:00 a.m. You get off the plane and have most of the day ahead of you. I take this flight a lot. Easy, often not too crowded, and, because it's early and most passengers sleep, quiet. About two hours into the flight, as I'm over Cincinnati and people are coming into the New York office, I call my producer. In the early aughts, a lot of first-class cabins had these GTE phones in the armrests. You pulled the handset out on a retractable cord, punched in your credit card information, and dialed. It cost a fortune, but it was useful.

"Hey. How you doing?"

"Um, I'm glad you called. Listen. The agency producer called…"

Odd tone of voice from my producer. It isn't that it sounds like someone has died, but something is definitely wrong.

"…we didn't get the job."

"What?"

"Yeah. The client decided he wanted to shoot with the other director."

"I thought the agency was recommending us?"

"The client overruled them."

"Wow."

There's a long pause, which, with the GTE calling rates, costs me almost five bucks. I am sitting in my plush, sheep-skinned, first-class seat, looking like a successful something, feeling like a complete fucking idiot.

"So what do you want to do?"

"Kill them."

"I mean, when do you want to come back?"

I have no reason to be in Los Angeles other than this job. Wasting money on a hotel room seemed like throwing good money after bad. Kind of like the GTE call I'm on.

"When's the next flight back?"

"Today?"

"Yeah."

"Lemme look."

Another pause as he puts me on hold. Another five bucks. I'm hoping the person sitting next to me is asleep and not eavesdropping on my public shaming. But I'm doing my best to keep my tone of voice nonchalant. I don't want my producer to know I am humiliated. You develop rhino-like skin in this business because you lose so many jobs. Losing to good directors is dealable. But you want to fucking kill yourself when the agency hires some knuckle-dragging mouth breather whom they told you they didn't want to work with again.

"There's a twelve fifteen and a two."

"I'll take the two."

I stew, pout, and explore new depths of self-loathing during the last three hours of the flight. Fucking asshole client. Spineless agency people. Making me look like a fool. In reality, it was entirely my fault. I broke a cardinal rule of the business. Never spend money until the contracts have been signed. I deserve what I'm getting.

We land in Los Angeles ten minutes early. I fly out there a lot, so I have a nodding acquaintance with some of the stewardesses who work this flight. As I get off the plane, one gives me a wave as she says goodbye.

"Coming back later in the week?"

"Yeah."

Actually, later today.

I walk up the boarding ramp, into the terminal, and head for the Admirals Club. I figure the least that would go right for me this morning is that they'll check me in there, so I don't have to schlep back to the terminal and do security again. Explaining my situation to the agent gives me yet another opportunity to publicly humiliate myself. I am truly a platinum-level asshole. Perplexed but accommodating, she prints me out a boarding pass for the 2:00 and wishes me safe travels. I grab some free Admirals Club lunch, drink a free Admirals Club beer, then head back to the gate I'd just left.

We're going to board in twenty minutes, so I just stand there. I'm scanning the faces of the other passengers when I see my best friend from Los Angeles sitting two rows ahead of where I'm standing. I go over, say nothing, and sit down next to him. After a beat, he turns to check out who has boorishly violated his personal space.

"What the…"

"You on the two?"

"Yeah. Were you here?"

"Kind of."

I tell him what happened. He thinks it's funny, which helps. We get on the plane and convince some people to move around, so we can sit together. We spend the flight back to New York catching up and having a nice lunch. It makes a uniquely degrading day seem like it has happened for a reason. One which I'll never figure out.

The car service drops me at the house in Hastings around midnight. When I go down to breakfast the next morning, the kids don't react to the fact that I'm there. Apparently, it doesn't seem odd that Dad went to California the morning before and is now back to put them on the bus the next morning. It's a good window into the magical way that kids experience the world. And a sidebar comment on how they've grown to accept how random my appearances and disappearances are.

Years later, during a dinner with my kids, I mention this story and how we'd all gone to some event later that night. My son gave me the stink eye and told me my recollection was bogus.

"You weren't there."

"I was."

"No, you weren't."

Then added for good measure,

"You were never there."

○　○　○

And, at that point, he was my biggest fan. It was a pretty clear marker that what I was doing, the weird ride I was on, was taking a toll. And that I was doing a much worse job of managing everything than I thought. My kids, my wife, what I understood to be my happy family, were all pretty fed up with what my dumb job entailed. Quite a bit more fed up than I imagined, as would become clear in three months.

I've Been Meaning to Tell You...

THE PHOTOS THE LOCATION SCOUT IS SHOWING ME ARE USELESS. I'M convinced he does everything wrong intentionally, so we have to hire him again to fix what he fucked up.

I'm in the conference room. From my seat at the south end of the big table, I can see all the way up Fifth Avenue, the top of the Empire State Building poking up fifteen blocks north. You only notice it the first few times you're in there.

The scout sits on one side of the conference table. He's in his forties, unshaven, wireless framed glasses, Pendleton shirt, Timberlands, lots of bracelets for causes and diseases, and a habit of never making eye contact, even when he's facing you. Also, he smiles at inappropriate times. There must be some diagnosis for this in the *DSM*. Like low IQ simpleton. The phone intercom buzzes. The receptionist says it's Neal.

Neal is my lawyer. My wife's and my lawyer. I've rarely had reason to use him. The biggest project I ever gave him was drafting the documents that make sure I die fast. I am terrified of winding up in a hospital like a rutabaga with its pants on, unable to speak but technically alive because of machines. Maybe he's calling about that. I walk over to the window and pick up the phone. Ten in the morning. Tons of traffic barreling down Fifth Avenue.

"Hey. How you doing?"

"I'm okay."

"What's up?"

"I'm just calling to say I'm sorry. We heard the news last night."

"What news is that?"

"About the divorce."

"What divorce?"

"Don't be funny."

"I'm not. Who's getting divorced?"

"Blanche was over last night picking up one of her sculptures. She told us."

"She told you we were getting divorced? She hasn't said a thing to me."

"You guys seemed so happy."

"I thought we still are."

I get off the phone and replay the conversation in my head. When I turn around, I realize the scout has overheard my end of things. And, of course, now he's making eye contact with me. Of fucking course.

"Gimme a minute, okay?"

I gesture for him to leave. He looks confused. Actually, he always looks confused.

He shuffles out. I close the door to the conference room. I pick up my cell and dial. After three rings, Blanche picks up. I can tell by the background whoosh that she's in the car.

"Hey."

"Hey."

Sounds neutral. Granted, "hey" is only one word. But it *did* sound neutral.

"I just talked to Neal."

Silence.

"Are we getting divorced?"

More silence.

"You there?"

Now a pause. Pauses sound different than silence.

"We'll talk about it later."

"Okay. But, just out of curiosity, is that what you told him?"

"I'm not going to go into it now."

"I mean, it'd be good for me to know if that's what we're going to be talking about."

"We'll talk about it when you get home."

She hangs up.

I walk back to the production manager's cubicle. The location scout is there. Five people now know I'm getting divorced. Blanche. Neal. His wife. Me. And this scout. And the scout and I found out at the same time. Last. I'm trying to remember what shitty band had a hit with lyrics about being the last to know.

I spend fifteen minutes telling the scout what I want him to do differently. Then I go back into the conference room and get on a call about a Midol job I shoot next. The agency team is all women. They think it's funny they're explaining period cramps to a guy. I try to focus on the call but can't. I choose to focus instead on the production estimate inside the job folder. It tells me how much money I'll make on this job. My focus returns.

My business partner sits across from me while I do this call. He is a ruggedly handsome, kind of dim, and incredibly effective salesperson. He's wearing an untucked Hawaiian shirt with a pair of Ray-Bans balanced on the top of his head. He reads the *New York Post* while I do the call. It takes him the entire twenty minutes I spend on the phone to get through Page Six and Cindy Adams. When the call ends, he tosses the paper across the table and points to a picture of some girl.

"I fucked her."

"Great."

"Seriously."

"I believe you."

He gives me a face-spanning, Tribeca realtor kind of smile.

"Remember, we're meeting up with Rich at five thirty."

"Can't do it. Sorry. Something came up at home."

"Hold on. This guy runs two big pieces of business. You'll be done by seven."

"Can't do it. Seriously cannot."

This new partner is not my friend. He's just a partner. I learned from my last business arrangement it works better this way. I'm on the verge of giving him a bit more detail about what exactly I have to deal with at home, then decide not to. Instead, I decide to just go.

My drive to Hastings is up the west side of Manhattan. I go past the redeveloped piers in Chelsea. Then the helicopter landing areas, tennis courts, basketball courts, and bike paths. Larry Flynt's Armenian-oligarch-inspired strip club slides by on the right. I'm always curious where the handicapped entrance is to that building. Then the traffic lights end, and I'm on the highway. It's mid-November. Leaves are almost all gone. It's bleak and beautiful.

I pull up in front of the house. It's a little after 4:00. The kids aren't home from school yet. I go in the back door, into the kitchen. The dog is really happy to see me. One day, someone besides me will walk her. I hear Blanche on the phone upstairs. Her voice is running quick. When she laughs, it's loud and sort of hysterical. I go up; she sees me and keeps talking. There's a window seat up there that looks out over the Hudson. I plunk down and wait. She doesn't seem interested in getting off the phone. Eventually, her conversation ends.

"You want to tell me what's going on?"

"You know."

"I don't think I do."

"Yeah, you do."

"We're getting divorced?"

A nod.

"Why did you think it was okay to tell someone that before you told me?"

"It just happened."

"Jesus Christ."

She turns to leave the room.

"You don't want to talk about this?"

She pauses. Silent.

There's a quick drum roll of feet as the kids climb up the front porch steps. The door bangs open, slams shut. No one's shouting gleefully that they're home. They dump their backpacks in the hallway and go into the kitchen, looking for television and food.

"We'll talk about this later."

Blanche heads down the back stairs to the kitchen.

I think about trying the "just give me one more year and it'll all be fine" monologue. But I don't. She doesn't seem inclined to give me any more time.

I try to start a conversation once the kids are in bed. I try the next morning. I try the next evening. I try the following morning before I leave for location. I try two days later before I leave for California. I try on the phone from California. By the time I get back a week later, it is clear I am going to lose something enormous.

Get Help.

I'M SEEING A THERAPIST TWICE A WEEK. SHE'S MY THIRD. THE FIRST GUY would show up late for our 8:00 a.m. appointments. It gave me a complex. The second one called me after two visits to tell me she couldn't see me anymore because one of her other patients had feelings for me. That gave me a different kind of complex. It's all worked out for the best. This third one is giving me some much-needed help.

Out in the real world, where there are no cameras, crews, or craft service tables, directors often struggle. As a general rule, we are not good at maintaining healthy personal relationships. Much of that has to do with not remembering that the back and forth in the real world is managed way differently than the back and forth on a set. Healthy relationships need give and take. You need to listen as well as talk. You just have to. One side doesn't get to give all the orders. Directors forget this. Especially when they get home. They know what needs to be done and how to do it and that it needs to be done immediately. Your wife and children often don't agree. Weird.

My life, at this moment, is a grab bag of unsettling, crazy-making experiences. My wife said our marriage was over, but I didn't believe her. I'd just left the big company in the midst of huge success to open a little company with a new partner. Business is going great: we're busy and working on better stuff. But my new partner checked into the hospital with some kind of crippling anxiety disorder after we'd shot two jobs. I'm mumbling to myself a lot about how people are just not fucking reliable. My sure things are all in question. My bets on stability are looking shaky. I am alternately confused, bombastic, or terrified a shit tsunami is about to destroy whatever I have left in one wet fell and final swoop. I am also starting to think I'm losing my mind and that my job might have something to do with that.

I explain to the therapist what directing entails.

"That sounds pretty fun."

"Yeah. It is, except I think it also has some bad side effects."

"Like?"

The example I give her involves immovable objects.

"I spend all day looking through a camera. If I see something I don't like, I ask people to move it. It might be a chair. Or a vase. Maybe a person. I might even ask them to move a wall. And they do. They move it right then, right there."

"That sounds efficient. And satisfying."

"Yeah. But I think I'm also behaving that way when I get home."

You can get away with behavior like this on a set. You can't get away with it in the real world. One person doesn't make all the decisions. Things don't always go your way. People don't always do what you tell them to. Walls don't move on their own. Directors don't get this memo. I didn't.

When things went kerflooey, I had coffee with my script supervisor. With two failed marriages behind her, I was sure she'd relate to my situation.

"Divorce fucking sucks."

I was full of original insights like that during this period.

"Yup."

Why I expected empathy and a pat on the back from this woman, I have no idea.

"She says I'm impossible to be around."

"She's right."

"Okay. Maybe in my personal life. But at work…"

"There too. The crew is kind of getting to hate you."

"Hate me? I thought they love me?"

"They love you because they get paid for ten hours and only work five. But they think you can be a real asshole."

"Jesus. Do you think that?"

"I think you're an asshole, but I like you in spite of that."

"Good to know you're in my corner. It's been this way for a while? Or is it just recently? With the divorce?"

"Years. Bruce. You've gotten to be a fucking crazy asshole."

"How come I keep working?"

"Very good question. Probably because you're so good at it."

I'd arrived at a schizo nadir. The moment when everything had simultaneously worked out perfectly and gone totally to shit.

Pimps and Gimps.

I'D SAID A MILLION TIMES I'D NEVER MAKE A MOVIE AGAIN AFTER *COLD Feet*. I put my head down hard and focused all my energy on making commercials. I thought I was better at them. Turns out I was a lot better.

The disruption caused by the divorce is making me content with just having plenty of work, quality be damned. And, because I'm getting the shit beat out of me by the whole divorce process, my tendency to be an asshole is quieting down a little. One thing I realize after thirty years of blowing my stack is that it's fucking exhausting. It's a lot easier to ask nicely but snarkily for what you want instead of starting the request with a list of everything that's bothering you that week and how the person you're talking to fits into all of it. Crews are starting to comment on the fact that I've changed. Secretly, I think they miss me as a prick.

Anyway, newly divorced, living in Chinatown, walking around in a distracted fog half the time, painfully separated from my kids, and feeling open to anything, I suddenly say yes to directing a movie called *Back-seat*. A young actor I'd cast in a spot had given me a script he'd written and asked if I'd be interested in doing it. Saying yes meant nothing. No money'd been raised. No cast was in place. I thought I was really just offering him encouragement. There'd been meetings every few months for two years, but nothing was coming together. I never thought about it. Until one day, the guy called me to say it was funded. All of a sudden, I'm making another movie. My life was sufficiently disrupted that I was actually up for this. I went to the office and told my producer I was going to take a few weeks off to make a movie. I thought he'd go ballistic. Instead, he was thrilled and had me move the production of the film into the office, so he could be part of it.

Backseat's about two knuckleheads who go on a road trip from New York to Montreal and their half-baked plan to have dinner with Donald Sutherland once they get there. The twist is that Sutherland skips dinner that night, so they can't crash his meal and meet him. But the plot point means they can constantly talk about Donald Sutherland, even though he'll never appear in the movie. During the drive, shit happens. One gets dumped by his girlfriend. The other gets them involved in a drug deal. There are encounters with oddballs. The girlfriend who walked away returns, pregnant. A number of scenes in the script take place in a shitty motel on the outskirts of Albany. The location scout found us an incredibly shitty motel in Yonkers. That's where we are on our first day of filming.

This is a tiny movie. A giant departure in scale from what I've been doing for the last thirty years. Instead of semis full of lighting, grip, and camera equipment and motor homes jammed with crew people like a commercial would have, this show has everything loaded into two Econoline vans. Instead of a production motor home, the crew works out of a station wagon or on a card table set up in a parking lot. The actors change in bathrooms. Everyone's nonunion. They don't know much, but they're enthusiastic as shit. I've chosen to celebrate by starting to smoke again.

That may be because I'm also a little nervous about what I've gotten myself into. I am a good problem solver. I can roll with almost anything. I know that a day on a set is going to be unpredictable. But the inexperience of the crew is shaking me. I ask for something simple, a light to be gelled, a prop to be moved, and no one knows whose job it is, and it takes forever. I did a nonunion job ten years ago in a small town in Texas. Standing in a parking lot at dawn with twenty crew members, I introduce myself. Then I ask who're the gaffers. Ten guys look at each other, then eight raise their hands. I only booked two. I ask about grips. Same thing. This is like that. The young ones are excited to learn. The old ones have nothing to teach them because they're no good at their jobs. So I'm smoking again.

I've set the camera up on a walkway connecting the ground floor rooms. I'm going to shoot the two main actors doing a walk and talk as they head to the room they've rented. As I sit down next to the camera, I look to my left and see a woman who appears to be in her late sixties peeking out through a big plate glass window. She has bandages all over her face. The bandages are not particularly clean. She's got the room's curtains pulled aside just enough to reveal her mummied puss. She doesn't move. She doesn't blink. She just stares. At me. Exceptionally creepy. But this is day one, shot one. I am not going to get flustered one hour into the job. I light a Marlboro instead.

We shoot the scene. The bandaged face never leaves the window. I take a sidelong glance at her every once in a while. Just weird. When we finish, we move to another camera position. Eventually she retracts her head, like a turtle just back from the ER, and the drapes close. We do two more scenes in the motel's lobby then break for lunch.

Somehow, even though this project has no money, the line producer has hired a great caterer to feed us. We are about to dig in to our first lunch. Numerous healthy salads, chicken marsala, a swordfish kebob, and amazing desserts cover the craft service table. I'm sitting with the two lead actors and the line producer. The sun is shining. The temperature is perfect. Four hours into the first day, three good scenes and we're already ahead of schedule. All is right with the world.

The sound of shattering glass interrupts whatever boring story I'm telling. Not the tinkle of a little window pane. It's the sound of a big, heavy, very thick slab of plate glass exploding as it hits cement. At least, I think that's what I hear because the blood-curdling screams of a woman are dominating everything. My first thought is that mummy woman tried to commit suicide by jumping out her window. But her room was on the ground floor. And the sounds are coming from above us, on the balcony.

One of the actors, gallant and possibly stupid, immediately begins running toward the sounds of glass and screaming. A few of the other males, crew and cast, follow, moving more tentatively in that direction. Maybe they just want to be able to say afterwards they also tried to save the woman. I stay seated. It strikes me that a good number of people staying at the motel are probably armed.

I see a very overweight African American woman standing by the railing on the second floor. She's the one who's screaming. There's blood on her hands and arms. She is not entirely dressed. She's gesticulating wildly, pointing back into the room, saying something about someone going out the back. The brave, possibly stupid, and perhaps about-to-be-murdered actor has run up to the second floor, gets next to her and, judging by his body language, looks to be thinking about going into the room she's vacated. I yell at the top of my lungs.

"Rob, *stop* where you are. *Now*. Do *not* go in there."

Fortunately, he listens.

Everyone's running around helter-skelter. It's just chaos. Suddenly, two cop cars speed in. Clearly, this motel has seen trouble before. Maybe on a daily basis. The black woman yells down to the cops that her "muthafuckin' client" has jumped out the back window. What caused the front one to shatter is not clear. One cop, gun drawn, goes up the stairs, the other, gun also drawn, goes around the back of the motel. The cops' walkie-talkies crackle.

A few of us walk tentatively across the parking lot to take a look at what's happening behind the motel. As we turn the corner, we see the cop standing over a middle-aged black guy dressed in a dirty T-shirt, jeans, and unlaced Air Jordans. He's sitting on the ground, back up against the motel wall, moaning and crying. Something's wrong with his feet. Very wrong.

That's because he jumped out the second-floor bathroom window, apparently after a dispute about his "fare," dropped twenty feet to the pavement and landed badly. So badly he broke both ankles. Now the cops need an ambulance. And now it's a crime scene, so the motel parking lot, which is where I'm supposed to do the next setup, is filling up with more cop cars and a couple of ambulances. This is not going to work for the shot.

My AD gives up without trying.

"We're not going to get this."

Oh, ye of little faith. I see a cop who, judging by how calmly he's barking orders into the shoulder mic on his walkie, looks to be in charge. I go over and introduce myself. He's quite interested that we're making a film. Especially that we're making one at this shithole where he comes on a daily basis to arrest hookers and crack addicts. I tell him that's why we love it. Texture. I then explain my dilemma. All the police cars, ambulances, and trucks are jamming up one side of the parking lot, and, for the next shot, I need to look in exactly that direction because of continuity. I've always found that cops love film argot. And, once I mention continuity and coverage, the cop starts nodding, like he understands everything. Then he tells the other cops and EMTs to move their vehicles out of the way. They do as they're told. I would take this guy with me anywhere.

The crew and cast rapidly lose interest in the crime scene. We're shooting fifteen minutes later. As I'm moving the camera to another setup, I see the African American working girl over by the craft service table. She's having coffee with the makeup woman, who's admiring her tri-colored nail polish with sparkles. And the mummy's window curtain is pulled back a few inches on the right side. Who wouldn't love this life?

More *Backseat.*

WE'RE IN THE FINAL WEEK OF SHOOTING, SO WE'RE WORKING A NIGHT schedule. We have three scenes scheduled. One in a restaurant. One on the sidewalk. One on the hood of a car overlooking a river. We're using SoHo as a stand-in for Montreal.

The first location is six blocks from my apartment in Chinatown, so I'm walking to work. When I turn right off Grand onto West Broadway, the AD spots me and hustles over.

"We have a little problem."

Pretty much every day on this movie starts like this. Today's first issue is the restaurant location. Initially, the owner said it's fine for us to shoot there while he's open. That meant we could start earlier. Now we can't get in until after he's closed, sometime after 11:00 p.m. That's not good because the guys are supposed to walk into a jammed restaurant expecting to see Donald Sutherland. In our low-budget-means-everything-for-free method, we were planning to have actual customers provide that rocking, overflow ambience. If we wait until the place closes, it'll be empty and, ergo, no sight gag.

I wander up West Broadway, trying to figure out how to solve this and why the fuck I've started smoking again after a twenty-year hiatus. I focus on the upside. I haven't been driven to drink.

I can only come up with one option: make the empty restaurant the gag. It's supposed to be the hippest place in town. Why would it be empty? A surprise visit from health inspectors? Signs of vermin in the kitchen? This might work.

I find the actor/writer/co-producer. I throw out my idea. Maybe. He starts working on some new dialogue. On to the next problem.

I was going to shoot day for night in the restaurant. By the time I was done in there, it'd be dark outside, and we could do real night exteriors. But now we can't shoot in the restaurant, so that means trying to do the day for night trick on the street. At six at night. In June. No fucking way. It's broad daylight out here.

I find the DP. As I'm trying to sell him on this plan, I realize I'm being stupid. Who cares if it looks like the guys pulled into town at dusk? No one. The audience will forget everything once the action moves into the restaurant. The DP agrees. We'll shoot it as is. On to the next problem.

The original schedule has us doing these two scenes in Soho then making a company move up to the Cloisters for the final setup. The view from the Cloisters at night looks like a view from a particular hilltop in Montreal. With all these schedule changes, we'll now be driving to the tip of northern Manhattan in rush-hour traffic, doing the scene, then driving all the way back down to SoHo for the restaurant interior. Poor time management.

I realize there are plenty of streets ten blocks south of us in Tribeca we could use. They'll be empty in an hour. The view's different, but who cares? Instead of a river and a hill, we'll see all the new office buildings across the Hudson in Jersey City. If I use a long lens, those buildings will get all sparkly and pretty and it'll look just like downtown Montreal in the distance. Everyone buys it. We just have to find a street and permit it.

Next problem. It's after 6:00, so the NYC film permit office is closed. I tell the producer he has to solve this. This guy is the cheapest fuck I've ever met. On more than one occasion during this movie, when I was getting bad vibes from the owner of a location we were shooting in, I'd turn to him and say, "Just give him a little more money."

And he'd reply, "I haven't given him any money yet, and I don't intend to start now. Just keep shooting."

He thinks we'll be cool.

"Go find a street you like, and we'll shoot there. If the cops show up, I'll just tell them the permit didn't come through the fax machine yet."

I have grown pretty comfortable with this style of working. It is nuts but liberating.

The location scout and I walk over to the area just south of the entrance to the Holland Tunnel. Plenty of wide, nondescript streets. I can put the car in the middle of any of them. If I look toward New Jersey, it's all high rises. If I do a reverse, it's older, red brick apartment buildings. I turn to the scout.

"It's a fucking perfect match for Montreal."

I say this having been to Montreal once when I was nine years old.

We go back to SoHo. I shoot the scene of the guys driving up to the restaurant. It's a tiny bit darker, so some of the interior lights in the stores and restaurants have come on. It looks like dusk. When we're done, we move to Tribeca.

We try to stay invisible. We're working out of a small van with just the essential equipment. We wait until it's dark enough to shoot then roll the car into the middle of the street. The lights and camera get set quickly. With no dolly or tripod to worry about, we're ready to shoot in fifteen minutes. The sun goes down completely. The actors climb on the hood. I sit down on a curb with the camera on my shoulder and we begin shooting.

Two hours later, we're back in Soho. I sit on the steps next to Cipriani with the actors as they run some new lines about the health inspection. We get inside the restaurant a little early, but the place is empty so the new lines work. We're done by 11:30 p.m.

Every piece of our original plan had gone to shit by the time I got to work six hours ago. We fixed the restaurant problem with a little rewriting. I realized the day for night thing didn't matter. And, in order to save two hours of driving, I'd switched us to a location downtown. The new location worked even better than the Cloisters would have.

We dealt. We had to. At certain points in the prior six hours, I'd gotten pissed at the low-budget way of doing things. Why the fuck can't we just spend a few bucks to do this right? But that isn't the MO on this job. And I had to adapt my MO to fit it.

I walk home, east on Grand Street, smoking a cigarette. I swear I'm going to quit as soon as I'm done with this movie. SoHo is deserted. Beautiful. A little Epcot-y with the cobblestones and fire escapes but beautiful. The elevator in my building opens directly into my apartment. I get out and find my middle kid in the living room watching television. She asks how everything went. I say fine. She asks me if I want to go up to the roof with her and smoke a cigarette. I tell her I'm trying to quit.

War Zone.

MARTIN SHORT IS STANDING IN FRONT OF ME WEARING HALF A FAT SUIT. A fat suit is a wardrobe contraption that looks like a baseball catcher's protective vest made out of five enormous down pillows. The front piece, the one that creates the huge belly, is two pillows hung from around his neck. The wardrobe lady is adjusting the rear pillows that balloon his butt out into two huge half-spheres. The makeup people have glued various rubber molds onto his face that give him jowls, bloated cheeks, and something they're trying to make look like a goiter. Short's telling a story about summers he spent as a kid on some lake in northern Ontario. He's doing different relatives' voices. He's funny. But the costumes are taking so long to get right, it's making me crazy.

We've been shooting a TD Waterhouse spot for the past three days. We have two days to go. Short is playing five characters in a boy band, as well as their manager. Through the magic of CGI, when you see the finished spot, there'll be five of him in most of the shots, interacting with each other, singing, dancing, mugging as he/they perform an NSYNC-ish song. Filming this kind of spot is grindingly dull. It's a slow, repetitive process that's totally unlike the way I normally work. Here's how a day goes: We do a series of setups with Marty dressed as one of the characters then stop for three hours while he gets completely re-created as a new one. Then we do all the setups again. Each character is a complex, time-consuming undertaking of makeup and clothing. There are facial prostheses, fake teeth, wigs, fat suits, beards, mustaches, colored contact lenses, and glasses. The upside is that Marty is very funny and keeps us entertained.

I'm having some personnel issues. One, my DP has a drinking problem. Clinically speaking, his drinking problem has returned. I wasn't working with him during the first episode. But I'm working with him now, during the encore. The last two mornings when I've gotten to set, I've found him curled up on the floor, wrapped in a sound blanket, sound asleep behind the set. I don't feel the job is in any jeopardy because the people around him, his camera assistant and gaffers, are used to dealing with it. In a dysfunctional piece of hierarchy-driven diplomacy, because of the DP's stature, we just pretend we don't see him lying there.

The second personnel issue is a bigger problem. The creative director hates me. Didn't want me to shoot the job. Got stuck with me because his boss demanded he hire me. Now, his boss made that demand for a reason. I'd done the introductory campaign for this client last year, and it made the agency famous. One year later, this guy's been hired, and he wants to put his stamp on things. This happens. When the new campaign is approved, he shuts me out of everything but one spot. And, just so I can be constantly reminded that I was not his choice, he behaves like a confrontational asshole every moment of every day. It doesn't bring out the best in me.

What I *do* have going for me is the guy's behaving like such a dick everyone hates him. Even his own people. I'm used to having people hate me during a job, but I always keep a few key folks in my corner. The creative director's got no one. On this job, my ace in the hole is Martin Short. We get along fine. That counts for a lot.

I met Short years ago, when I made a film for *Saturday Night Live*. The premise was everyone knows how the Olympic torch gets to the games, but no one knows how it gets back to Athens. The film's a series of gags about people who have nothing to do with sports getting stuck with the torch. A housewife pulling it out of a mailbox, a wino using it to light a cigarette, an arm holding it out a Greyhound bus's rear window. Martin played the first torch returner, a guy struggling to get across the West Side Highway holding the flame aloft. The cars don't slow down, forget about stopping.

I thought it'd be funny if we did a take where Martin actually steps out into the highway. Dumb. My suggestion resulted in a narrowly averted five-car pileup, a driver calling the cops to report a lunatic holding a torch in the breakdown lane of the West Side Highway, cops rushing to the scene, me explaining the *Saturday Night Live* thing, and Martin and James Belushi bailing me out by giving the cops autographs. As I said, dumb. But we have history.

Martin is ready. Finally. I walk over to where the camera's set up on the floor. It has to be placed in the exact same spot for each of the different character's setups, so the computer can merge the different takes together afterwards. Various grip stands and a levee's worth of sand bags have the thing locked into position. Even a small earthquake won't budge it. The DP, glazed and inhaling black coffee, sits by the camera. He seems better. Meaning he's upright.

I walk over to my chair by the monitor. I've pretty much stopped checking in with the agency because the creative guy is always trying to make a scene about something. Better to just ignore him. The AD yells for quiet. Suddenly, the creative director is standing next to me.

"C'mere."

He leads me over behind the set walls. We stand in a narrow space cluttered with scenery jacks, electrical cable, grip stands, and apple boxes. Without any preamble he's in my face.

"Listen to me, you fuck. This is my job. Not yours. I'm in charge. And you better start treating me that way. 'Cause, if you don't, I'll shut this whole shit show down. I don't fucking care."

I stay quiet. He continues.

"I never wanted you shooting this job. Never. But you are. And you better do what I tell you to."

I stay quiet a little longer. Some other venom spews out. There are jabbing fingers and some flying flecks of spittle. This guy is a freak. My turn.

"I'm sorry you see things this way. I think the job is going fine. Everyone seems pretty happy. Your client. Your producer. Martin. And Steve."

Steve's his boss.

"How the fuck does Steve know what's happening here?!?"

"I spoke to him last night."

"You called him?"

"He called me."

"He called you?"

"Yeah. And I told him things are going very smoothly."

This triggers more finger pointing and spittle flying when, because it's gotten really loud, the agency producer comes around the corner, looking to see what's happening. Just as he appears, the creative director finishes up.

"You are a piece of shit."

The producer looks back and forth between us, trying to figure out what's going on.

"What's the problem here?"

The creative guy points at me.

"Him."

"What're you talking about?"

"This is a fucking disaster."

The producer looks at me, squints, then directs his attention back at the creative guy.

"What? I think everything's going really well."

The creative guy stands there fuming and framing his next attack. I jump in.

"This is a complicated job, everyone's under a lot of pressure. It's hard. I think we should get back to shooting."

Which we do. No makeup sex. The good news is the guy stays completely away from me for the next two days. When we wrap, he simply disappears. At least he owed Martin Short a thanks.

A week later, I'm in an editing room. I've just looked at a horrible cut of the spot. Instead of letting me put one together, the creative guy's gone to the editor two days early and started cutting himself. And created a total botch. Maybe intentionally, so I'll look incompetent. The only option is to start over, from scratch. But the creative guy has staked his claim.

"This is my edit. I don't need you here."

Territory successfully marked and urinated on. I leave the edit suite. This is going nowhere good.

A month later, I'm location scouting in Toronto. As I finish lunch in a downstairs bistro on York Street, my producer calls from New York to tell me Martin Short called and left a number. It's a Toronto number. I call, Marty picks up, we figure out he's staying two blocks from where I'm sitting. Then, diplomatically, cautiously, he asks whether I've seen the spot.

"Yes. It sucks, right?"

"Yeah. It's not…"

I try to explain how this happened.

"They finished it without me. I was not allowed in the room. They didn't include any of the gags. And, worst of all, they didn't do the effects work, so, instead of seeing five of you dancing around, there's just one of you, looking lost."

"It looks soooo cheesy. How the hell does that happen?"

I gave him a thumbnail of how my business works. How directors are hired guns. How sometimes people actually try to undermine a director, and the job, in order to protect their place in the world. How clients sometimes see half-finished work and think it's great as is. How a lot of these factors had come together in a perfect storm on our job.

I had covered my ass, though. I'm not a total idiot. After I'd been tossed out of the editing room, I had a duplicate set of the dailies secretly made and cut a version of my own. It wasn't finished, but it was a better representation of what I intended. I told Martin I'd send him a copy. Four days later, while I'm in a nightclub filming a woman blinding her date with her toothpaste-enhanced smile, Marty called. He was confused.

"How's it possible they wouldn't want to use this? It has everything. All the idiot characters. Dancing. Me as a screaming thirteen-year-old girl. It's hilarious. Why isn't this the version on the air?"

It's complicated. Most of what you see on television or in a movie theater is often not the best version of the ad, the show, or the film. It is a version that, because too many people have thrown in their two cents, is a muddle and therefore not as interesting or funny or dramatic as it could be. Which is amazing. Because the whole point of the ad or the show or the movie is to hold people's attention. This is why they rarely do.

How to Be an Asshole.

WHEN I STARTED, I WAS REALLY DUMB. I FOCUSED ON IMPRESSING THE wrong people. Because I figured everyone on a set thought I didn't know what I was doing, I would suck up to the crews. This was rational. I needed these experienced technicians to do what I told them, so I tried to curry favor with them. My favorite method was to complain loudly about how inept the agency was. Sometimes within the agency's hearing. The crew guys found this endearing. Hilarious. The behavior of a real up-and-comer. Someone with talent and confidence. Oh. And someone who was loudly and obnoxiously biting the hand that was feeding him. The fucking crews didn't care if I committed career suicide. And it never occurred to me that, because I was paying them, maybe, probably, definitely, that was why they were laughing.

This was bad for business. So I started to rein it in. I'd still lose my temper or give some agency person I particularly disliked a cold shoulder. But, whenever an agency asked me to shoot something a different way, I no longer said:

"Fine. We'll shoot it your way. Then we'll shoot it the right way."

Lethal. To my continued career.

Anyway, I started getting tactical. I was an asshole from time to time, but I did it to save my ass instead of commit suicide.

If a commercial sucks, the director fucked it up. If it comes out great, it's mostly the agency's doing. You might get a little credit. But not much. Which is amazing, considering how rarely the final product resembles the storyboard you bid on eight weeks before. And really amazing how all those changes, which you'd fought tooth and nail to make, are now everybody else's ideas.

It's part of the scam that successful commercial directors have to pull off. You create this illusion that there's a lot of collaboration going on. There's not. Not if you're doing the job of the director properly. Done right, you have to be something of a tyrant. Something of a general. Something of a narcissistic egomaniac. Something of a fucking asshole.

The best reason to stick your neck in the noose and be a dick is when you're shooting something that can be great and the agency doesn't realize it. Remarkably, agencies often don't see the potential in what they hatched. I never worked in an agency, so I have no idea how they create and judge stuff, but I've seen so much shitty work I have to assume there must be a big career upside in creating crap. But, as a director, if you consistently deliver crap, not only is there no upside, you're out of business.

I shot a campaign for NY Telephone. One of the commercials had the potential to be amazing. Three brothers on a three-way call but only two know they're on. As the oldest bitches about the youngest, who he doesn't know is listening, all hell breaks loose. A great, emotional screaming match. It was a good idea, but no one in the agency actually realized it. I cast a trio of Italian-American guys. The agency fought me about "ethnic" casting. I did some odd things with camera angles, so the viewers were confused at first about who the third guy was. It also confused the agency. I had to get in a fight with the client to explain that we didn't need to spend five seconds of screen time watching one of the characters dial a ten-digit number because viewers understood how dialing a phone works. Then, when I'd finished shooting, I went back to my in-house editor and cut a rough version of the spot, so the agency could use it as a guide. If you're not in this business, you don't know that commercial directors are rarely, if ever, involved in editing what they shoot. Many times, they're not even invited to the edit. They see the final product when it's done. To me, it's nuts. So I always figure out a way to do a cut that I can get in front of the agency before it gets fucked up.

I sent the rough cut I did to the agency producer. About four hours later, one of the sales people walked into my office looking ashen. She said the producer had just called and screamed at her for ten minutes. I was an asshole. A fuckhead. What was I thinking doing a cut of the spot myself? Agencies edit, not directors. What kind of insanity drove me to do that?

Let's see. One, my career continuing. Two, my responsibility to show these people what I'd intended when I did all this casting and shooting they didn't understand. And, three, it's my job. I'm a director. What's happened is my so-called vision. Great spot or stupid spot.

I had to fix this. I took the producer out to lunch. For two hours, I scraped and bowed. Apologized for overstepping my bounds. Asked her forgiveness. This was particularly difficult because I'd seen the editor's cut just before lunch. The producer hadn't shown him mine. Their editor had worked his own magic. And it sucked. Just stand-out bad. The agency thought so too. So, after the kiss-the-ring lunch, the producer reluctantly showed the editor what I'd done and, wouldn't you know it, he basically copied my edit, called it his recut, showed it to the client, and that's what went on the air. The spot did well. Suddenly, I was in demand to do a lot of phone company ads here and in Canada and Europe. I pulled an asshole move with the people who hired me, but the risk was worth it.

It can also go the other way.

O   O   O

I am shooting a campaign for one of the large car rental companies. The spots suck. But it's an enormous job. Sometimes you take a big pay day, make the stuff look pretty, and keep your mouth shut. The last part is hard for me.

Casting is going badly. Fifty actors have already auditioned, and none of them can make us forgot that these things are terribly written. Finally, the creative director says to the fifty-first and fifty-second actors to take a shot at it, "Can't you act better? Jesus."

I already don't like this guy. He's arrogant, vain, and borderline illiterate. I've bitten my tongue so much on this job that blood's caked around my mouth. Which I now open.

"You're not allowed to speak to actors that way."

"What?"

"Don't speak to actors like that. You think the reason this stuff sounds like shit is because all the actors are bad? Trust me. It's not the actors."

I've hung myself. I mean, maybe if…nah, I'm fucked. Ted ignores me and pouts for the rest of casting and the next three days. Refuses to speak to me. I feel like I'm back in third grade.

The next morning, we start filming. I'm setting up the first shot. A woman is at a window, watching as a car drives in. Simple. Just before we roll, I go over to video village to explain to the agency and client what I'm planning to do.

"You can't do the shot that way."

First thing Ted's said to me in four days. I ask him what the problem is. "The window's wrong."

I look at the monitor. Window looks okay to me.

"What's wrong with it?"

"It has six panes. The window in the storyboard has four."

"The storyboard is a cartoon. This is the real world."

"You have to shoot the board."

Storyboards are the simplistic, illustrated versions of a commercial. They're drawn by illustrators long before actual locations or cast members or even directors have been hired. They're suggestions, at most, of what will be in a frame once a spot is being shot.

I protest.

"Nothing in these storyboards is drawn to scale."

"Shoot the board. That's your job."

So, for five days, I do. The art department goes insane. If the storyboard shows a mailbox with the flag shaped like a pinafore, they have to fabricate one. If the board shows a woman's scarf blowing left to right at a ninety-degree angle, they have to rig fans so close and run so hard that it almost blows the actress over. If the board shows a sign in a body shop with hand-drawn letters instead of a font, the sign has to be custom fabricated with hand-drawn letters. It is crazy. And useless. And makes the shitty commercials even shittier. All because I humiliated this putz in front of a couple of actors. I actually knew enough at this point to have kept my mouth shut. Or at least to have done it in private. I was doing the job strictly for money. These spots were going to suck, no matter how much I tried to improve them. Poor time to make a moral point. Longest five days of my life in commercials. Also, when I finally understood the expression, "Who do I fuck to get off this picture?"

Never Heard of Him.

THE LOCATION SCOUT DRIVING ME TO MODENA THINKS I'M FROM MARS.

"You've never heard of Michael Schumacher?"

That's the guy starring in the commercial I'm shooting.

"Nope."

"How is that possible? He is the highest-paid athlete in the world. He is a god."

I don't follow sports much, but I am 100 percent sure that some fucking basketball player makes more money than Schumacher. This stupid Italian location scout doesn't know what he's talking about.

"Michael Jordan's the highest-paid athlete in the world."

"Schumacher is. He makes, like, five times more."

The scout keeps explaining how much money's involved in Formula One as we drive to Modena. Ferrari has their test track there. Schumacher and the rest of the Ferrari's Formula One team practice there. The scout is really excited that he's going to be able to see the place. It's like Mecca or something to Italians. And he's shitting himself at the thought that he'll be in the physical presence of Schumacher. I don't care. No

263

doubt making me the best director to shoot this job. Well, maybe the second best. The guy they really wanted to direct it, another American, is a fatuous putz who gives grades to the storyboards he gets sent. Storyboards are the crude cartoon renderings agencies draw up to present their ideas. If he thinks the job is a B, the agency has to woo him. The Italians decided that, if they're paying you seventy grand for three days' work, they don't do wooing.

I'm working for Fiat, making a spot introducing the Multipla, a new family sedan. In the spot, Schumacher is having dinner with friends in a crowded restaurant. They've heard about the Multipla and pepper Schumacher with questions about what it looks like. Every answer he gives only confuses things more, so he starts moving the restaurant's furniture around, building a representation of the car with dessert carts, chairs, tables, and serving trays. Why has a Formula One driver agreed to do this? Because Fiat owns Ferrari and, therefore, owns a piece of him. And, according to the scout, they pay him $200 million a year to drive a Ferrari and do a few ads. On top of that, he makes another $200 million endorsing shoes, shirts, beverages, phones, and whatever else he'll agree to stand next to or hold in his hand. As we pull off the highway outside of Modena, I'm coming around to the idea that he just might be the highest-paid athlete in the world.

Working with Schumacher is a challenge. There are weird availability rules. He drives all day. So he can only shoot at night, after he's done practicing. I'll get him for three hours a night for three nights. Not much time to shoot a spot where Schumacher's in every scene. But I came up with a simple solution. Cast a double. Someone who looks just like Schumacher. That way, when he leaves each night at 10:00, I can put the double in his place and keep working. I'll shoot the double from behind or from the side and he'll be out of focus, so I'll get away with it. They do it on movies when the star is an asshole and won't hang around to do their scene partner's coverage. I came up with this solution because…it seemed like the obvious way to solve the problem and get the job. Everyone else said they needed five days to shoot it. My solution solved it in three. The other challenge is his personality. According to everyone, Schumacher's rough. He hates making ads. He's known to call directors fools and dispatch them. Another really good reason to get the job done in three and not five days.

We pull into a hilltop estate five miles out of town. It was built in the late 1800s. Two castle-like turrets are on either end of the main structure. There's a circular gravel driveway abutting a grand entrance. Off to the right is a ballroom-sized space with floor-to-ceiling windows. We go in there. It looks like a giant wine cellar where some marchese ages his vintage Barolos. I love it. My production designer does too. At least, I think he does. He speaks no English and looks like Marilyn Manson. He makes friendly hand gestures. I probably say, "Fantastico." I can be that stupid and guileless an American asshole.

My producer clicks off his cell and walks over.

"We're going over to the track. So you can meet him."

"Good."

"He's giving you an hour. A royal audience."

"I don't need more than fifteen minutes."

I wander back into the ballroom. My AD starts telling stories, all of which have to do with him being Bertolucci's AD. For example, when you shoot in Bhutan, where it takes an hour to boil water, Bertolucci still demands his pasta al dente. Good to know. The guy's a Roman caricature of the name-dropping, film business jerk. I'm certain he'll be telling these stories and dropping these fucking names for the next five days.

The producer hustles back in.

"*Andiamo.* Schumacher's going to see you in ten minutes."

We speed down the hill and into Modena. I stink up my producer's BMW with a cheap Tuscan cigar. As we pass the center of town, the road starts a long, slow left turn, hugging the perimeter of the test track. There are tons of people jammed up against the chain-link fence, peering through it.

"What's going on there?"

"They're watching."

"Watching what?"

"Schumacher."

As we get to the heavily policed entrance to the track, hundreds of people crowd around our car. My producer gently steers us through the crowd, up to the gate, next to a cordon of security guards. Something happens in Italian, walkie-talkies crackle, the gates open, half the crowd tries to push in with us, the police push them back, and the gates slam shut behind us. It feels vaguely menacing, definitely not like you're outside Giants Stadium trying to get an autograph.

"Is it really that fucking interesting to watch a guy drive?"

"Yes. He's the best in the world."

We park next to a flat-roofed, one-story, cinderblock building. Along one side of it, five semis are neatly parallel parked. One's covered with satellite dishes. Two are covered in tightly wrapped tarpaulins. One carries oversized tires. Another carries vehicle skeletons. When I get out of the car, a deafening roar of engines moves from left to right, like the way Hendrix's version of "All Along the Watchtower" is mixed. My producer smiles and makes one of those hand gestures Italians make that means they did something disgusting to your sister.

"The music of Ferrari."

I guess. Another weird thing that has religious meaning to Italians.

A guy in a light-gray suit comes out of the cinder block building. He and my producer yammer away, and I follow them toward another building, a two-story brick house. It's ringed by cypress trees and a manicured lawn. We're in the middle of a racetrack and there's a little suburban house. When we get to the front door, the guy in the suit knocks. As he does this, he kind of quivers. Like there's a chance a grenade's going to go off on the other side of the door. More timid knocking, then a shout comes from inside. He opens the door very slowly, and we go in.

We head down a bare hallway and enter a tiny living room. There's a fireplace with no fire. Two armchairs and a couch. The walls are wood paneled. There's a guy standing over by the windows. He has short, dark hair that requires blow drying. He's on his cell. In one of the armchairs, slouched, long legs stretched out, a plate of food balanced on his lap, is Schumacher. He's wearing what looks like a fireproof space suit. It's off-white, long-sleeved, tight-fitting. There are a lot of zippers. The one on the front is pulled down halfway. He's got a T-shirt on underneath. The guy who walked us over inches hesitantly over near him and says something. Schumacher responds gruffly in Italian. Maybe it's just that his first language is German, but he sounds pissed. The Fiat guy gestures toward me. Schumacher gets up, shakes my hand, and switches to English. I begin to dance.

"Thanks for letting me fuck up your lunch. Sorry about this."

Celebrities assume commercial directors are fools. Which is often true. I find, if I call myself an idiot before he can even think it, I come out ahead. Also, I'm convinced that swearing in front of a person you've just met is an effective icebreaker.

"That's okay."

I detect the glimmer of a Teutonic smile.

"I'm not sure how much they've told you…"

"Not much. A Multipla ad. In a restaurant."

"Right. It'll be simple. And I'm sorry about the whole working-at-night business. It's a pain, but it's the best way to do this."

"I get it."

"You know the premise?"

"Yeah."

"You're in a restaurant. Your friends are asking you questions. You wind up moving furniture around to show them what the car looks like."

"Can I ask you something?"

"Sure."

"Do you think that'll work?"

"What'd you mean?"

"Do you think it'll look stupid?"

I hate this moment. When I have to defend an agency's dumb idea. I didn't come up with this premise. I'm just getting paid to shoot it and make it seem less stupid. Agencies don't sell their ideas to the celebrities first. They sell them to the clients who are going to pay the celebrities. The celebrities only give a shit about one thing: whether they'll look dumb.

"I think it'll be odd. Plus, it's you, so people won't be expecting you to be so..."

He smiles. Maybe Teutonic, maybe not.

"They won't expect me to be what?"

"Funny. Rumor has it you're a pretty serious guy. People treat you like you're dangerous or something. I figure if we make you look a little goofy, it'll be great."

No doubt this is the first time the words "Schumacher" and "goofy" have been used in the same sentence.

He smiles again.

"Okay. How do you deal with my schedule?"

"I have three hours each night."

"How do you get that done? I'm in every scene."

I treat Schumacher like an adult who's done this before.

"I cast a guy to be your double. When you're not there, I'll use him, and it'll look like you're still there."

Another small smile. This is going good. Or maybe that was a sneer and he thinks I'm a douche. I don't know yet.

"You have a picture of him?"

I turn to my producer who, amazingly, is prepared. He takes a folder out of his briefcase, hands me the double's headshot, and I show it to Schumacher.

He laughs.

"That's what I look like?"

"Close enough for me to make the trick work."

"Okay. You're the director."

Bingo. The talent, apparently the world's highest-paid athlete, decides I know what I'm doing and can be in charge of this miserable phase of his life. I'm done. And Schumacher's got other things to do.

"So...see you tomorrow. We'll do a quick wardrobe fitting when you get to location."

Everyone's smiling. Nothing's exploded, Schumacher included. But, because I can't keep my goddam mouth shut, I keep talking.

"I was amazed seeing all those people standing at the fences, watching you practice."

"You into Formula One?"

"I don't know much about it."

"You interested?"

"I'm interested in anything."

Schumacher gets up and grabs a pair of gloves off the coffee table in front of him.

"C'mon."

The Fiat guy reacts like I've been given a personal invitation by God to do a walkthrough of heaven. Schumacher leads us back to the cinder block building. I prattle on, convinced if I keep asking questions, he'll stay interested. I point at the satellite dishes.

"There's a lot of technology here."

Dumb observation. What am I thinking? That these guys want an excellent cell phone connection?

"It's all technology."

He opens the door and points me in. I'm suddenly in something that looks like a NASA ground control center. Except everyone is speaking Italian, German, French, and Spanish, not Texas drawls.

"Jesus."

"Not what you expected?"

"I had no idea."

Schumacher explains it all. And he's an excellent teacher. The vehicles are equipped with sophisticated transmitters. They send a constant stream of data about how the car is operating into this control center. Technicians monitor tire pressure. Others watch oil temperatures, how it's performing and whether it's stable. Still others watch readouts about wind resistance as cars go in and out of corners. Everyone wears headsets. The roar of Ferraris pierces the walls every forty-five seconds.

Schumacher heads toward a set of airlock doors. I follow him as he goes out toward the track. We step into a covered vestibule where three Ferraris are being prepped. Schumacher's lead pit man helps him into another fireproof outfit that covers the one he's wearing. He speaks in Italian to one of the mechanics then switches to German for a conversation with a different one.

My sensory apparatuses are overwhelmed. The engines rev. Pneumatic wrenches scream as tires are changed. All of this bedlam is topped each time a car goes by on the adjacent straightaway, blurring past at 175 mph. Schumacher comes over next to me, checking my reaction.

"Very cool. Chaos. But cool."

"No chaos. We know exactly what we're doing."

A giant, lumbering truck comes into view. It's one of those beasts that drive slowly down hot, city streets in the dog days of summer, spraying water out the back to cool things down and quiet the dust. Two of these, one behind the other, pass us. Water sprays everywhere. Two of the pit crew jump back so they don't get soaked. Schumacher, still standing next to me, puts his helmet on. I'm confused.

"Where're you going?"

"I'm going to drive."

"Don't you wait until the track dries before you go out?"

He smiles. A Teutonic prince who's now going to explain something to an American idiot.

"We race in the rain. If I don't practice that, I can get hurt."

This guy drives a vehicle set ten inches off the ground, powered by a V-10 engine cranking out 1,000 horsepower, moving at more than 225 miles per hour on a track that is soaking wet. Jesusfuckingchrist. No wonder they pay this guy so much money.

Schumacher climbs into the vehicle. He's so low to the ground his helmet is between my knees and waist. The pit crew belts him into place. He speaks into a microphone inside the helmet. His gaze goes toward the track then back to one of the pit crew. I wave. He gives me a thumbs-up.

He pulls the car out, onto the wet road, a fine mist of water, oil, and gasoline filling the air. The thing makes an ungodly noise.

Schumacher shows up promptly the next evening at eight. He changes into a suit, takes a seat at the table with the six actors sharing dinner with him, and I begin to shoot his lines. He starts out a little stiff. I just let the camera roll, don't tell him when I'm shooting, and, when I'm not, he forgets to be nervous. I'm happy after five takes.

"Great, Michael. Let's go on to the next line."

"I can do that better."

"No, no, no. You did great. Let's move on."

"Let's do it again. We have time."

And that's the way it goes. For three days. The man who I'd been warned was Satan incarnate, who would not work one minute longer than he was contractually obliged to, who'd want to beat me into submission, always wants to do another take. He wants to do better. He has me demonstrate how I do the body double thing. When I change the camera position and put the Schumacher doppelganger in his place at the table, he stares at the monitor with a big smile. When the double feeds Schumacher's line to an actor, Schumacher listens closely. After two takes, he goes over and speaks to the double. Tells him how he would say it. Makes a joke with him. The double is shaking he's so nervous.

I'm done with Schumacher at 10:30. He stays until midnight. He just wants to see if I'm doing him right.

When I
Went Blind.

MY RIGHT EYE FELL APART ONE NIGHT DURING DINNER. MEDICALLY
speaking, the retina detached.

It was a Saturday night. I'd driven my son back to college in Troy,
New York, and taken my youngest along for the ride. We took a carload of
my son's friends out for dinner. No one turned down an invite to Jack's
Oyster House. Seven of us gorged on food. Platters of oysters. Gigantic
steaks. Broiled lobsters. Midway through the steaks, things got exciting.
Waiters started running around helter-skelter, yelling for a doctor. The
packed dining room went instantly silent. An elderly woman had keeled
over in the ladies' room. They thought she'd croaked. When it turned
out to be just a case of the vapors, the all clear sounded, the entire room
exhaled, and the place lit up again.

But the excitement was about to continue. As I redirected my attention to my New York strip, I noticed the vision in my right eye was terrible.
I could only see the very center of things. Everything on the left and right
was black. I'd had cataract surgery in each eye. So, at first, I thought one
of the replacement lenses had slipped out of place. I didn't say anything.

Just kept rubbing my eye, seeing if I could make the replacement lens go back where it belonged. Like a dislocated shoulder. It didn't work.

The next morning, the little one and I drove back to New York. My vision was awful. And it was raining opaque gray sheets the entire way. Driving was not a great executive decision. When we got to the city, I figured I should call a doctor. By some stroke of luck, my ophthalmologist's answering service connected me directly to his cell phone. Why are doctors surprised when you tell them you're calling them because there's an emergency? I described what I was seeing, or technically not seeing, and, without a pause of any kind, he told me to get in a cab and go the hospital. Immediately. A doctor would be expecting me.

She was. Jasmine. Doctors with names you'd expect to be those of people selling T-shirts and beach balls at a Phish concert aren't—for me, at least—folks I have immediate confidence in. Anyway, Jasmine did a quick exam and told me the retina was detached. She tried her best to present this all calmly, but it was clear that this was not good. Twenty minutes later, a retina surgeon came in, took a peek in my dilated eye, and said he needed to operate. Right away.

"I can't do that. I'm a single dad at the moment. I need to find someone to look after her."

"Where's her mother?"

"It's complicated. We're divorced."

We're so more than divorced it's not funny.

"You need to figure something out, Mr. Van Dusen. Quick."

"What about doing this tomorrow?"

"If you wait that long, you might permanently lose the sight in the eye."

My youngest was in the exam room with me listening to all this. She was flattered that I used her as an excuse to delay surgery, mortified that I told the doctors her mother and I don't communicate, yet weirdly calm about the fact that I might go blind in one eye. Her main beef, as she now will tell anyone who asks, was that I drove us down from Albany with almost no eyesight, during a monsoon. Which is a legit beef.

My daughter and I left the hospital. I was sporting an eye patch to keep the bad eye from getting worse. She didn't think I looked cool at all. I organized a hand-off of the child to my angry ex and had the surgery the next afternoon.

Recovery from retina surgery is challenging. You sit in one of those upright massage chairs, your face resting on an oval foam pad, staring at the floor. For two weeks. Fourteen days and nights of looking at the ground. There's a clinical reason for this. During the operation, they inject helium into the interior of the eyeball. The gas forms a bubble that presses the retina against the back of the eye socket, helping it to reattach. If you don't keep looking down, the bubble won't push the retina in the right direction and you might lose sight in the eye. The threat of going blind gives you a lot of incentive to stay in that chair.

Before I left the hospital, I asked the doctor for painkillers, figuring I'd just get stoned for two weeks. No can do. Painkillers would mask the symptoms of an infection. If they don't catch an infection immediately, the retina doesn't reattach and…you lose sight in the eye. Pretty much everything the doctors said ended with "…and you'll lost sight in the eye."

I asked what my eyesight would be like after I recovered.

"Assuming the operation's successful?"

"Yeah. Let's assume I look at the floor nonstop for fourteen days. What then?"

"A good outcome would be 20/400."

"That's a good one?"

"Yeah. You'll see, not like you did before, but that can be partially improved with glasses." Boy, would those be some serious glasses.

My close friend's wife was kind enough to sit in the waiting room during the operation and then bring me home around 10:00 p.m. Judging from the fact that neither she, the cab driver, nor my building super would make eye contact with me, I knew I looked pretty bad. I didn't sleep much. I kept thinking about how I made my living with my eyes and one of them might be done for. Then I realized what a stupid observation that was. Pretty much *everyone* made their living using their eyes for something. Everyone on earth. I was now on the fence about whether I could even continue the "woe is me" riff until the morning.

I took my recovery super seriously. I never looked up for more than thirty seconds. Even in the shower. If I had to go out, I stared at my shoes and watched my feet shuffle along. After going to the deli on Crosby Street one afternoon and noticing that the owner, a grumpy old Chinese woman, kind of puked in her mouth when she got a look at my eye, I decided to invest in some tinted glasses.

A week into my recovery, my executive producer calls. A job we'd been bidding on a few weeks earlier had been awarded. To me. My producer knows I've had an operation. But I've kind of downplayed the severity of it. Time to level.

"I don't know if I can do this."

"What d'ya mean? You sound fine."

"I'm pretty much blind in one eye."

"You mean it's kind of fuzzy, right?"

"It's not fuzzy. I can't see out of it. I'm blind in one eye. Plus, if you saw the eye, you'd gag."

"Get some glasses."

"I did already. But, if I go into a meeting with these glasses on, it won't take long before people'll realize something's wrong."

"Like what's wrong?"

"Like I'm blind."

"We'll figure it out."

We did. I went out and bought even darker glasses. I looked like a pretentious asshole. Or one of many busy directors working at that time. I told the agency people that I'd gotten hit in the eye with a tennis ball. I had a producer next to me at all times. I had to because I couldn't see much other than weird, nondescript blurs. Even if I knew where I was, my depth perception was all fucked up, so I'd bang into stuff.

Woody Allen made a film about a director who goes blind as he starts making a movie. He doesn't tell anyone other than his agent and the script supervisor. It's very funny. I continued looking for the humor in my situation.

During casting, I normally sit at a desk and watch the actors audition from about ten feet away. I couldn't see anything one foot away, let alone ten feet. I had my producer put a tiny television monitor on the desk right next to me. The agency was sitting at the other end of the table, watching on the big monitor. I would turn away as subtly as possible, then lean in very close to the tiny TV and watch. My producer freaked.

"Don't do that!"

"What?"

"Put your face up to the screen."

"That's the only way I can see anything."

"Don't. I'll show you the tape after. You'll freak everyone out."

I stumble through casting, scouting, and the rest of preproduction. Finally, we're shooting. When I got to the set, the crew all looked at me strangely. I'd worked with most of them for thirty years. They knew I didn't wear glasses. Let alone tinted wraparounds. Indoors. I had to take someone into my confidence. So, just like the Woody Allen movie, I picked the script supervisor. She and I were pretty close friends. She's smart, hilarious, and nasty. My kind of girl.

"I have to talk to you for a sec."

We went off to one side of the location with our coffees.

"Your glasses look stupid."

"Thanks. I had an eye operation."

"Lemme see."

"You don't want to do that. Listen. Because of the operation, I can't see that well."

"Welcome to old age. Blurry, right?"

"Blurry would be an improvement. It's dark and gray. Mainly dark. I can't really see."

"Jesus."

"So I need a little help. I need to have the monitor next to me. Instead of next to you. And I need you to not say anything when I stand right next to that fucking monitor and touch my nose to the screen because that's the only way I can see. And I need you to tell me if there's anything going on in the frame that shouldn't be, because all I can really make out are some blobby shapes."

"Fuck. You're, like, handicapped."

"Kind of."

"Why are you even doing this job?"

"Because it's a good job and they're paying me a lot of money. Just help me out. And don't say anything."

The two actors were great. Whatever they did was funny. This made me look like a genius. We flew through the day. The last shot was out at the end of one of the giant piers in the Hudson River. The couple were in a romantic restaurant set we'd built, saying mushy things. I really needed the script supervisor's help for this because, at night, I couldn't see anything at all. My producer guided me out to the end of the pier, I parked myself in my chair next to the monitor. Normally, I go over and talk to the actors every few takes. I couldn't risk doing that tonight because, with the wires, cables, and stands everywhere, I was sure I'd trip and fall into the river. Just for the record, we finished an hour early.

I asked the agency to give me a day or two to put together a cut. They were graciously willing. I'd never worked with the editor they'd hired, but I was a fan of his work. He'd done two very well thought of features, so I figured he'd do great. I went to look at the first cut and was completely bummed. It was terrible. Bad takes, bad construction, bad rhythm. He didn't get it. This was not the job I wanted to start recutting from scratch. But I had to. Fuck it.

I spent two days standing with my face six inches away from an eighty-two-inch LG HD monitor recutting, trying not to enrage the editor because I wasn't using his work. The agency producer showed up the second day and never said a word as I worked with my nose shoved against the screen. The rest of the creatives appeared later to take a look at the cut. They liked it.

The spot went on to be one of the most successful the brand ever made.

It's interesting to review the what-ifs and the whys. Initially, I'd thought the best thing would be to tell the agency I was "sick" and beg out. But, because it was a great job, I rationalized the shit out of it. I wasn't completely blind, so, fuck it, I could do it. I think I did the right thing.

Over the course of a year, my vision returned to almost 20/20. This is a rare outcome for detached retina repairs. I can see almost perfectly, work, read, and play tennis. Kind of amazing. Less amazing is that, despite the success of the commercial, I never heard from the agency or the client ever again. I figure they were secretly a little skeeved out seeing me smush my face into the monitor all the time. Or maybe humiliated when they learned that the most successful spot they'd made in years was done by a blind guy.

The Surge.

IN THE SUMMER OF 2008, I MADE A DOCUMENTARY CALLED *THE SURGE.* It's about the tactical change the United States made in 2007 in a last-ditch attempt to stabilize the chaos in Iraq. As we were finishing editing, I wondered whether viewers would accept what the film revealed. The media had painted the Surge as a failure. In fact, by many metrics, it had largely been a success.

The initial invasion in 2003 was a tactical success that quickly turned into an operational disaster. The Bush administration engaged in an enormous amount of backtracking and deception. Victory was claimed when it never happened. Iraq by 2005 was an ever-worsening, dangerous mess. The idea that a calamity of those proportions could be fixed, even fixed a little, is really hard to believe. But it pretty much had been. US military deaths fell from a peak of 127 per month to 11. Iraqi civilian deaths fell even more dramatically. From 1,700 per month to fewer than 200. All lost lives were tragic but the precipitous falloff in the death toll was remarkable.

But, if you read the papers, spent a lot of time on the internet, and watched television, you didn't know that. I consume ungodly amounts of media, and I didn't know it. I also carry around a healthy skepticism about what I consume. When my kids were young, every morning at breakfast, I'd lay out the three papers we had delivered and ask them to notice how different the headlines for the same events were. Everyone's got an agenda. Figuring out what actually happens is just really, really hard. So, with the Surge, when we got all this positive information, it was hard to accept and incorporate.

We needed to add a postscript to the film that addressed this. Just presenting the data would not change people's minds. And, in some ways, the words of the military personnel, reporters, civilians, and diplomats who lived it would have the opposite effect. I needed to find normal people who had their own first-hand experiences with what had happened and put them on camera. The answer was right in front of my face. Iraqi civilians. I arranged for a camera crew to go out onto the streets of Baghdad and Ramadi to ask cab drivers, students, merchants, mothers, whomever they came in contact with, what the result of the Surge has been. I didn't want any of the crew to be Western, thinking that might affect the responses. I gave the Iraqi crew a simple brief. Iraqis wouldn't know the operation had been called the Surge. But they would know what their lives were like before and after a certain date. So I told the crew to pose one question, the same one to every person.

"What was it like here in 2005? What is it like today?"

The crew interviewed over fifty people. When the footage arrived in New York, we hired a translator to help us, a Palestinian woman whose day job was at the UN. She was in her mid-thirties, smart, charming, and excited to help us. After explaining the back story, we played the dailies for her. I asked her to do a little translating on the fly because the editor and I were so curious about what the Iraqis were saying. She started off interested, translating a phrase here and there, but, after the third interview, she suddenly stood up and started yelling. At me.

"These people are lying. They're reciting propaganda. They're being forced to say these things. Possibly at gunpoint."

"This was all done by a civilian Iraqi crew. There's no soldiers, no government people with them. They're just wandering the neighborhoods, asking people what happened."

"Impossible."

"What makes you think they're all lying?"

She paused, trained her eyes on me with contempt, making sure I knew she thought I was a moron.

"It's completely obvious."

"Right. But tell me why?"

"Because nothing they say is what I read in the *New York Times* or see on Al Jazeera."

She either quit or we fired her, depending on whom you ask. We hired another translator and eventually learned what the Iraqis were saying. Not one person in the fifty said things were worse. Everyone said things had changed dramatically for the better. They felt safe. Life had gone back to almost normal. None of the responses made mention of US forces or what the United States had done. The Iraqis' answers simply described their lives. Which all were better. Actually, there was one complaint. A guy who owned a record store said he was pissed because rush-hour traffic had gotten so much worse since the violence stopped and now it took him an hour longer to get to work.

$$\bigcirc \quad \bigcirc \quad \bigcirc$$

I'd finally made a documentary. About a challenging, polarizing topic. I'd tried really hard to make the film completely neutral and fact-driven and keep my assumptions out of it. There was no narrator, no one tilting the balance. I'd allowed all the talking to be done by the people who lived it. I wanted the film to speak for itself. I was proud of it. Maybe most proud that it confused and angered so many people. Frederick Wiseman would probably not have chosen a topic with as many political hot buttons. Predisposition is tough to overcome. People stop listening pretty quickly when what they're hearing doesn't fit with their assumptions. Today, Wiseman picks much softer topics: ballet, small towns, department stores. *The Surge* was a hard topic. But, if you watch it, you learn. Not what you think happened but what actually happened.

61

Show Me the Money.

Whenever I meet someone from the real world, they're always curious about my job.

"Boy, that sounds like a fun job."

"Sometimes. It's different."

"Must be exciting."

"Can be. Then, you know, it's a job."

Eventually, they ask if I went into directing because I always had some deep-seated desire to express my creativity.

I'm always honest.

"No. I had a deep-seated desire to make money."

I'm comfortable with the creative stuff. I've learned to manage the production process well and spend my budgets judiciously, and I got very good at telling stories. But my real focus is on getting paid. It's a little more layered than I make it sound. Getting paid matters because it means something. It means I'm good at my job. It means I'm not a fraud. It means, by doing something so competently so often, I am something. So I get the trifecta. I get the monkey of being a fraud off my back. I get the money. And I get the stability that money provides. Which is what I've been trying to create from that first day in Roosevelt Hospital, pitching stab-wounded Crazy Eddie. It's a very logical sequence to me. And it's helped me stay busy for longer than all but four or five other guys doing this.

I've never seen myself as an artist. I see myself as a businessman. Not a great one. But good enough to understand that my business is me. I am a creative commodity. And I measure whatever success I have more in monetary terms than artistic ones. I guess that makes me a hack. Fine by me.

When I'm around most other kinds of creative people, I get confused.

"What do you direct?

"Commercials, a couple of movies, I've done a documentary. Mainly commercials."

"Do you do anything you're passionate about?"

"I'm passionate about all my work. What about you? What do you do?"

"I'm a composer."

"Oh. That's cool. What kind of music?"

"Hard for a non-musician to understand. I'm just finishing a piece for guitar, soprano sax, and performance-specific feedback loops."

My iPhone creative language app translates this as follows: I spend all day in a dingy coffee place in Bushwick, I'm starving to death, and my parents are trying to figure out a nice way to tell me they're not covering my rent anymore.

"Like Andrew Bird?"

"Well…not as commercial."

God forbid it's commercial. Artists often behave like commercial success is a bad thing. Like being able to pay your rent from doing your art is a failing. I can never figure this out. In their worlds, success isn't correlated with a paycheck. Critical success, they say, is enough. It is? Who would want to spend three years of their lives on something, anything, unless there's a big potential upside? And, at least the way I understand it, big potential upside has got to include making some money. Song-writers, directors, actors, painters, novelists, even poets, all want fame and fortune. It's not a failing. It's logical and rational. The fact that so few of them cop to it is where the problem, for me, lies. Successful creative output, whether songs, books, pictures, or films, ideally will wind up reaching a wider audience than your girlfriend and parents. Admit it. That's what you're praying for. A wide audience that pays you. You may claim you don't care about all that. I don't think you're telling the truth.

62

Marty and Me.

ONCE A GOOD LOCATION HAS BEEN DISCOVERED, LOTS OF PEOPLE START using it. Location scouts share info. Particularly about places that are hard to get into. Like offices, schools, and hospitals. Hospitals are really difficult. Most of them don't want anything to do with film crews. For good reason. We're disruptive, and the lives of people in hospitals are at stake. They don't need us making bad situations worse. The only ones that will even think about allowing filming are the hospitals that are stone-cold broke. Fortunately for film crews, there are a couple of these in New York.

For this job, I'm trying to find a hospital with a specific look. Big, bright hallways, oversized patient rooms, and a nice exterior. And it should feel a bit classic and upscale. Ivy-covered exterior, nice windows, mature trees. Like a college administration building. I really like one the scout's found in the Bronx. It's in a tough neighborhood, and the emergency room's always busy with a combination of uninsured people, women in labor, victims of criminal violence, and chronically sick old people. Needless to say, the hospital's on financial life-support.

Some savvy administrator figured out that parts of the unused eighth floor can be closed off, so film crews can work there without getting in the way of the day-to-day operations. I'm walking through that space with the guy whose bright idea this was. He's had ten shoots since he hatched this idea and now thinks of himself as a studio executive.

As we stroll down a hallway, I ask if there are any places that look back toward the city skyline.

"Yeah. Over here. That's an angle Marty likes."

"Marty?"

"Scorsese. He did some of the *Wall Street* picture here. Nice guy."

"Oh."

"So's Leo. And Matt."

"DiCaprio?"

"Yeah. And McConaughey. Nice guys. I did a little scene with them. Fun."

"You're an actor too?"

"You're a riot! No way. Marty just thought I was perfect for this one thing."

He stops me and points down the hall.

"This is the place he likes to put the camera. Check out that angle from down low."

I bend my knees so I'm seeing things from a foot or two off the floor. Apparently, that's not Marty's angle.

"You wanna get right on the ground."

I get down on one knee.

"See the city? Nice, right? You two want the same thing. Very similar creative minds."

My understanding of Martin Scorsese is that we are not at all similar. As a friend of mine who's done many films with him puts it, "Remember the guy in fifth grade who was so weird you sort of steered clear of him all the time? Well, he grew up, and his name is Marty Scorsese." That and he's a great movie director and I'm not.

We book the place. When we come back to shoot a week later, the administrator's with us all day. Every time I set up a shot, he's over by video village checking it out. If he approves, he nods his head and gives me a little thumbs-up. If he's not impressed, he keeps his arms crossed and avoids eye contact with me. I assume that the angle I've picked is not one Marty liked.

63

Brand-New Day.

My producer's driving this morning. We're in Danville, a little town in central Pennsylvania that's home to Geisinger, a giant health care system. I'm making commercials for them. Danville's six streets wide, with all the north-south ones dead-ending at the Susquehanna River. For no discernible reason, the planner who laid the place out decided to make all the streets one way. Getting most places requires driving three more blocks than it would if the guy'd understood two-way streets. The Waze lady keeps telling us to make a U-turn.

I'm sixty-two. I get up to pee during the night at least once. Shuffling back and forth to the bathroom, my head can get a little busy. If I'm shooting in the morning, I'll often get caught up in a loop about what might go wrong. This particular job's loop is about the cast. They're all real people who've used the hospital. I'm supposed to get them saying nice things about the place. What if they say terrible things? What if they all clam up and say nothing? Well, I guess I'd just have to figure something else out, wouldn't I? Because I'm the fucking director. Fuck it. I fall back asleep quick.

I work less these days. Which I'm okay with. I knew this would happen eventually. All through my career, I was like an annoying Chicken Little, telling anyone who'd listen that my career was about to end. I figured, if I kept predicting the worst, it wouldn't happen. The only person who really believed me was my ex-wife. She scheduled things involving alimony, child support, and division of assets to coincide perfectly with the highpoint of my career.

A normal career span for a commercial director is ten years. And that's assuming you even get a span. You decide to do it, find a company to put you on their roster, get a few jobs, do them well so you get more jobs, start shooting with some regularity, and then, at the five-year mark, things start to go south. You rely too much on one client, and they dump you. You think you're the shit, so you price yourself out of the market. You actually are the shit but create a really expensive operation, and the financial pressures crush you. Even if all the stars stay in alignment, unless you're always developing new clients, updating your style, doing visible work, directing stuff that sells some product, the whole thing can, just as suddenly as it took off, be over. Somehow, I've had a much longer run than most of the guys I competed with. It didn't always look like that would be the case.

Originally, my plan was to segue from commercials into movies. Movies would be my second act. But, because my first movie didn't do great, there was no segue. I stuck with commercials. Because I had to. I had no other options. Some years I made progress. I shot better commercials. I did my job with more skill. I worked with bigger budgets. Other years, there was no forward motion. Some years, I'd expand the company, adding directors and satellite offices; then, if the volume of work didn't support it, I'd shrink the business. I never took bet-the-company risks. When I made mistakes, and I made plenty, they weren't catastrophic. I was always able to hang on until I got another job, which would lead to another job and so on and so on, and I survived. When I did make big mistakes, like suing my largest client, pure luck kept me in business. I have been very, very lucky. I am definitely the least talented of the guys who've had long runs.

You have to keep changing to keep working. If only for your own entertainment. And I was always willing to change. This past year, I've been trying to totally rethink the scale of my productions. I've spent my life running sets with sixty or seventy people. Four or five big trucks full of equipment out on the street. Generators making a racket and spewing diesel exhaust into blue, suburban skies. Fancy catering. Motor homes full of movie stars, famous athletes, or politicians. The first couple hundred times, it's exciting. You feel like a master of something. Then it becomes a giant pain in the ass. I finally decided it was time to change.

So, today, instead of seventy people, I'm working with a crew of eight. Instead of a fleet of trucks, there's just one small van parked in front of the location. No one is over the age of thirty, except me, the producer, and one camera guy. We're using two small cameras. We've only brought two lights because I want to shoot everything naturally. Our setups, even with the inexperienced but enthusiastic kids we've hired, will each take less than an hour. I am looking forward to this.

I walk into the house we're using as a location. Unlike the old days, we haven't scouted the place the day before, so no one knows where to put any of the equipment. I have to show up early to tell the crew what to do. Fine by me. I show the two camera operators where to put the cameras. We're doing a simple interview with one woman, so I put one camera in front of her and one to the side. I'll sit next to the camera in front of her and ask the questions. I won't operate a camera for two reasons. First and foremost, I need to have a conversation with the woman. If my eye is pressed into a viewfinder, she won't think I'm listening to her. Second, I can't make out shit on these new digital monitors. When a person in front of the camera moves two or three inches, you have to refocus. I can't see well enough to do this with the new, tiny cameras. After sitting in editing rooms and cringing at yet another soft, unusable shot, I've ceded all the operating to the young guys. Their eyes work.

They're fluent with all the new technology. I'll use my brain to do what I can still do, get a performance out of someone.

I head into the back of the house where we've set up a stripped-down version of video village. The agency and client are there having breakfast. I give them a quick rundown of how the morning's going to go, what I'm hoping to have the woman say, and how I'll shoot it. Most important, I remind them not to panic during the first five minutes of shooting. Working with real people takes time.

Another thing I like about this new working method is the drastically simpler approach to food. Shoots used to be three-ring circuses of never-ending gourmet meals. It was a world where people got pissed if their latte was lukewarm or we'd run out of the croissants they like. We don't play that anymore.

I pour myself a Dunkin' Donuts coffee from a Box o' Joe and grab a donut. I say hi to the other six people in the crew. I'm hoping they've ignored whatever stories they might have heard about me biting crew people's heads off. That was the old me. This new style of work is going to chill me the fuck out.

I find the woman we're interviewing. A very sweet, older lady who's recently lost her husband. I want her to tell that story today. It's moving and human. As long as I can keep her calm and distracted, she'll do great.

Another benefit of working small is not bothering with complicated hair and makeup. This is a real person, so we don't need it anyway. We probably never did. Most people look just fine without being powdered, combed, and blotted. I ask the makeup person to not do anything other than brush her hair and walk her out to the camera. We're ready to shoot in less than half an hour.

With digital cameras, you don't need to use slates, the white plastic boards with the scene, take, director, and camera info on them. You just roll. The woman has no idea we're filming. I start chatting with her. I steer her into the story of her husband's death. She's very solid. I ask her about something she'd told me when we first talked. About how she and her husband met. She spins it out. They happened to both be in the same greasy spoon grabbing dinner after working the three-to-eleven shift in adjacent factories. They were standing near a counter looking at pies. There was one piece of coconut cream left. She wanted it. So did Charley. He asked if she was going to take it. She said, "Yeah, but I'll share it with you." They were married a year later. As I'm hearing this, I'm adding shots I'll do later in the day. One will be a slice of pie.

I guide her through different stories for about half an hour. Digital allows us to do long takes instead of changing film magazines every eleven minutes. It's another thing I like about the new technology. I think we've got just about everything we need. So I go back to check in with the agency. They're a nice group. Only one bad apple. The producer. He's old, meaning my age, and nasty, also like me, but worse. He's a blamer. Only looks for mistakes. Someone else's. Any comment he makes is either critical or disruptive or both. Which I now have to deal with.

Without asking anyone, he's told the makeup person to fix a problem he's seen with the woman's hair. But there is no problem. She looks perfect. But, because the makeup person is young and inexperienced, she assumes the producer is important, so she does what he tells her. When I get back to the camera and see her fussing with the woman, I ask, "What're you doing?"

She barely looks at me and keeps fussing with her goddam brush and comb.

"The producer wanted me to fix the hair."

"Stop. C'mere for a sec."

She follows me over to the front hallway. Midtwenties, rough, inked, lots of ear piercings, gum. I've never seen her before in my life.

"Listen. Don't do anything like that unless I ask you to. Even if the agency asks you to do something, talk to me first."

She gets furious. At me. This tends to happen with inexperienced crew people. They don't make mistakes. Ever. How can I be telling her she's done something wrong? I was like this when I was twenty-five. Shit, I'm still like this.

I go back to video village and ask, completely disingenuously, what was the problem with the woman's hair. The producer, the blamer, says there was a flyaway hair he wanted fixed. I suggest it doesn't matter. The producer starts a testy rant about not wanting to deal with our mistakes during editing. The assumption being I've done something wrong. Hmmm.

I start a monologue on the radio show I host in my head. I mainly do insult comedy. I'm riffing about how amazing it is that this guy, who is really overweight, could have even noticed a flyaway hair when, from the moment he got here, he's had his face and mitts buried in donuts and danish. He hasn't seen anything other than the crap he's crammed in his fucking piehole. Until just now, that is, when he stopped trying to find a bucket of cream cheese or a production assistant to refill his coffee and decided that was a good moment to say something producer-y. I remind myself how fortunate I am to work less. And that I've learned to do these bits in my head.

My idyllic new-style, low-key-working environment now ruined, and my blood pressure elevated enough that I'm hearing timpani banging in my ears, I refocus on finishing the interview. We start shooting again, and I ask a few more questions. I get the woman to clarify a few things. She's great. I'm done. I check with the agency, and they're good. The producer says nothing. Perhaps because his mouth is full. We move to the next setup.

Ten minutes later, we're shooting in the small kitchen. I've put the next performer, another real person, in a shaft of natural light coming in the kitchen window. It looks great without us doing anything. Just then, one of the young tech geniuses comes up to my producer. Very mature and capable for his age. Quietly, but loud enough that I can hear, he tells the producer that, while he was downloading the memory card with all the footage we just shot, it erased itself. My producer absorbs this, thinks for a moment, and then turns to him.

"Are you fucking kidding me?"

That card held forty minutes of one-of-a-kind footage. Of a real person talking. We cannot redo this. Young, inexperienced crew plus imperfect digital technology plus working fast plus not supervising closely results in gigantic fuckup.

Maybe this new style of working sucks.

I've brought along one guy who's not a kid. Neal, an Australian in his mid-thirties. He's old enough to be comfortable with both film and digital cameras. And he's standing right next to me, hearing what I'm hearing. When we exchange a look, it has history.

Two years ago, he and I were on a steamboat floating down the Mississippi River. I was following Mitt Romney around for a few days as he campaigned for president. We started the day at an insulation factory in Janesville, Wisconsin, swung by a feed plant in Rockford, Illinois, and then drove to Dubuque, Iowa, for the boat ride.

The paddle wheeler was coming in to dock. I wanted to get a shot of Romney diving into the crowd waiting for him there. Neal asked how much shooting I'd do. Five minutes, max. He thought it would be a good idea to change the memory card because the one I was using was almost full. While he did that, I looked toward shore and took in the scene. Campaign buses, black Silverados, network television vans with satellite dishes, police cars, Secret Service, supporters with signs and autograph pads, staff cars, and all the other mess that is a presidential campaign trail. Right then I heard Neal say, "Fuck."

"That doesn't sound good. What happened?"

"I just erased the card."

"Erased? Like gone erased?"

"Yeah."

"That sucks."

When you experience a massive technical problem that appears capable of destroying the job, a variety of things happen. They include your gut reacting like you've eaten lunch purchased from a street vendor in Mogadishu. My personal default reaction is really dumb.

"We can probably fix this, right?"

I always say this. Glass-half-full kind of guy that I am.

And, going forward, my contribution to "fixing this" will be asking if it's fixed every ten minutes.

An hour later, I was driving us south toward the airport in Iowa City. I'd asked whether it's fixed yet at least five times. The mood in the car was like the one you experience in a hospital waiting room while a relative is having a surgery with bad odds. Fake optimism camouflaging unspoken dread. Just as we hit the outskirts of Iowa City, the wheel that told us the program was running stopped, the screen re-formatted, Neal clicked on a folder, discovered a ton of files, opened them and, boom, there it all was. Mitt was back.

A year later, on a different job, it happened again. I finished shooting a scene, walked over to talk with the DP about what we'd do next and heard a camera assistant say, "Fuck."

I'm now an expert on this erasure shit. I calmly instructed the AC to stop what he was doing. Then I scanned the room looking for Neal. He was over by the window putting a bazooka-sized zoom lens back into its case. I walked over to the window.

"The guy running B camera just erased the card. We can fix this, right?"

Neal smiled.

"Probably."

"Probably definitely?"

"Probably."

We parked Neal in a back room with a laptop and the card in question. Again, the hospital waiting room angst mixed with Somalian food poisoning gut cramps. And me asking every ten minutes if it's fixed yet. Forty minutes later, we were fine.

Now, standing next to Neal in this dinky kitchen in Danville, I'm simultaneously certain we'll be okay and panicked that, this time, my luck has run out and we actually *are* fucked. Whatever. We start the retrieval process. Initially, the young tech geniuses manage it. Neal's looking over their shoulders as they search for a program that'll restore everything.

They should be able to handle this. It's simple. Go online. Find a program. Download it and run it. Which they do.

Moment of truth. They click open the folders. Huh? We're looking at tons of kung fu footage. Fuck. They download another program. Start running it. This one'll take three hours before we know anything. At this point, I run an options list in my head.

I've decided the young tech geniuses are in over their heads. If they've ever had a card erase, they probably just said fuck it and reshot what they'd lost. I change the command structure. I pull the young geniuses off the retrieval mission and put the wizened, thirty-five-year-old Australian in charge. Out of everyone's earshot, I ask him if he really thinks we'll find it, or should I assume the worst, bite the bullet, and reshoot the interview.

"It's there."

Somehow, I also hear, "…and I'll find it in an hour and we'll be good. Relax."

He didn't say that. If I wasn't experiencing audio hallucinations, I'd know his answer just means the information, the ones and zeros, is somewhere on the card. It does not mean we'll be able to put it back together. But I choose to hear it my way and decide not to reshoot the scene with the widow. Potentially dumb as shit.

I keep working, totally believing the footage will reappear. As I travel around Danville during the afternoon doing different setups, I periodically text Neal. "Fixed?" Over the next five hours, I copy and paste that message four times. Around nine that evening, I'm out at an amusement park doing the last setup of the day. I want some shots of Ferris wheels, merry-go-rounds, summer's night stuff. I have a sense they might work in the part of the story where the woman talks about her and her husband going on a first date. As we're doing the last shot, I feel my phone buzz. A text from Neal. "Sleep well, mate. Footage transcoding. Synced in the morning."

I love young, inexperienced tech geniuses until something happens. And then I have no use for them. They seem to understand everything and then, suddenly, they go all dumb on you. When there's a problem, experience, which usually also means age, pushes youth to the back of the line. And experience doesn't always mean gray hair. The person who solved all three of these disasters is thirty-five. In your mid-thirties, you're in the sweet spot of experience, instinct, and wisdom. Younger than that, you're just hoping you know. Older than that, you're the guy saying, "We can fix this, right?"

I spent three days editing the spot. The woman's performance, half of it retrieved from erased footage, was great. We put it together with images of her house, downtown Danville, her doing errands, fishing in a little creek, and the amusement park rides. And a slice of coconut cream pie. It worked pretty well. The agency was happy. No one remembered the flyaway hair. Or the cold Dunkin' Donuts coffee. And they'd never remember that most of the first day's footage, the scenes they're so in love with, had gone missing for eight hours. Because they never knew.

I remembered all of it.

How Did This Happen?

64

WHEN MY MARRIAGE ENDED, I SORT OF CAME UNMOORED. I WASN'T DOING the stability thing well at all. I knew stability mattered more than ever, that it was essential to getting through what was happening, but I couldn't keep a grip on it. I had a nice, new apartment. A good group of friends. I was a hyperattentive father. But sometimes I'd find myself standing in a doorway, on the way to work, my face turned toward the building so no one could see I was crying. Very tenuous grip.

I changed companies every few years. After saying I'd never do another one, I shot two more movies. I finally made a documentary. I kept a close eye on my kids and, just when I was accepting that this was the pleasantly disconnected life I'd lead, I met someone.

I was a bad date. Like some way too extroverted person in a twelve-step program who overshares the shit out of everything. Victoria listened to me describe every terrible thing I'd ever said and done. I could recite them all from memory, chronologically. Then she listened to the even worse stuff I hadn't done but had been accused of. When I wrapped up that fascinating portion of the evening, I asked her why that didn't make me the world's worst choice for a boyfriend. She razzle-dazzled me with some kind of enlightened wisdom about life being a story and perspectives changing and how people make and learn from their mistakes. Oh. And she also liked that I was still starved for stability.

I got lucky. The woman I did all this confessing to was smart, beautiful, accomplished, and pretty stable. And the timing was good. Things had calmed down. I was less of an asshole, I was less busy and around more, and, because I was less of an asshole, she didn't mind having me around. And I wanted to be around her all the time. Everything was nice and funny and easy. After a year or so, I knew I'd spend the rest of my life with her. I figured we'd just keep going like we were. Two apartments, lots of independence. Modern and mature. I dumped that plan when she went to Italy for a month. Man, oh, man, did that throw everything into focus. Two days after she got back, I made my move. I got out of the shower, walked into the living room, asked her to get off her computer for a minute, and then asked her to marry me. In the enthusiasm of the moment, I forgot to get dressed, so I was standing there in a towel, dripping wet. I told her she couldn't give me her answer for two days. I didn't want a yes or no she could later blame on jet lag. Victoria didn't follow the rules. She only waited a day to say yes. What was a great relationship became a greater one. I miss one thing about our life before marriage. I loved introducing Victoria to people as my consort. Things are good. My three kids are all married and do cool things. My stepsons do cool things too and seem to be tiptoeing toward the altar. I have three grandchildren with weird names. Everyone, Victoria included, thinks I'm more laughable than embarrassing. And, for all the toes I stepped on, I still shoot.

Most commercial directors aren't so lucky. They wind up divorced, shell-shocked, financially wobbly, struggling to accept that it's gone south, starting new families at sixty, dressing like idiots, making pleading phone calls to people they shot four decades ago looking for work, wearing porkpie hats indoors, talking about some movie they've been developing for twenty years that never gets made, and, if they had some real success, getting divorced a few more times. It's like painfully slow drowning. With lots of people on the beach watching. Many rooting against you. This line of work isn't nice to people.

A lot of the observations I've included in this book are pretty obvious. Shitty things follow good things. Then good things follow bad. You get smarter once you admit you're not. You don't know anything when you're twenty-five. And you're scared. You barely know something at fifty. It's a long race. Honest to God, anybody who can get out of bed in the morning, brush their teeth, and figure out how to turn on a Mr. Coffee already knows this stuff.

I went into a business I didn't know existed. Every choice I made was about creating a stable, predictable life. Turns out stability isn't tangible, reliable, or definable. Turns out life is about surprises and wrong turns and good luck and bad choices and showing up on time. I wonder how things would have turned out if I'd been trying to really fuck it up.

ACKNOWLEDGMENTS

A TON OF PEOPLE MADE THIS THING BETTER.

The connected dots: Victoria asked me to stop talking and write something; Harry Stein read what I wrote and suggested that I write it again; Mary Blakemore and Alex Smith knew someone named Web Stone; Web said he'd try to sell it but I had to write it again; Ann and Kipp Sylvester invited me to dinner, where I met my brilliant and put-the-story-in-a-place editor Will Dana, who had me rewrite it a final time.

My early readers, Richard Davies, Stan Schonholz, Craig Jacobson, Clea Colangelo, Brian Schneider, Gabrielle Lasting, and Ethan Podel, helped enormously. And a big thanks to Honor Moore for loaning me her desk.

Thanks to the supremely organized, tight ship that is Post Hill: Anthony Ziccardi, Michael Wilson, and especially Maddie Sturgeon, Devon Brown, and Seane Thomas.

Thanks to all the people, over the years, who came to work and dealt with me being an asshole: Mark Molesworth, David Frankel, Tad Van Dusen, Leslie Larson, Richard Fink, Robin Fried, Paul Riccio, Chuck Pfeifer, Biff Johnson, Marty Gillen, Mark Kovacs, Steve Shor, Bob Fisher, Joy Saylor, David Feikens, Maria Stenz, Alexis LePage, and Julio Rodriguez, who believes my success is a result of a conspiracy. A special nod to Danny and Judy Michael and to my friend and script supervisor, Liz Maas, for always being in on the joke.

Thanks to the people who paid me to go to Italy so often: Giorgio Marino, Luca Fanfani, Silvana Gabelli, Giulia Buffa, and Caterina Tempestini.

This weird business will continue. Gloria Colangelo, Sam Wool, and Pete Dever are the rock stars who'll run it.

Of all my producers, Mike Salzer looms largest. Thanks to Wynn and Charlie's love of the Knickerbocker Bar and Grill for reuniting us.

Thanks to Gavin Cutler, David Cornman, Jeff Dell, and Bryan Moak, the amazing film editors who turned so many of my messes into something great. Thanks to my fellow directors at Assembly and MacGuffin, especially Julian West, Kevan and Chris Bean, Nick Fugelstad, Marie Constantinesco, Mike Rowles, Gary McKendry, and Jeff Fleisig. And to Stuart Stevens, Russ Schriefer, and Ashley O'Connor for adding new categories to my résumé.

Big thanks to the writers who let me shoot their stories: John DeCerchio, Steve Fechtor, Bonnie Bohn, Greg Steward, Margaret Elman, Steve Crane, Joe O'Neill, Bill Heater, and Tom Messner.

All of the above helped make this book better. My stepsons, Jonah and Gabe, think I can improve personally. My kids, Zane, Dara, and Wynn, and their partners, Ellen, Magnus, and Shea, seem to have given up hope on that happening but remind me anything's possible. Fortunately, my grandkids, Falcon, Ellis, and Sky, think I'm the greatest.

Finally, my biggest thanks of all to the one who made everything better, my wife, DarkBird9.